# Date Loaned

| | | | |
|---|---|---|---|
| DEC 10 1933 | | | |
| JAN 4 - 1934 | | | |
| FEB 1 - 1934 | | | |
| OCT 21 1934 | | | |
| MAR 31 1935 | | | |
| OCT 27 1935 | 146 | | |
| NOV 10 1935 | 146 | | |
| JAN 5 1936 | 146 | | |
| | | | |
| | | | |
| | | | |
| | | | |
| | | | |
| | | | |
| | | | |
| | | | |
| | | | |
| | | | |

# ONCE UPON A TIME
# AND TODAY

Maud Nathan

# ONCE UPON A TIME AND TODAY

by

MAUD NATHAN

*Author of "The Story of an Epoch-making Movement"*

WITH 28 ILLUSTRATIONS

G. P. PUTNAM'S SONS

NEW YORK : LONDON

1933

PRINTED IN THE UNITED STATES OF AMERICA

I dedicate this book to the memory of my husband, the Fairy Prince of this tale, and to the memory of my little daughter, whose brief life taught me the measure of human joy and human sorrow.

## AN ACKNOWLEDGMENT

No words can express my thanks and gratitude for the constant encouragement, sympathy, and coöperation given me in the writing of these chapters by my comrade and friend who prefers to be nameless.

# FOREWORD

THE Woman Movement did not come into being, as many think, for the purpose of securing the vote; instead it was and still is a world wide awakening, protesting, uprising of women of all races and nations to a comprehension that in the organization of human society a "square deal" had not been meted out to their sex. The understanding, when it came, led to diverse demands for a fairer and less discriminating distribution of the privileges as well as the duties of life. Throwing off the veil in Egypt and Turkey, unbinding the feet in China, struggling for education in India or Timbuctoo are all as integral parts of the movement as the more familiar and picturesque suffrage campaign in the United States.

Destiny seized many a woman in this far-flung uprising and made her a heroine, often to her own astonishment. One such was Maud Nathan. Her background was the traditional domesticity of her race coupled with an environment, including a large family connection, presenting determined resistance to any departure from the old order. The exception was her devoted husband who gloried in her every achievement and honor won. She was slowly lured into social work by the desire to serve, and timidly began to feel her way in the great outside world.

The Jewish women of our country were slow in awakening. When the women of her own synagogue formed a sisterhood or auxiliary, it was Mrs. Nathan who became its first president. It was not long before a National Council of Jewish Women was organized (now a powerful body of splendidly self-reliant and intelligent women) and after the first president resigned, Mrs. Nathan was asked to be the candidate for that office, but she declined. Always true to her faith and loyal to the particular work of Jewish women, one of the first Jewesses to preach in a synagogue, the broader interests of all human society made a stronger appeal to her.

One finds her in her early years serving as a director of Mt. Sinai Hospital Training School for Nurses, the New York Exchange for Women's Work, organizing schools for immigrants on the East Side, serving in the Women's Auxiliary of the Civil Service Reform Association and speaking for a reform candidate for mayor. Investigation into conditions in mercantile establishments led Mrs. Josephine Shaw Lowell, the noted philanthropist, and others to organize the "Consumers' League" of which Mrs. Nathan became a director, and after the retirement of Mrs. Lowell, succeeded her as president. Here she served for many years and did her most heroic work. Women employees in department stores the nation over owe to this organization the fact that stores are closed in the evening, hours of work have been shortened, seats provided behind counters, and a weekly half holiday granted in summer. The infinite patience, the long hard endeavor to achieve these seemingly simple ends of justice are well-nigh incomprehensible to those who coming later find them established facts.

Naturally Mrs. Nathan was drawn into the Municipal League and into the suffrage campaign. She began her speaking in parlors where she plead for the working woman. Her talent expanded into decided platform power and she became a familiar and popular speaker for many causes. She never babbled words; she said things that made her hearers reflect and eventually change their minds. One recalls her presence and her pleas in Albany at many a hearing for reform measures, including the suffrage and in many a congressional battle in Washington as well. As the campaign for suffrage whirled faster and faster, she kept pace with it, responding cheerfully to every call. On the street at an open air meeting, on the East Side in a small stuffy hall, in luxurious parlors, or Carnegie Hall, her practical speech and her charming personality were frequent features. As delegate and speaker she attended conventions of the International Council of Women, the first great effort to unite the women of the world. She went also as a delegate, speaker and interpreter to conventions of the International Woman Suffrage Alliance.

A busy life she has lived, an heroic life of achievement. The world today is an utterly different one from that she found when, looking out upon it timidly in her youth, she made her first choice between the claims of the "new woman" and the resistance of the old order. In the struggle that wrought the change Mrs. Nathan was a forceful, dependable, always helpful battler for the right.

CARRIE CHAPMAN CATT.

# INTRODUCTION

THE author of this book is one of those exceptional persons who are entitled to write an autobiography and who are able to make the record of their experiences in life interesting, illuminating, and representative.

Mrs. Nathan is a New Yorker of the old stock, born and bred in the best tradition of Sephardic Judaism, loyal to her ancient faith and her own people, but yet a woman of intensely modern spirit, eager to devote her talents and her charm

> To the long, long toil and the strenuous fight
> Of the human race to win its way
> From the feudal darkness into the day
> Of Freedom, Brotherhood, Equal Right.

In this brave adventure she has not only been an inspiration to other women (and to men also, if you please), but she has rendered fine practical service to the cause of humane progress—service which Christian churches could not fail to recognize and value without being false to their own best traditions and ideals.

I first became acquainted with Mrs. Nathan when she was the leading spirit of that remarkably efficient society known as "The Consumers' League"—a modest name which provided a protective coloration for a combative and liberating enterprise. Its purpose was to expose and destroy the cruel and demoralizing conditions under which working girls were employed in many of the shops in New York; after that the enterprise could be widened to embrace the whole country. But how to begin? With a Black List of shops where conditions were bad? No. That would be a boycott; illegal. But there was no law against a White List of shops where conditions, after careful investigation, were found to be good. So the League was wise as a serpent and harmless as a dove. Its members voluntarily followed the White List in their shopping. The Black List became unnecessary. Economic forces were enlisted on the side of humanity and fair play for the working girls in the shops.

Mrs. Nathan came to me to ask if one of the early meetings of the League might be held in the Brick Presbyterian Church in New York, of which I was then the young and unseasoned minister. I accepted with an alacrity which probably made her head swim. She made one of the best speeches at the meeting that I have ever heard—womanly, persuasive, eloquent. Ever since then we have been friends. That is probably why she has asked me to write this brief introduction to her book.

But the reader will find much more in these pages than the record of philanthropic enterprises. They give the picture of a personality, fine, courageous, lovable; a Jewish girl, woman, lady, who never forgets her heritage, and never makes it a weapon of offense. The story of this life, first in the New York of Edith Wharton's *Age of Innocence,* then in a midwestern town, then in the New York of the 'Eighties and 'Nineties, and then in the cosmopolitan range of contacts into which Mrs. Nathan's humane and energetic spirit led her, is full of interest. It is well told, too, with simplicity, with vividness, and with that clarity which is the first mark of good writing. To modernists who do not despise the past, to feminists who admit that men have their virtues and uses, to Jews who do not hate Christians and Christians who do not hate Jews, I commend this book.

HENRY VAN DYKE.

Dr. Henry Van Dyke

# CONTENTS

# ILLUSTRATIONS

# ONCE UPON A TIME
# AND TODAY

# CHAPTER I

## ONCE UPON A TIME

ONCE upon a time! Mysterious magic lies in this phrase! It visualizes the wonderful fairy tales that quicken youthful imagination. It transports us back to childhood days—the days of the green and gold fairy-tale book! "There were giants in those days." There were wonderful princes who broke the spells cast over beautiful princesses by wicked fairies; there were enchanted castles, thrilling adventures. The fairy tale of life has its giants and its dragons, its good fairies and its wicked fairies, its handsome princes, its beautiful princesses, its enchanted castles, its amazing adventures.

Therefore, what more fitting beginning for the annals of a human life than: "Once upon a time"?

This open sesame carries me back through the centuries across the far-flung sea, Homer's sea, to a land of enchantment and romance—a land where beauty, poetry, learning, culture were the heritage of its people; where lived men who combined the scholar's persistence of purpose with the idealism of the dreamer. They were men and women of courage, of faith, of deep spirituality, who dreamed of a land of hope, a land of promise. My ancestors were men of this caliber. They were victims of the religious fanaticism rampant in Spain. Rather than give up their faith, their religious principles, they preferred to be exiled, to break up their homes and seek freedom and liberty of thought in a new world, even as the Pilgrims did. A new world had been discovered by a Genoese and the Jews of Spain and Portugal eagerly followed in the new path. First they had fled to Holland, then to England, and eventually they came west. They crossed the fearsome sea, and when they reached the little Dutch colony of New Amsterdam they halted their wandering steps.

The basic principle which inspired the Pilgrims to found a colony in the new world was the desire to worship God in their own way, unhampered by restrictions of a state dominated by the church. The basic principle which actuated the Sephardic Jews [1] to leave their homes of comfort and luxury was the same yearning as was felt by the little *Mayflower* band for the free expression of conscience. In addition to this was the longing for civic liberty. In Holland and England they had found religious tolerance, but not complete political freedom.

In contrast to the Pilgrim settlers, the Jewish settlers had no desire to found a colony; their desire was to take an active part in the upbuilding of the civic life and become an integral part of the community. They had been debarred from the full rights of citizenship in the old world; from this unjust restriction, their manhood revolted. In the new world they saw their opportunity to live their religious life side by side with their ideals of citizenship.

Nearly three hundred years have passed since that little band of twenty-three Jews came over on the *St. Charles* in September, 1654, and settled in New Amsterdam. This was only thirty-four years later than the Pilgrims landed from the *Mayflower*. Surely the descendants of these Jewish Pilgrims are entitled to consider themselves one hundred per cent Americans equally with the descendants of the *Mayflower* Pilgrims.

The rights of citizenship sought by the *St. Charles* group were not attained without a struggle, but they came eventually in full measure. Their ideal to become an integral part of the community has been realized. It seemed as

[1] The descendants of the Jews who were expelled from Spain and Portugal.

Grace Seixas Nathan
My paternal great-grandmother.

Simon Nathan
My paternal great-grandfather.

though the old world ghetto had been left behind forever, and that on this new continent no such group barrier would ever be raised. The old ghetto gates were built of stone and iron. Alas, that the centuries have wrought in the new world ghetto gates of prejudice and bigotry!

The Pilgrims established their struggling little colony on Massachusetts Bay; there they built their house of worship immediately after providing themselves with necessary shelter. It was but a few years later that they established a house of learning for their youth.[1]

The Jewish settlers suffered neither from cold or hunger, nor were they obliged to build themselves log cabins, but they, too, felt the necessity for worship. There were only a handful of these Jews, not enough to form a congregation, so the members of the Dutch Reformed Church offered them the hospitality of their house of worship, and here services were conducted until the group was large enough to have its own synagogue.[2] It was the second religious congregation established in New York, the Dutch Reformed being the first.

I have tried, in these few paragraphs, to establish a setting and background for this story. Genealogies are dry reading, even to those directly interested, so for those who wish to dig and delve into the roots of the past, the appendices will provide this opportunity. Here it is only necessary for me to say that my earliest paternal ancestor, of whom I have accurate knowledge, was my great-grandfather, Simon Nathan, who came to New York from Frome, Somersetshire, England (see Appendix I). My father was the next to the youngest of a family of fifteen children. He was named after a close friend of my grandfather's, Robert Weeks of New York. He was an ancestor

1 Harvard University was established in the year 1636.

2 It was in a corner of a grist mill on Beaver Street, near Mill Street (now South William Street), that the congregation Shearith Israel (Remnant of Israel) was organized.

of Robert Weeks de Forest, the late president of the Metropolitan Museum of Fine Arts, who was one of New York's leading citizens.

In my possession is the silver mug which Robert Weeks presented to his namesake, my father, on the day he was named, in 1831. This mug was given to me when I was a baby. My brother, Robert, was older than I, but he had received a new silver cup from his godfather. I, being merely a girl, my father's cup was passed on to me. I remember that as a child I resented the fact that the old battered mug was considered good enough for me, while my two brothers, the one who preceded me and the one who followed me, were each the proud possessor of a shiny new mug, which had been specially bought for him. It was only in later years that I realized that my cup was more valuable and precious than theirs and that there was some compensation, after all, in being merely a girl! I wonder whether this childish feeling of resentment, in being given an old mug while the boys had shiny new ones, was not the germ of that ardent feminism which was to develop and later influence my life.

My maternal great-grandfather was Gershom Seixas,[1] born in New York, January 14, 1745. He was a Rabbi and an ardent patriot. He was among those who protested against taxation without representation, and when the British were about to enter New York he closed the synagogue, rather than fly the British flag. His fellow citizens appreciated his judgment and elected him a trustee of King's College of New York (afterward renamed Columbia College) and he remained on the Board for twenty-eight years. In this connection, it is interesting to note

[1] George Washington had a warm regard for this benign Jewish clergyman, and extended to him an invitation to his inaugural ceremonies in New York, 1789, together with thirteen other clergymen. At these inaugural ceremonies, Rev. Gershom Mendes Seixas offered a prayer invoking God's blessing upon the First President, and upon the new nation. He died in New York, in 1816.

that Rabbi Seixas' great-granddaughter, my sister Annie Nathan Meyer, is a trustee of Barnard College, affiliated with Columbia University. And indeed it was she who started the movement to found this college for women. The family tradition has been further emphasized by the election of Judge Benjamin Nathan Cardozo, former Chief Justice of the Court of Appeals of New York State and at present a Justice of the Supreme Court of the United States, as trustee of Columbia University—Judge Cardozo being a great-great-nephew of Rabbi Seixas.

My maternal grandmother, Myrtilla Seixas,[1] married William Florance of New Orleans. Later the family moved to Philadelphia, their home being on Rittenhouse Square. This house must have been a fine old mansion from the description given in a book published recently of old Philadelphia homes.[2]

From the slight genealogical data I have given in the Appendix it will be readily seen that my father and mother had a mutual ancestor—Abraham Mendes Seixas.[3] So it was natural that when as a young man my father went to Philadelphia on business, he was cordially received by his cousins on Rittenhouse Square. In these days of which I am writing—the days of once upon a time—it was considered more decorous for the daughters of a family to marry according to age, the eldest first, and so on down the line. If there were many daughters, the younger ones felt aggrieved if their older sisters did not marry without delay and so give them a chance. This may account for the extremely early marriages made by our mothers and grandmothers.

My mother's older sister had married a Charlestonian; it behooved my mother, therefore, to follow her example and make way for the youngest sister. So it was fortunate

1 The daughter of Gershom Mendes Seixas and Hannah Manuel.
2 *Rittenhouse Square, Past and Present,* by Charles J. Cohen.
3 His will is given in Appendix II.

that just at this time the handsome, debonair young cousin from New York came into her life. They fell in love, and although she was only seventeen she became his bride in January, 1857, and left Philadelphia for her New York home. This home was in West Fifteenth Street, which was then a fashionable neighborhood. There was born, almost two years later, their first child.

Even as early as 1860 the inherent progressiveness and restlessness of New York was shown by the upward trend of business and the forcing of the residential district farther and farther north. No better illustration can be found than the following incident: About the year 1835, when my father's eldest sister required a change of air, she was sent from the family home on Crosby Street way up to the country—the locality that we now know as Twenty-ninth Street.

My parents left the Fifteenth Street home and moved to West Twenty-first Street, where I was born on October 20, 1862.

I have no recollection of this, my first home, because we moved from there when I was only two years old. So that my first recollection of a New York home is the house that was known as 6 West Thirty-sixth Street—the first house west of Fifth Avenue. Here I had my three-year-old birthday party and here came into my life the wonder of a baby brother and later of a baby sister. How could one forget a home which held such epochal memories!

At the southwest corner of Thirty-sixth Street and Fifth Avenue was "Barmore's," the fashionable caterer of that day. The building was considered quite wonderful at that time, because it combined a hotel, restaurant, confectionery shop, and ice-cream parlor. There were windows in some of the apartments facing west and overlooking the small court which separated the building from our house. We, too, had two windows on this court, facing east: one on the second floor and one on the third floor.

Rabbi Gershom Mendes Seixas

My maternal great-grandfather.

His portrait hangs in Columbia University, with those of other former trustees.

Seixas Nathan

My paternal grandfather.

One day, my mother found a plank placed across the narrow court, one end resting on our third-story window sill, the other on the window sill of the opposite apartment. She discovered it just in time to prevent me from crawling across the plank on a "dare." My older brother and an opposite neighbor, Harry Fanshawe, had, at great trouble and with great difficulty, procured the board and had placed it there because they had made a wager that I would not dare play acrobat with them and go across the dangerous plank. Never have I been able to resist the temptation of accepting a "dare."

Some venturesome, indiscreet imp has always urged me on, even to the brink of folly, when suggestion has been put in the form of a "dare." Analyzing this incident in the light of mature self-knowledge, I realize that this trait has been an impelling force to urge me forward. The childish taunt, "You daren't do what I've done," has always made me feel: "What others have done, I too can do."

Another story comes to my mind in connection with my inability to refuse a "dare." When about five years old, my playmates, my older brother and his chum, Harry Fanshawe, having jumped four steps of our brownstone stoop, dared me to follow. Nothing daunted, I poised with a sinking heart on that fearfully precipitous height of four high brownstone steps and gave a glance at the flagstones that seemed at an abysmal depth. I jumped—result, a severe sprained ankle and torn ligaments producing a weakness which has hampered me all my life. Moreover, this unfortunate incident was the cause of great humiliation and mortification, for I was unable to walk for some time and my mother sent me out in my little sister's baby carriage, which according to her ideas was making the punishment fit the crime. If I behaved like a baby, I must be treated as one. She lost sight of the psychology involved, for I can still feel the sting of shame at being demoted in the eyes of my playmates. Years later this ankle again caused me a mortification which was ludicrous in spite of my discomfort. I turned my foot on my way to market one morning and was forced to sit down suddenly in the middle of the sidewalk. The street was thronged with passers-by, but I, in my extraordinary attitude and disheveled appearance, only provoked disgust, rather than sympathy. The women pulled their skirts aside and carefully avoided me. The men looked amused, even interested, but did not offer any assistance. It was evident that I was taken for a drunken woman, and drunk very early in the morning.

The years of childhood unfold themselves in my memories, marked here and there by certain poignant recollections which stand out more vividly than others. Is this because the impressions made by incidents were prophetic of later development of character? Could my childish mind have been puzzled over the problems of class distinction and the status of working women at such an early age? Was it pondering over these that makes the following incidents seem so vivid in my memory?

One evening my father, who was an excellent whist player, had invited a few friends to the house for a game of whist. My mother, who never played cards, suggested calling to see a friend who lived in the neighborhood. My father demurred at her going out alone even at dusk and offered to leave his game to escort her. To this my mother would not consent, but said she would take one of the maids with her, and let her call for her again. With childish curiosity, I asked my mother why she couldn't go out alone. Was she afraid? She was too big to need a nurse to accompany her! She explained that some rude man might insult her if she walked alone at night. The maid who escorted my mother was young and pretty. Why was there no danger of *her* being insulted? She was permitted to return alone and go out alone at a later hour to call for my mother. I pondered over this and found no solution to the vexing problem.

On another occasion my parents, having decided to take a little holiday and visit Niagara Falls, considered the desirability of taking the two older children with them. My brother jumped at the suggestion and was overjoyed at the prospect of the adventure. I, too, was delighted to learn that I was to be included in the party. However, when I was told that my nurse, Margaret (who had been with me from birth and was my foster-mother), would not be asked to go, I loyally declined to leave her. "If Mammy's not invited, I'll stay home with her!" That was my decision. What would "Mammy" do without me? She would be so lonely! And besides, it did not seem fair, in my youthful opinion, not to let her, too, see the wonders of Niagara. So I remained at home and it was not until I was fifteen years of age that I had the privilege of beholding that marvelous waterfall.

We always said our prayers at night at our mother's knee. These prayers were said partly in Hebrew and partly in English. When my mother and father were going out to dinner, we said our prayers a little earlier. When my parents went to Niagara Falls without me, I said my prayers to "Mammy." It was then that I missed my mother most. I missed her maternal blessing; she always placed her hand gently on my head and blessed me; then she always embraced me tenderly, while I, with my arms clasped around her neck, would hug her closely. My mother was a beautiful and brilliant woman. I know she was the recipient of much genuine admiration, but I doubt whether she ever had any greater admirer than her own little daughter. I was a very proud little girl of five years of age the Saturday that my mother took me for the first time to Sabbath service at the synagogue. The building at that time was on Nineteenth Street, just west of Fifth Avenue. We were brought up to keep the Sabbath day holy, according to the literal rendering of the Commandments. Therefore, we walked to and fro, in order that no horse should be compelled to work for us. I was dressed in my blue Irish poplin dress (a dress which has become historically important in my memory, because I also wore it to my first matinée: *The Black Crook*).

In our orthodox synagogue, the women according to oriental custom, are relegated to the gallery, while the men sit below. My mother and I toiled up the high flights of stairs and I was told to sit on the steps of the aisle, next to my mother's seat. And here my memories carry me twenty-three years ahead of my story when I took my own little girl to synagogue for the first time.

My little girl was following with rapt attention the same service I had followed so many years before. She sat on the steps of the aisle right next to me, and as I watched her, it seemed as though I were looking at myself and living through once more my childish experiences. After my little girl's first service, we lunched with an aunt who asked the child how she liked "shule." [1] My little daughter replied, "Oh, it was very nice, but I like the circus better."

To go back to my own childhood impressions, I was much interested in watching the services conducted by Rabbi Lyons, my aunt's husband (who was Rabbi over a period of fifty years), dressed in his long black gown, with a wide "talith" (praying shawl) over his shoulders and a high silk hat on his head. The chanting in Hebrew was melodious and I was able, in my childish piping voice, to join in the singing of the familiar hymns. After service, the boys, who sat below with the men, were blessed by their fathers and by the Rabbi. Then we all met in the vestibule and Sabbath greetings were exchanged. The most interesting synagogue service for us children was that of "Succoth," when the annual celebration of the harvest

[1] The customary Jewish term for synagogue.

occurs. This harvest festival of thanksgiving antedates by many centuries the New England Thanksgiving festival. In memory of the days of the Exodus, when the children of Israel dwelt in booths, a booth is erected in the court between the synagogue and the vestry house, decorated with foliage, flowers, and the fruits of the harvest.

A short service in this booth follows the regular service in the synagogue and the participants break bread, eat olives and fruit, and drink the juice of the grape—this wine being sent from Palestine. How well I remember my impatience at being obliged to sit through the long service in the synagogue, with the many repetitions of prayers and the slow, measured responses in Hebrew, when I was anxious to get into the fairylike booth fragrant with flowers and heavily scented with luscious fruit. The bread—small twisted crisp rolls, covered with poppy seeds —always tasted better than any bread served at home. The olives were more juicy and the Palestinian wine had a flavor all its own. It was only at Succoth and Passover seasons that we children were permitted to sip wine and it was nectar to us.

The Passover service was distinctly a home ceremony. We invariably held the "Hagodah" [1] service on the eve of the holy day in our own dining room. My father would chant the prayers in Hebrew and we all made the responses together and sang the hymns and psalms in unison. This home service was specially adapted for children. There were questions which the oldest son and the youngest son were supposed to ask their father, and his replies explained all the symbols used.

The "matzoths"—the unleavened bread—which we ate during Passover were, to us children, the most delicate and appetizing of all crackers. It was no hardship for us to be denied bread through Passover week. We often begged to be allowed to continue substituting matzoths for bread

1 A memorial service symbolic of the Exodus from Egypt.

after the week had passed. The only hardship for us lay in the fact that Good Friday usually fell in Passover week, so we could not eat the hot cross buns which our playmates ate with so much gusto.

There were other hardships which seemed to differentiate us from our little playmates. My mother was very strict as to Sabbath observance; we were not allowed to attend parties on a Friday night (our Sabbath Eve) or go to matinées on a Saturday. These deprivations may have strengthened our characters, but they were a great source of annoyance at the time. For all our companions, outside of the large family circle of cousins, were Christians. The small group of Sephardic Jews who had settled in the United States in the seventeenth and eighteenth centuries had intermarried from generation to generation, because they did not wish to give up their faith. But the business and social fabric of their lives had been interwoven with their Christian neighbors—as they had hoped for—and their friendly intercourse was but natural. They were actively participating in the civic and national life and had become a strong power in the community.

On Sunday mornings, my older brother and I were sent to Sunday school, where we were taught the history and principles of our religion and were also taught to read Hebrew. All this training in Jewish ritual, Jewish principles, and Jewish traditions has formed the background of my spiritual life. I can well remember how irksome at that time seemed these religious observances. The long walk back and forth from synagogue, instead of riding, the being debarred from social functions other than family gatherings on Friday nights and Saturdays; the insistence upon the rigidity of certain dietary laws, all seemed to me, at the time, so unnecessary. I longed to live the same life as my playmates. Although I secretly resented these little things, which made me seem different in the eyes of my playmates, it never occurred to me to rebel. In this feeling of resentment I can now see the sense of group consciousness, the desire to be part of the dominant group, rather than of the minority group. I felt particularly resentful because we were debarred from joining in the festivities of Christmas and Easter.

We children not only learned the traditions and principles of our own religion, but we were also taught to respect the customs and conventions of other religions. We were not permitted to practice our exercises on the piano on Sundays—out of consideration for our neighbors. In the country we were not permitted to play croquet on Sundays.

In the light of the present, I can now appreciate the value of this training. If I have been able to express in my life, standards, ideals, a code of ethics, that have spelled helpfulness to others, has it not been because the roots were laid in a distinctive religious background? Does it make any difference whether our youth have, as a religious background, Jewish principles, Christian principles, or the principles of any of the great religions of the East? Is not the essential thing that they have a real spiritual background upon which to build character? It is possible to be moral, ethical, without having a spiritual background; but mere morals, and a code of ethics, cannot, by themselves, develop a certain fineness of feeling, the lack of which is felt by those who have spiritual tentacles.

It was the custom in those days for New Yorkers to stroll up and down Fifth Avenue after church, displaying their best hats, clothes, and manners before going home to a two o'clock Sunday dinner.

We children, returning from our Sunday school in Nineteenth Street, would join our companions as they came from their fashionable churches on the Avenue. Fifth Avenue was the promenade par excellence not only on Sundays, but on every day of the week. Our daily walks with our nurse were on Fifth Avenue. Occasionally we went as far north as Central Park, when we took sandwiches with us for refreshment, lest we return home late for supper. Sometimes we walked down as far as the Fifth Avenue Hotel at Twenty-third Street. Here we were allowed to rest a short time—in the lobby of this, to our eyes, magnificent hotel.

In our daily peregrinations we occasionally stopped to play hide-and-seek around the huge blocks of stone which were lying loosely in front of St. Patrick's Cathedral, then in the course of construction—sometimes carrying home in triumph a wonderful chip of marble as a memento. There were no lordly traffic officers in the middle of the highway, but an occasional friendly policeman on his beat would courteously escort the timid across the Avenue—much narrower then than now—but considered even at that time a crowded thoroughfare. One of our favorite walks was around the top of the reservoir which flanked Fifth Avenue from Fortieth to Forty-second Streets, now the site of the New York Public Library. After that perilous and fatiguing journey, we would sit and rest in the Forty-second Street park, back of the reservoir, now called Bryant Park. It was in this same park, many years later, that I participated in the ceremony of unveiling a fountain dedicated to the memory of my dear friend, Josephine Shaw Lowell.

Opposite the reservoir on Fifth Avenue was a block of houses, different from any I had ever seen. They had turrets and battlements and didn't resemble in the least the typical New York brownstone houses. I didn't know at the time that they were reminiscent of Tudor architecture. I only knew that they held for me a charm and mystery quite inexplicable. In one of this row of houses lived "the Widow Chase," a well-known New York character who—in those days—was considered very wealthy. Little did I think at that time that her granddaughter would call me "Aunt Maud." She married my nephew and has endeared herself greatly to me. Rutgers Institute, a school for girls, was in the center of the block—and because of the fascinating exterior—I wanted to attend that school. But it was considered too far from home, so I was sent to one on Thirty-eighth Street, west of Fifth Avenue, presided over by Mrs. Ogden Hoffman and her two daughters. I was very proud of being allowed at the age of seven to walk two blocks alone.

I had learned to lisp my alphabet, and to read and write, at my mother's side, and it was with some trepidation that I went forth from her protecting wing to study in a classroom. However, several of my playmates on Thirty-sixth Street attended this fashionable school. I remember Minnie Saulsbury, afterwards Mrs. William Read, and Minnie Fraser, who later married Rev. Dr. Thompson, the rector of the Episcopal church at Greenwich, Conn. Other schoolmates were Alva, Jenny, and Mimi Smith—later, respectively, Mrs. O. H. P. Belmont, Mrs. Perry Tiffany, and La Marquise de Fontenilliat; the Sutton girls, the Secor girls, the Hoyts, the Van Aukens, and the Gilbert sisters of Gilbertsville, New York.

While we were living at 6 West Thirty-sixth Street, I was considered by my schoolmates socially correct, but after we moved to 307 West Forty-sixth Street, west of Eighth Avenue, I was regarded as being outside the social pale! I can recall how the girls lifted their eyebrows superciliously and tilted their noses. Human nature is always the same. New Yorkers still catalogue their acquaintances according to the localities of their homes. An intellectual giant might live in oblivion on Third Avenue. Whereas a wealthy nincompoop living on Park Avenue would have her daily doings chronicled in the newspapers and all the world flocking to her teas!

Mrs. Hoffman and her daughters were much loved by their pupils and it was with a pang of dismay that after two years we found the school was to be taken over by

Mme. de Silva and Mrs. Bradford. Schoolgirls have a tendency to be hero worshipers and I soon found my affections transferred from the dignified and sympathetic Miss Virginia Hoffman to that delightful French lady (literally of the old school), Mme. de Silva, and to her charming daughter, Olio, who was my playmate. Mrs. Bradford's daughter, Clara, was in our class, too, so we felt we could always get favors through the daughters of the principals.

My next school was Gardiner Institute. Imbued as I was with the spirit of New York's social directory, I felt that I was progressing, since the new school was on Fifth Avenue! No one who did not live in New York in the eighteen-seventies can realize the magic that lay in those two words: Fifth Avenue. At that time, no shopkeeper had dared to desecrate the dignity of those rows of "brownstone fronts." Those who were known and those who wished to be known walked up and down that thoroughfare. The leaders of society drove in their coupés and victorias. Occasionally a coach and four passed up the Avenue on its way to Central Park or to Jerome Park. The equipages rolled down leisurely of an evening to the Academy of Music, Irving Place, where opera was given, or to Daly's or Wallack's Theaters on Broadway. Afterward these carriages might be found outside of Delmonico's on Fourteenth Street, where friends would meet for a champagne supper and for friendly greetings.

My brother and I were sent to Dodworth's dancing school. I inherited my love of dancing from my mother. At the age of three I was dancing fancy dances. These I danced sometimes with my brother as partner, and sometimes with a golden-haired, blue-eyed little boy named Willie Taylor. Willie was my first beau! I liked his blond type and in those days some little gentlemen preferred brunettes. At home when the family wanted to see me blush, they only had to tease me about my beau, Willie.

Thirty-three years later when, as President of the Consumers' League of New York, I sent my annual report to the Department of Economics of the various universities, I received a long communication from Prof. W. Langworthy Taylor, Department of Economics, Nebraska University, acknowledging the receipt of the report and also asking me whether I recalled dancing with him at Dodworth's and Hlasko's dancing schools in New York. Charlie Rushmore was another of my favorite dancing partners and many years later we happened to sit together at a dinner and enjoyed a reminiscent talk of our childhood days.

Every child dreams of her future. In my early childhood, I was undecided whether to be a second Casabianca, or be a world-renowned cantatrice. All through my life these two figures have stood as symbols of a dual nature. They have remained in my subconscious mind, the one dominating me to perform acts of sacrifice, the other urging me on to a broad rich life through which I could make my influence felt. These two points of view hold the eternal question so well expressed by Henri Frederic Amiel in his journal: "I wish to fulfill my duty—but where is it, what is it? Here inclination comes in again and interprets the oracle and the ultimate question is this: Does duty consist in obeying one's nature, even the best and most spiritual? Or in conquering it? Life, is it essentially the education of the mind and intelligence, or that of the will? And does will show itself in strength or in resignation?"

# CHAPTER II

## GIRLHOOD DAYS—LIFE IN A MIDDLE WEST TOWN

When I was twelve years of age, my father, having met with business reverses, decided to leave New York, and accepted a position as General Passenger Agent of a small railroad in the Middle West, with its headquarters in Green Bay, Wisconsin. He had been a member of the New York Stock Exchange and upon leaving the city, he sold his seat for about $10,000. It is a significant comment upon the difference between the financial standards of fifty years ago and today, when $625,000 was paid for a seat a few years ago.

The excitement incident upon moving our "lares et penates," making the long journey, finding a new home, making new acquaintances, and going to a new school in an entirely new environment was a wonderful adventure for us children. We could not understand why our mother seemed so depressed and unhappy at the thought of leaving New York. We were unable to realize the situation from her point of view. She was to be suddenly transplanted from her accustomed New York milieu, where she had been the center of a brilliant literary and musical coterie, to an obscure village life, surrounded by strangers who would look at her askance, as though she were from another world, and with whom she would have no interests in common. I speak of her circle having been literary and musical, because my mother had the faculty of drawing literary lights about her. As a girl she had written charming verses, and it is amusing to remember that in those days it was not considered modest for a young lady to have her name appear in print. So, when some of her poems were published in the Philadelphia paper, they were signed by a male friend of the family who had chivalrously allowed his name to be appropriated for this purpose! My father had a particularly sweet, rich baritone voice and often sang duets with well-known sopranos and contraltos, both amateur and professional; my mother frequently playing the accompaniments. I recall many musical evenings at our New York home where professionals and amateurs mingled with a certain feeling of camaraderie, that was not often found at that time. I also recall that Edmund Yates, the English author, Clara Morris, the tragedienne, A. M. Palmer, the well-known theatrical producer, and his handsome wife, and Mrs. Barrymore, mother of the popular actors, were visitors at our home. This Bohemian atmosphere did not prevent society leaders from sharing our hospitality. My father was a member of the Union Club, and his friend, "Willie" Wharton, and his wife, were among the guests; also the Travers brothers, the Remsens, the Schuylers, the Johnsons, the Mulocks, the Van Burens, Paul du Chaillu, the Van Rensselaers, Mr. and Mrs. "Winnie" Grey, as well as "Buck" (J. Buchanan) Houston and his wife. These are a few of the well-known names that come to me from a hazy past.

My older brother and I were sometimes allowed to greet our parents' guests and remain a short time in the drawing room or foyer hall to listen to the music. On one occasion we were upstairs, dressed and impatiently waiting to be sent for; when the message finally came, we were so eager to get to the party that we went down the stairs, hand-in-hand, too rapidly, with the result that we fell with a crash and our screams and yells resounded through the house. Because of this misbehavior, we were punished by being sent upstairs again at once, and we were obliged to go to bed without ever having a glimpse of the guests or, much worse, a taste of the party: the ice cream.

My mother's literary taste led her to write plays, as well as verses, and she had decided dramatic ability. She belonged to a club of amateur actors and often took the leading part in theatrical performances given for the benefit of some philanthropic organization. When my father lost his money, my mother was prevailed upon to present an original play and take the leading part herself. Her friends encouraged her and came nobly to her assistance. The play was given at Terrace Garden. Although I was only twelve years of age, I was very tall and precocious for my age and I begged my mother to allow me to act the rôle of the soubrette, a very small part. There were not many lines to memorize, but I was alone on the stage when the curtain rose, and it was a very terrifying moment—the opening night of the performance. The play was repeated once or twice and I believe my mother netted a sum large enough to help pay part of our traveling expenses.

From this cosmopolitan atmosphere, my mother was exiled—saddened by my father's wild speculations in Wall Street, which had been the cause of his financial downfall. She was also full of forebodings for the future of her children.

Up to this time I had traveled very little, so that the railroad trip, which included night travel, was the first journey of my life. Since then I have traveled far and wide to many distant lands and have seen many strange sights. But that first journey from New York to the little western town of Green Bay had in it the thrill of the explorer. I was going into a new world, a new home, a new school, and was to meet new friends. What would I find? What would it all mean? Oh, the contrast between the happy, eager expectant child and the heavy-hearted mother! As I watched the swiftly passing scenery from the car window, my mother, rousing herself from her depression, said: "Now we have said good-by to New York. We are already in another State—this is Connecticut." "No, Mamma," I quickly retorted, "I've been carefully watching for the red border line and I haven't seen it yet!" Such a remark would have been impossible today even from a child much younger than I was. For today, atlases which stress political divisions do not form the main feature of a child's lessons in geography, as they did in my day.

My parents found, in Green Bay, a frame house in a desirable neighborhood, and after adding a wing, it housed not only the family comfortably, but also our Chickering concert grand piano, which my mother had shipped out there, being unwilling to sell it. An amusing incident is connected with that piano. When it arrived, my mother called at the only music store in the village and asked to have three men sent to the house to put the piano in our music room. She emphasized the fact that three men would be necessary as it was a grand piano. Later on, two men called and said they thought they could manage it. However, when they saw the size and shape of the piano, they threw up their hands. My mother said: "I told you it was a *grand* piano." "Yes," they said, "we know you did. We've handled many a grand piano, but never one of that *shape!*" They had supposed that my mother was merely boasting of the quality of the piano!

The freer life of the small western village suited the buoyant spirits of us children. Life out there was far different from the conventional and prosaic life we had led in New York. There were no pangs of regret for us and we could not understand our mother's sad eyes and continued depression.

As soon as we were settled in our new home, a school had to be found for the children. This was a very easy matter, not involving the problematic element of choice, as there were no private schools and the children all attended the one public school. My older brother and I entered the high school, the younger children went to the grammar school in the same building. I experienced the first great contrast to my New York school life on my first school day. It was strange to walk to school with my brother, to have him enter the same building with me, but to find that we were to sit in the same classroom was bewildering. And strangest of all was, that it all appeared to be perfectly natural, simple, and matter of course to the people among whom we were living. It took me a little time to adjust my mind to this new condition. It was a startling experience for a little girl who had attended a fashionable, conventional New York private school "for young ladies." After I became accustomed to the new order I thoroughly enjoyed it. The boys sat on one side of the schoolroom and the girls on the other, and many a roguish glance was sent across that center aisle which separated us. The girls far exceeded the boys in number, as most of the boys at that time were sent to work as soon as they had completed their grammar school course. The girls, however, were kept at home to assist with household work, and this they were able to do after school hours. Therefore, most of them had the privilege of a few extra years of education. Few professions were open to women; some of the girl graduates became teachers, some became saleswomen. One girl was considered quite audacious because she wanted to learn to paint and went alone to New York to pursue her studies at the Art League. I found it quite stimulating to be taught by a man, instead of by women. In New York, not only had my teachers been women, but the principals of the schools were also women.

In Green Bay, Professor Briggs, a dignified, rather severe looking Scotchman (in spite of the twinkle in his eye), was principal and also taught some of the higher classes.

Annie Florance Nathan

My mother, née Annie Augusta Florance.

The parents of the first white child born in Augusta, Georgia, were named Florance, no doubt my mother's ancestors. Hence the middle name.

Robert Weeks Nathan

My father.

Named after his father's friend, Robert Weeks, an ancestor of Robert Weeks De Forest.

Reproduced by Hollinger, from old daguerreotypes.

I also found it stimulating to compete with boys as well as with other girls. In our debates and spelling bees, the girls were often pitted against the boys and our delight at winning was increased a hundredfold, because our triumph seemed to vindicate our belief in the equality and perhaps even the superiority of our sex! At least it prevented us from having an inferiority complex. In this connection I well remember how Professor Briggs, in giving out the Latin lesson for the following day, warned us that the declension of "hic, hæc, hoc" would be difficult to memorize, and that probably no one would be able to repeat it accurately. Here was the old-time challenge —the dare—that I had never been able to resist. I learned to recite the declension of "hic, hæc, hoc" so glibly that I have never forgotten it. Other lessons of far greater importance have been consigned to oblivion.

The curriculum was different from that which had been in vogue at the private schools I had attended in New York. There, I had studied French and rhetoric, and had been given a cultural smattering. In Green Bay, the only language taught was Latin and we were grounded in mathematics. We made an intensive study of local geography and history. We were able to draw the map of Wisconsin with our eyes closed, but we knew little or nothing of the Greek archipelago, of the French renaissance, or the history of the Medici. Moreover, we were taught the fundamentals of the Constitution of the United States, which in a young lady's school in the East had been deemed entirely unnecessary, since girls would never become citizens and, therefore, did not need to cumber their minds with these non-essentials!

At this time, the vote had already been granted to women in Wyoming. Therefore, it did not seem such a distant goal to the women of Wisconsin. In the East, however, the women had not yet felt the stirring of the new spirit; that is, with the exception of that small historic band of pioneers who met in 1848 in Seneca Falls, New York, to demand their rights.

Little did I dream in those days of co-educational classes that my latent feminism was being developed in a way which would lead me to participate in the Fiftieth Anniversary celebration of the Seneca Falls reunion.

One feature of co-education appealed very strongly to me; this was the freedom that resulted in regard to social relationship. When school was over, the boys took the girls home in their sleighs—perhaps taking them for a sleigh ride first—or they walked home with them, chivalrously carrying their books for them. These girls and boys, having been brought up together from babyhood, naturally called each other by their Christian names. My parents were shocked to find that I was sharing in this familiarity. They thought that the boys ought to call me "Miss Maud," and that I should address them by their surnames. The traditions of our former New York social life continued to be the standards for my parents. But for us children, these traditions ceased to exist. They had been left behind in New York, with many another hampering convention of daily life, such as daily walks with a nurse, being waited upon by servants, formal visits to aunts and uncles, and supper in the nursery when there were dinner parties.

In Green Bay, my parents' hospitable spirit was shown by occasionally inviting their new acquaintances to dinner. These dinner parties, however, were quite different from the formal New York functions. We children, instead of being relegated to the nursery, formed part of the company at the table. One of my mother's greatest trials was her difficulty in securing servants. The only ones available were the daughters of well-to-do farmers who would condescend to be "helpers" but resented being called servants. They expected to be treated as members of the family circle and to sit with the family at meal time. This condition my mother, with her New York traditions and southern background, refused to comply with. But when she found that she would have a cookless kitchen unless she could effect a compromise, she yielded to the extent of permitting the maid to eat in the dining room after she had served the family.

One of the great joys of our new life was the fact that we were permitted to have dogs as pets. They, instead of nurses, were our companions on our walks. Instead of being obliged to walk miles past stereotyped brownstone houses to reach the trees and grass and open spaces of Central Park, we would swing our gate behind us, walk at once under trees, up hill and down dale, taking our sleds with us when there was snow on the ground.

I was graduated from the high school two years after my entrance, at the age of fourteen and a half years—an age much lower than any of my classmates. My older brother had been graduated a year ahead of me. Thanks to my facile memory, I passed one hundred per cent in all my examinations and stood with five other girls at the head of our large class. Again my feminism—I remember the great glee I felt that none of the boys in the class stood so high. Many of the girls made their own dresses for graduation day. I was never an adept with my needle, but my mother insisted that I learn to sew and I was obliged to assist the seamstress with my dress. We all wore white. As the day approached, I was greatly excited. The graduation exercises were to be held in the large public hall where the concerts, theatrical performances, and dances were held. I was selected as salutatorian and read my essay to the large audience. The title was "Awake, 'tis day!" Recently, in looking over a box full of old papers, I came across this girlish essay. I reread it with interest, for in spite of its flamboyant style and the youthfulness of its diction, I felt in it that call to action which has been a strong urge all through my life—overcoming in a measure my natural tendency to inertia. Senator Howe of Wisconsin, who was at one time Postmaster General, was asked to address the class and give us our diplomas. It seemed a terrible ordeal to walk across the stage, receive the parchment,—tied with white ribbon,—curtsey gracefully, and return to my seat. Often in later years, when facing a large audience, about to give an address, the picture of that frightened little high-school girl would flash before my eyes, and the contrast between the past and the present would help me to the desired poise.

I was truly sorry when my happy school days were over. Yet I was thrilled at the thought that now I was considered a "young lady in society." There was no thought of a college career, for my mother had very decided views in regard to colleges for girls. She always contended that as the daughter grew older the more she needed the constant care and devotion of her mother. In her opinion, a mother's brooding care and the exchange of daily confidences were essential to the sympathetic relationship that ought to exist between mother and daughter. When a girl was sent to college, my mother felt it was a sure sign that the girl's mother had lost control over her and had felt it necessary for her daughter to be disciplined by college life. It is difficult to conceive that such opinions could have been held only sixty years ago. My mother was considered a broad-minded woman, but in these views she was merely reflecting the opinion of the women of her class at that time. But few girls went to college in those days and nothing can better emphasize the difference between the then and the now than the fact that today it is as natural to ask a young woman from what college she had been graduated as to make inquiries as to her brother's alma mater.

So for me, my education was finished at fourteen and a half years! Of course, I took piano lessons and later singing lessons. I also read history, literature, and French with my mother, in order to round out a cultural outlook. The French reading was the beginning of my love for the language. Later, when I found myself in France, it took me little or no time to become accustomed to the rapid speech of the French people and to acquire the accent and a certain proficiency which much practice through the years has developed, and has been a great source of pleasure.

It is interesting to compare the attitude of mind of those days with the present-day attitude in regard to a young girl entering business or a profession. Although my father was by no means in affluent circumstances, and although my mother found it necessary to economize in many ways, there was no thought or suggestion of my adding to the family income by taking a position. I was permitted to assume certain domestic duties and to take charge of the pantry and keep the pantry key, much to the disgust of my younger brother and sister who preferred the pantry door ajar, so they could pilfer cookies. They rebelled at the thought that I had free access to the shelves, while they had to cajole me in order to snatch a stolen bite between meals. Where, today, would we find a housekeeper with her bunch of keys or the traditional key basket? I was taught to cook and to sew and was sent twice a week to a convent to learn to embroider.

As I was no longer a schoolgirl, I was allowed to go on boating parties, sleigh rides, and dances with the older circle. Though only fifteen, I looked much older. I was permitted to "put up" my hair and to wear a "train." What a contrast to present-day styles, when the older I grow the more abbreviated become my skirts, and the grandmother of today instead of decorously wearing her hair smoothed out under her cap, proudly shows her bobbed hair!

There was a choral society in Green Bay which gave

public concerts on special occasions. I was a member and enjoyed both the rehearsals and the concerts. Private theatricals were greatly in vogue, and taking part in these performances gave me much pleasure. One rather amusing incident stands out in my memory: An attractive Englishman was given the rôle of an ardent lover, who in one scene was to bribe me—a soubrette—to carry a missive to his lady-love, my mistress. During the rehearsals he bestowed a very proper "stage" kiss upon my cheek. Since there is no such thing as a "stage" kiss today, perhaps I had better explain its definition. A "stage" kiss was one that was really given in the air and did not touch the face of the recipient. The Englishman warned me, however, that on the night of the performance, he intended to be more realistic. I begged and entreated him not to give me a real kiss, for I feared my mother would blame me for having permitted him to take this liberty, and would bar me from taking part in future performances. He refused to believe this, however, and yielded to the temptation of teasing me and carrying out his threat. I, too, gave the scene a more realistic turn by giving the surprised man a genuine, sharp slap on the face, which was so unexpected (not being part of the action in the play) that our acting in consequence was hugely applauded.

Occasionally an operatic or theatrical "troupe" came to the town and then the attendance was general and was made a gala occasion. I remember that my mother entertained the leading singers of one opera company and it was a great social event. They sang for us in our large music room, which had the distinction of containing the only grand piano in town. The leading tenor of the company was Charles Clark. He was young, good-looking and had a sweet voice. I lost my susceptible girlish heart to him at once. The fact that his wife accompanied him and was the leading soprano did not in the least interfere with my aspiration to join the company and eventually elope with him. That he looked upon me as a mere child, my pride refused to allow me to believe. He gave me a kiss, upon leaving, and that seemed sufficient proof to my mind that he reciprocated my ardent passion. In after years, I met him and his wife many a time in New York musical circles, and we discussed with much merriment my early impressions and ambitions.

At a time when moving pictures were unknown, even a temperance lecture was considered a form of entertainment. One of the lecturers who placed Green Bay on his schedule was John B. Gough, the well-known temperance lecturer. Although I was not feeling very well, I did not want to miss anything in the line of entertainment, so I begged my mother to allow me to join a party which had reserved seats for that evening. The hall was very warm and lacked proper ventilation. In the midst of the lecture, I suddenly fainted and was carried to an anteroom. While the lecturer was exhorting his audience never to touch a drop of liquor even under the guise of medicine, brandy—quickly secured from a nearby saloon—was being poured down my throat, with the purpose of reviving me. Perhaps this incident explains why I have never been a prohibitionist!

There was no synagogue in Green Bay. The only Jewish family with which we came in contact attended the Presbyterian church, and in spite of their marked Jewish features they disavowed their Judaism. This was a shock to us. We had always been brought up to be proud of our ancestry and of our religious background. We frankly spoke of our Sabbath and our family prayers at home. My mother expected us to remain at home on Friday evenings, and many a dance or boating excursion was changed from a Friday evening to a Saturday evening in order that my brother and I could join the party. For on Friday evenings—the Sabbath eve—my mother lighted the Sabbath candles at sunset and repeated the Sabbath blessing. My little sister, being the youngest, was permitted to blow out the match, which was done with much unction and fervor. Then at supper we had "grace before meat" and after the meal we grouped ourselves around our mother while we all took turns in reading a portion of the Sabbath evening service.

The little town, so far as I could judge, was entirely free from any spirit of intolerance. We stood alone as the only Jewish family in the town. Yet we were made part of the communal life and the difference between our religious backgrounds was never stressed. I dwell upon these friendly social relations because of an incident which occurred in New York in later life. One of my schoolgirl friends married and came to New York to live. Her husband had inherited a fortune and she found herself the chatelaine of a Fifth Avenue mansion and a Tuxedo estate. At first she was delighted to renew the acquaintance with me—her old-time school friend—and visits and hospitalities were exchanged. However, it was not long before she came under the influence of New York's growing anti-semitism. Our former intimacy gradually assumed more formal relations.

As I look back, I can understand one of the causes of my mother's unhappiness in the Green Bay life. She was an ardent Jewess. She had instilled in her children the principles and traditions of their faith. She looked forward to seeing them marry and carry on these traditions into future generations. Obviously there would be no opportunity for these hopes to be realized in the Green Bay setting, and she must have dreaded lest her children marry outside their faith.

Yet my mother was very liberal in spirit. She encouraged us to go with our neighbors and friends occasionally to the Presbyterian church, where we could listen to a sermon and hear the hymns sung. She had confidence

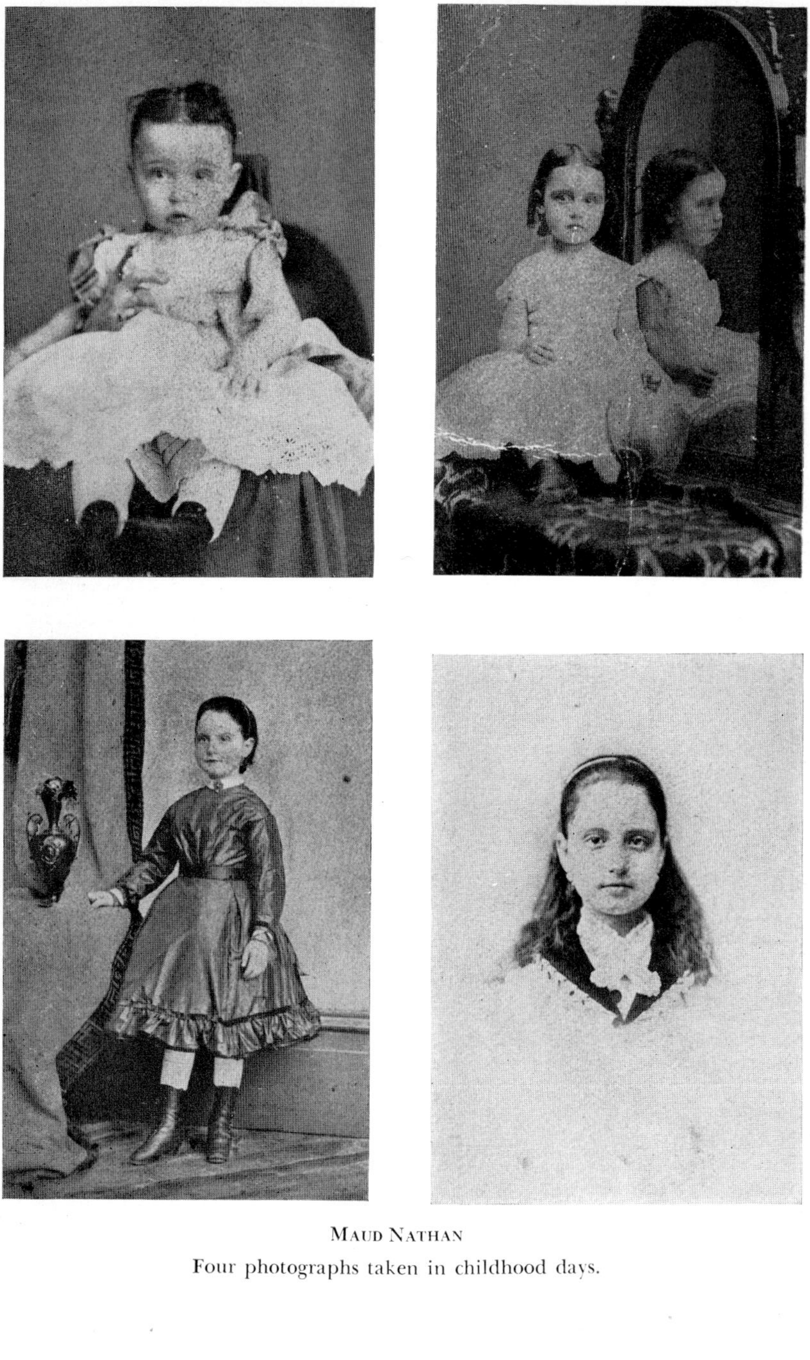

Maud Nathan
Four photographs taken in childhood days.

that in no way would our loyalty to our own faith, in which she had so conscientiously trained us, be shaken. She had given us the background. She grasped at the opportunity to give us broader contacts. In this, I feel, her judgment was right. I can see now how this experience prepared me for a future which was destined to carry me along broad lines. Had these formative years been spent in New York, I should have missed much of this broadening influence.

My loyalty to the traditions of my faith, my pride in the record of my ancestors in New York City has always remained firm, but my life has not been bounded by the walls of the synagogue. Because of this fact, whatever of use I have been in the world has been increased tenfold. I have been thrown with people of all races, nations, and creeds and have been able to meet them on their own plane, without any dividing sense of difference coming between us.

The happy life in Green Bay was soon to end. My father had decided to go back to New York. We were sorry at the thought of leaving. The four years we had lived in the little town had been joyous ones. They had been freighted with far greater importance than could be realized at the time. The freedom from conventionality taught me to consider conventions in their proper proportion and to cast aside those that seemed insignificant. While the life of Green Bay was in itself provincial, it took me away from provincialism and gave me a broad outlook. Up to the time of my leaving New York, I had in a vague way considered that a certain superiority attached itself to a person belonging to New York, and that the prizes of life could only be won by such cosmopolitan affiliation. This new experience taught me that from the very humblest beginnings in a small village, life may develop along the broadest lines. I am often interested in taking up a newspaper and reading of some former Green Bay schoolmate having attained a position of responsibility and honor.

The New York of the early 'seventies was narrow, provincial, smug, self-satisfied. Edith Wharton in her novel of that period, *The Age of Innocence,* shows this quite plainly. As I remember the social standards of my mother's circle, I appreciate the truth of the picture Mrs. Wharton has drawn.

My spirit rejoices that during these impressionable years I came under other influences.

## TO MY DAUGHTER MAUD

(Written by my mother on her thirty-third birthday.)

I am gaining years, my darling,
Yet do not say I'm growing old,
All that Time is taking from me,
He gives to thee a hundred-fold.

As a rose whose leaves are falling
Midst the buds on selfsame stem
Shares the homage and the culture
Which alone is due to them.

So while thou art young, my darling,
I shall bask in thy Youth's sun,
Never missing charms so fleeting
While counting thine come one by one.

If an essence twice distilled
Doth strength and sweetness gain,
Content am I with withered leaves
Thy purity retain.

Annie Florance Nathan.

March 27, 1875.

# CHAPTER III

## THE FAIRY PRINCE AND THE LAND OF ENCHANTMENT

My father left Green Bay for New York some time before the rest of us, telling my mother that he would send for us as soon as he had secured a home for the family. In the meantime, my mother decided to move to Chicago, so we again packed up our household goods and moved away from the quiet village to the great throbbing busy city on Lake Michigan. We had only been there a short time and were scarcely settled in our new home when my mother was taken very ill and my father was recalled by telegram.

Those were my first dark days, after a happy childhood. I remember lying all night on the floor of the hall, at my mother's door, unseen by any of the household, praying and sobbing and pleading with God to spare her all suffering and permit me to suffer in her place. When she was taken to a private hospital, my grief knew no bounds. It was only because I felt assured that she would soon recover that my father was able to persuade me to go at once to my grandfather Florance's home in New York City, taking my younger brother and sister with me, to wait there for our parents to join us when my mother would be strong enough to travel. My older brother had secured a good position in Green Bay, but was to follow us later.

So, at the early age of sixteen, I undertook the charge of my thirteen-year-old brother and my twelve-year-old sister on that never-to-be-forgotten journey back to our birthplace—New York. The four years' absence seemed but an episode—New York was *home*. I have traveled in many lands, have lived for many months at a time in France, I have left New York for long periods, but it has always been *home* to me. This trip to New York filled me with an almost overwhelming sense of responsibility. I was proud of the confidence that had been placed in me in having been given charge of my young brother and sister. Had any accident happened, such as a railroad wreck and either my brother or sister injured, I would have felt that I had not been a competent protector of my wards. It was, therefore, with a great sense of relief that we reached our destination in safety.

The day after our arrival, it was at my grandfather's home, that I met my "Cousin Fred," whom I had not seen in many years.[1] He was a handsome man of thirty-five years of age, a member of the Union, Knickerbocker, Manhattan, New York and Racquet Clubs, and of the Seventh Regiment Veteran Association. He was very popular with the ladies and much sought after by members of old New York families. His loyalty to his faith was very strong; although he had many opportunities to throw aside his religious traditions and marry one of several charming New York belles, his pride of lineage kept him a bachelor. His father's home, as I have already said, had been established along the lines of Jewish tradition. Subconsciously he felt that if he ever had a home of his own, his wife would be framed in the same picture with his mother, and his children carry on the ideals which had come down to him from his forbears.

"Cousin Fred" called at my grandfather's home the day after our arrival to inquire whether he could do anything for us. He was fond of his uncle—my father—and because he was so much older, he felt a paternal interest in his young cousins. It was with great surprise that he greeted a tall, mature-looking young lady of sixteen long, long

[1] See Appendix III.

Frederick Nathan
1880

years; her hair dressed high in a Psyche knot and managing a "train" with dexterity. That train lent so much dignity to the occasion that I declined to allow the cousinly kiss offered me. I explained that as I had been absent so many years from New York, my cousins were apparent strangers and should not, therefore, claim cousins' privileges.

Perhaps my shyness was not entirely due to my newly-acquired dignity. Perhaps there was also a note of coquetry in my attitude, for I remember thinking what a handsome man my cousin was and what fun it would be to have a jolly time with him.

Two score and ten years later, I can now attest that he was not only a handsome man, but was "beautiful within" and that his constant companionship has been the richest blessing of my life. Years before that meeting, my mother's prophetic soul had selected him as my mate. When I was a baby on her knees, she had told him jestingly, "Wait for Maud. She will make you a good wife." And the night before our arrival in New York from the West, as he lay awake in bed, he had recalled the incident, and with amusement reflected that although he was still a bachelor and in his thirty-sixth year, he was not likely to lose his heart to a child who happened to be his cousin. His feeling was all the more emphatic because of the opposition he had openly expressed in regard to his older brother's marriage several years before. This brother had married a first cousin on his mother's side. It was not likely that Fred would follow a course against which he had strongly protested. But the old Shakesperian maxim, "Pity is akin to love," was no doubt true in this case, as it has been in similar cases. He lavishly gave me his sympathy and pity when the sad news of my mother's death reached us a short time after our arrival. It was he who was asked to break the news to me. It was he who carried me, fainting, upstairs to my room and laid me on the bed.

It was he who sat with me daily and urged me to eat my food. Indeed, he was so attentive and solicitous for me that my aunt told him that she feared I would miss him too much when his daily visits ceased. And she warned him that he ought to give me assurance that his affection for me was merely cousinly and—owing to the discrepancy in years—entirely paternal in attitude. He acted upon my aunt's suggestion, and one day he said to me, "You must not lose your heart to me, because, whereas you are a dear little girl and I am very fond of you, I am old enough to be your father." My pride was wounded. He implied that there was a strong chance of my losing my heart to him, but not the remotest chance of his falling in love with me! My obstinate, perverse disposition made me rebel at this attitude of his. I remember making a solemn vow to myself that I would bring him to his knees to woo for my hand, in order to remind him that he was old enough to be my father and that I, therefore, scorned him as a lover!

It has always proven dangerous to play with Cupid's tools. The arrow that one shoots from his quiver is apt to prove a boomerang, which returns and overwounds the sender. Within a month and a half after my solemn vow had been made, I had the sad satisfaction of reiterating his words to me. I say sad, because I would have much preferred accepting him at once as my cavalier and lifelong comrade. I had a horrible fear that he would take my answer as final and that then I should be unhappy for the rest of my days. At first he admitted that it would be unfair to take advantage of my youth and inexperience, so he decided to leave me free, but assured me that *he* would never marry any one else. If, after a year, I had met no one else whom I preferred to marry, then we would overcome our scruples in regard to the marriage of first cousins, and would be married in spite of the difference between our ages. So, for nearly eleven months while I was free to accept attentions from others, and actually did receive two proposals of marriage, my heart was really betrothed, and I was deliriously happy when, on Thanksgiving Day, 1879, our engagement was announced.

The diamond solitaire ring which had sealed our engagement, I wore under my glove for a few days before we announced our betrothal. I felt its brilliancy almost burning a hole through the glove and feared it would reveal the secret. I kept silent, however, eager though I was to show the beautiful ring and proclaim my happiness.

Those wonderful months of our engagement! Never was there a more devoted lover. I lived in a whirl of excitement, breathless, receiving gifts of flowers, of bonbons, of jewelry. There were supper parties at Delmonico's, family dinner parties, theater parties, and my first introduction to the opera in New York at the Academy of Music. I was fêted on all sides. These were days before the automobile, but my fiancé's coupé was at my disposal, so that shopping for my trousseau had an added thrill. The contrast between this life and the simple pleasures of the social life of Green Bay was so great, I marvel now that, young as I was, I did not lose my head. The steadying influence must have been the deep and powerful love for my fiancé that filled my whole being, so that while I had the natural joy and pleasure of a young girl in all the attentions which suddenly came to me, I knew even at that time that this glitter was secondary to the sense of confidence and mutual love which existed between us.

Trousseau buying in those days was quite a different matter to what it is today. The bride-elect had to be supplied with dozens of every article of underwear and household linen. Girls at that period wore many more undergarments than does the girl of today. So there were numerous shopping expeditions to A. T. Stewart's and Arnold, Constable's—famous stores of that time. Those were the days of ruffled and be-flounced muslin petticoats, of embroidered flannel petticoats, of long, lace-trimmed chemises, of corset-covers, high-necked and long-sleeved nightdresses. There were no bloomers, no step-ins, no brassières, no pajamas! In place of the modern girl's variety of sweaters and sport suits, my trousseau contained a bustle, a camel's hair shawl, and a soft white cashmere shawl.

It was an exciting moment when the first wedding gift arrived. This was soon followed by hundreds of others, for our family circle was large and my fiancé had many friends and acquaintances. In those days most wedding gifts were of silver, so the display of silverware was bewildering. The few mirrors and sets of china and glass lent some variety to the overloaded tables which filled completely the living room of our apartment.

Always it had been my dream to travel. One of the great excitements of my engagement was the planning of the wedding trip. It was to be a trip to Europe—a visit to that wonderful land of magic and enchantment. I was so thrilled over this prospect that it apparently transcended the climax—the wedding day.

I remember that our wedding day, April 7, 1880, was an unusually cold day for that season of the year. In fact, there was a flurry of snow during the afternoon, which was quite unseasonable. Truly I have been one of the fairy queen's snow-maidens. The most epochal events of my life have been heralded through a white snow mist. My baby came to me in a swirl of snow. She died while the silent flakes fluttered against the window pane; the soft blanket obliterated the bleakness of her last resting place. I was so impressed by the coincidence that I had snow-flowers chiseled on her tombstone. Many, many years later, the lover to whom I had been mated in a

Maud Nathan
1880

snowstorm was taken from me in one of those blizzards which occasionally has paralyzed the life of New York.

The wedding took place in the Shearith Israel synagogue on Nineteenth Street, west of Fifth Avenue. As I drove up to the door, I found the usual crowd of sightseers, curious and eager to catch a glimpse of the bride. I heard frank and disconcerting remarks, upon alighting from the carriage. My wedding dress was the conventional white brocade and satin gown and I wore the long tulle veil and orange blossoms which every well-regulated bride wore in those days.

An orthodox Jewish wedding is an interesting ceremony —with its traditional customs. The "tabor," [1] where the prayers are read during the service, is in the center of the synagogue and was our marriage platform. Over it was stretched a white satin brocaded canopy—the canopy of happiness—supported by four standards. These standards are held by the groomsmen during the ceremony. The bride and groom stand beneath this canopy facing each other, the rabbi at right angles to them. The groom stands between his parents or their representatives, and the bride is similarly supported. The marriage service is chanted in Hebrew. The few questions addressed to the bride and groom are asked in the language of the country and the address to the married couple is in the modern tongue as well. There is no music other than chanting and singing in an orthodox synagogue, but for a wedding it is permissible to have musical instruments. The groom places the wedding ring on the bride's finger and gives her his first marital kiss. Two unique symbols are specially noticeable in an orthodox Jewish marriage service. They are the "canopy of happiness" and the shattering of a wine glass. After the bride and groom have sipped the

[1] The "tabor" is a square raised platform to which steps lead on either side; it is inclosed by a low railing. At one end is a reading desk, at the other a bench. At the four corners are candelabra.

consecrated wine from the glass, the groom places the glass on the ground and smashes it with his heel. I recall having asked the Rabbi his interpretations. One was that no other could drink from the glass in which the bride and groom in sipping the consecrated wine had consecrated their lives. The other was, that as difficult as it was to put the pieces of glass together so difficult was it to separate man and wife whom God had joined together. Alas, that this interpretation seems a mockery today! In these days of heedless marriages, multitudinous divorces, and precipitate remarriages, one might assume the interpretation of the shattered glass to be: as easily as the glass is broken, so easy is it to break one's marriage vows!

Forty-three years after my marriage when I met a compatriot at a tea in Rome, she came to me with outstretched arms, and reminding me that she had been at my wedding, spoke with enthusiasm of the vivid impression it had made upon her—the beauty and simplicity of an orthodox Jewish wedding ceremony.

I never hear the rhythmical melody of Mendelssohn's wedding march, even now more than half a century later, without feeling a peculiar gulp in my throat, and recalling how my Seventh Regiment drill-trained husband whispered, "Right, left, right, left," as I took his arm and we descended the tabor in perfect step together, typical of the way we kept in step all through our wedded years. Under the bower of flowers we walked, but I was walking on air, sailing through the ether to the land of

Never-never mourn or sigh
Never-never weep or cry!

I and my Fairy Prince, to live happily forever after!

Thirty years later we celebrated our wedding anniversary at our home by a remarriage ceremony. I had borrowed the same "canopy of happiness" from the synagogue. The same Rabbi who had performed the ceremony in 1880—Dr. H. Pereira Mendes—awaited us in his clerical robes to repeat his blessing. Many of the same guests were present. But instead of facing a rather frightened looking, pale-faced groom, I faced a man whose blue eyes showed the love and devotion which had but deepened with the years.

# CHAPTER IV

## THE NEW LIFE AND THE OLD WORLD

SURELY no young girl started her married life under happier auspices than I did. Everything seemed to conspire in my favor. I had youth, people called me good-looking, and I had a young girl's natural love of admiration; a vivacious temperament, eager to enjoy life at every point; a husband who adored me, ready to gratify every whim and wish—and I was going to Europe! Even today, as I write of it, the thrill of that first sailing away into the unknown comes over me. I see again the wharf crowded with a sea of faces; my father's rather serious face, my sister's—with tears in her eyes—and all waving good-bys, while my heart was singing—singing in the present and exulting in what lay before me.

Our boat, the *Scythia,* was small and unpretentious compared with the modern, mammoth, luxuriously furnished floating palaces. During stormy weather, it rolled and pitched to such an extent that ropes were placed on deck for passengers to grasp in order to steady themselves while taking their constitutionals. The mountain-high waves gave me a sense of exhilaration. I persisted in staying on deck on one occasion when all passengers were warned to go below. I had the deck steward strap me in my steamer-chair and lash the chair to the railing. The waves dashed over me and I reveled in the wonderful experience. There was no thought of seasickness for either my husband or me. Even when it came to crossing the much dreaded Channel, we were not daunted. But alas! I met my Waterloo several months later on an anchored warship in Villefranche harbor.

Several years afterwards, at Manchester, Vermont, this humiliating experience was recalled to me in an unexpected way. I had just been introduced to a young clergyman and his wife. The conversation of our little piazza group drifted into experiences at sea. The lady whom I had just met told the following anecdote:

"My father used to tell a good story about a little American bride he had met and for whom he had given a luncheon on board his ship, the *Quinnebaug*, when he was stationed at Villefranche. This young bride had boasted of being such a good sailor that she felt she was absolutely immune from seasickness. But the swaying of the anchored ship proved too much for her. And my father used to relate with glee how she turned first pale, then green, and finally had to be assisted to his cabin, where she threw herself helpless on his bed."

I listened to the full recital of this story and joined in the general laughter. Then turning to the raconteuse, I said:

"Your maiden name evidently was 'Casey.' "

"Now, how could you tell that from the story?" was her reply.

"Because," I sheepishly retorted, "I was the little American bride, and your father, who was then Captain Casey, honored me by giving me the luncheon."

Thus, the humiliating phantom of my Waterloo stalked after me through many years from Villefranche and finally caught up with me at Manchester, Vermont!

The crossing of the Atlantic took longer in those days than at present. It was ten days before we landed at Liverpool. It was there that my ear first recognized the difference between the *English* language and the *American* language. The intonation and phraseology were so strange that it was difficult to understand. When the porter asked about our "boxes" I didn't know that he was referring to our trunks. To "throw up" a window was bewildering. To go up in a "lift" was puzzling. The cockney speech was quite unintelligible, but hardly more so to American ears than Oxford English with its deep throaty enunciation and rising inflection at the end of a sentence. This Oxford English in its exaggerated form has always been somewhat difficult for me to take in rapidly. This brings me to an amusing incident which occurred when I was visiting London in 1899.

We were dining at Surrey House, the London residence of Lord and Lady Battersea. I was seated between the host and a son of Sir William Vernon Harcourt, M.P.—Bobby Harcourt, a recent graduate of Oxford University. He was naturally interested in the "States," his mother being a daughter of John Motley, the famous American historian. He plied me with questions, and because of my inability to understand his enunciation, I was obliged to ask him constantly to repeat his question. I grew both embarrassed and weary and found it easier in listening to his opinions to appear to agree, even though ignorant of what he was saying. Finally I was caught! Having stated that I was absolutely of his opinion, he suddenly exclaimed, "Really now! How extraordinary!" And turning to the other guests at the table, he again expressed astonishment that I, an American woman, should be in sympathy with such a British point of view. To this day I don't know what the point of view was, and if "Bobby Harcourt" ever scans these pages, I hope he will enlighten me.

London in 1880 presented a strong contrast to a young woman whose experiences had been limited to New York and Green Bay. The spectacular evidences of royalty, the palaces, the picturesque guards in brilliant uniforms, the royal equipages on Rotten Row in Hyde Park—with the outriders and postilions—all made me feel that I was strolling through a fairy tale. Queens, princes, the Beefeaters of the Tower in their ancient costumes, the Guards in their scarlet coats and plumed hats, the evidences of class distinction everywhere—how could all that be reconciled in my mind with democratic New York or the simple village life of Green Bay?

I had a sufficient knowledge of English history and literature to have a real appreciation of my visits to places which had been well known to me by name. But my strongest impressions were made by the differences that confronted me on every side. The solidity of the architecture with its very evident hoariness of age. The small gardens and parks, the number of window boxes with bright flowers, which counteracted the dull grayness of the buildings. The air of leisure on the part of the top-hatted, frock-coated, white-spatted men who walked down Piccadilly. The picturesque buses which rolled along so many streets and stopped at the various "circuses," the hansom cabs and the frequent whistling which was heard to summon them. The strange money with its guineas and sovereigns, shillings and farthings, pennies and ha'-pennies which made shopping an extraordinary and literally an *additional* adventure!

I had some English cousins. My mother's cousin, Rowena Florance, had married an English barrister, Joseph Guedalla, a great-nephew of Sir Moses Montefiore. Through them my mother had years before met Sir Moses, the great philanthropist. My mother had said that she would rather meet him than any member of royalty—not excepting Queen Victoria. This was repeated to Sir Moses, and he was so flattered that he sent her—as a souvenir of their meeting—a handsome gold bracelet, enameled in blue and set with a pearl. This bracelet contained a photograph of the donor. Upon my first trip abroad, I carried that bracelet with me, hoping to be presented to Sir Moses, and hoping to make a sufficiently favorable impression as to lead him to present me with a companion bracelet for the other arm. But alas, the aged philanthropist and traveler had been failing in health and the time was not propitious for a visit to him. So my hope was unfulfilled.

My cousin's husband, Joseph Guedalla, was honored by the friendship of the then Prince of Wales—later King Edward the VII. The night that Mr. Guedalla gave us a dinner and opera box party, I remember his wearing a beautiful pearl and diamond shirt stud which had been given him by his royal friend. That box party stands out in my mind as one of the thrilling incidents of my first London visit. Among the guests invited to meet us was Lord Aylesbury—one of the Prince's friends. We were opposite the royal box, which was occupied by the Prince, Princess, and their two daughters. The Prince had been leveling his opera glasses upon our box in a way that would have seemed to me presumptuous, persistent, and pronounced had he *not* been a royal Prince. During an entr'acte, he beckoned my host to meet him in the foyer, so Mr. Guedalla and Lord Aylesbury left our box. Before they went, however, a wager was jestingly made between them—one wagering that the Prince would ask to meet me and the other that he would not. In either case I was to be the recipient of another dinner and theater party in my honor—the loser of the wager to be the host. I was, therefore, in a great state of excitement when, upon their return, I was told that the Prince not only asked who I was, but begged them to bring me to a breakfast on board the royal yacht. The day was fixed. It was all arranged that we stay at my cousin's house at Ryde during the yacht races and then drive over to Cowes and go on board the royal yacht. I was told that I would, of course, meet the Princess too. Is it a wonder that this box party stands out in my mind above all other box parties—even now—half a century later?

We paid our week-end visit to my cousins at Ryde and on the eventful day the heavens opened and we had a deluge of rain. My cousin had only open vehicles and I was told that it would not be practical to drive so far in the heavy rain and arrive drenched. Another day would be fixed upon later on, and all would be explained to his Royal Highness. My disappointment was all the keener because my husband's satisfaction and joy were so apparent. His jubilant spirit seemed to mock and jeer me. It was only later on that I understood his point of view so well. He had been actually afraid lest my head be turned by royal flattery. He realized the danger, owing to my youth and inexperience. My disappointment soon wore off, however, as there were so many other worlds to conquer.

After a few weeks of sightseeing in London, and participation in the whirl of its social season, a strong desire to see Paris led us to cross the Channel. I began to fear that something might happen to Paris before I could lay siege to it and conquer it. Suppose some terrible devastating fire should destroy it! Suppose some fearful explosion should demolish its most beautiful buildings! It seemed better not to linger on in London when the Grand Prix races and the Champs Élysées beckoned to me alluringly. So we left for the Continent.

If London interested me, Paris enchanted me. Many, many times have I revisited the beautiful city on the Seine and always have I recaught the glamour of that first visit. I learned to know Paris very well. I went about at first as though in a dream. In some vague way I seemed to have been there before. I acquired a knowledge of the topography of the city as if by magic. I was able to scold the cochers in their own language when they took me by the longest routes in order to increase their rates.

My husband insisted that I have a French maid and that I should be accompanied by her when he did not go out with me. This seemed to me not so much a matter of precaution as a silly convention, against which I rebelled.

After the freedom of my girlhood in Green Bay, and the lack of special chaperonage in New York, it seemed to me an absurd restriction for a married woman to endure.

An adventure that might have ended disastrously proved to me the wisdom of my husband's point of view. Leaving the maid at home to do some sewing, I went out one day alone. I soon found I was being followed. To escape the young man's unpleasant attentions I jumped into a fiacre. He promptly followed in another. Thinking it wiser not to go to my hotel I decided to call on some friends. After a somewhat lengthy visit, I returned to my waiting fiacre to find my cocher asleep and the persistent cavalier pacing up and down in front of the door, smoking a cigarette. He shook the cocher to arouse him, opened the door of my fiacre and helped me in, then raising his hat, he jumped into his own waiting fiacre and I heard him give in a loud voice the order: "Suivez cette dame jusqu'à ce qu'elle descende chez elle–Ne laissez pas perdre de vue ce fiacre." My cocher, however, managed to give him the slip and when I reached the hotel, my pursuer was nowhere to be seen. But as I got out I spied a billet doux tucked in the corner of the cushion. I decided not to leave it for the cocher to laugh over, so I took it with me. It was brief and to the point. I was implored to meet my unknown admirer at a certain hour the following afternoon at a certain corner of the street near the Magasin du Louvre. I threw the note into the fire that was cheerily burning in our sitting room at the Hotel de l'Athenée. My adventurous spirit was so keen that I actually had to stay at home the next afternoon lest I might not be able to resist the temptation to take a peep at the "rendezvous" just to see whether my flirtatious Frenchman was really waiting for me!

We spent the summer in Belgium, Germany, Austria, and Switzerland. Then we returned to Paris, where we passed some time before going to Italy and the Riviera for the winter.

Europe unfolded itself in magnificent vistas, presenting to my eager spirit a panorama which in some peculiar way (indigenous to youthful impressions) always seemed to make me the central figure, discoverer, and explorer. My verdict was quite contrary to the fiat of a young nephew, Robert Nathan, whose first trip abroad was made when he was about ten years of age. His first quest upon landing in Italy was for a pop-gun with which to shoot beans and thus celebrate the Fourth of July. He failed to find one. "I don't think much of Europe," he wrote home. "It is very much overrated. They don't even have pop-guns and bean-shooters." But at seventeen, a young bride does not look for bean-shooters. She sees everything *couleur de rose.*

The Italian sunsets were the most brilliant ever seen in the world and were, of course, especially gorgeous as a salutation to the bride. The waters of the Mediterranean were bluer than they had ever been known to be. The mountains of Switzerland were higher and more covered with snow than ever before. The castles in Germany were more full of romance and more picturesquely perched on wild precipitous crags. A new world opened up, peopled by giants, intellectual and social. Instead of feeling like a pigmy in consequence—such is the aplomb of youth faring forth in a spirit of adventure—I seemed suddenly to grow in my desire to reach their heights.

After the strenuous weeks of London and Paris and the still more strenuous weeks of rapid traveling, I was rather miserable and the doctor advised my taking a "cure" in the little German village of Elgersburg. When my husband and I were deposited at the station and I saw the train steam away, I could have sat down on the platform and wept. The village seemed to be the most dismal, God-forsaken place in the world. It was raining, there was mud everywhere, no sidewalks. Boys were driving flocks of geese along the road. There was no room for us at the "Kurhaus." We were sent to a cottage and given a large, cold, bare-looking room—no rugs to cover the concrete floors, no blankets on the beds—merely feather beds. The cure was a strenuous one. I was awakened at six A.M. by having cloths that had been wrung out in cold water flung on me. Then I got a good rub-down to increase the circulation. I used to shiver in anticipation of this early morning treatment, but my health improved, and before we left I was able to walk several miles—to the next village and back. As the only Americans in the place and probably the only ones the villagers had ever seen, we were the cynosure of all the other "Kurgäste."

One day I did not appear at the Kurhaus for breakfast and the German women were most solicitous. They inquired for the absent "husband." They thought that husband was "gemahl" or "gemahlin" and were amused when they discovered their mistake. I remember the shock I experienced the first Sunday I spent there. I had discreetly refrained from taking my embroidery to the Kurhaus gardens, for although Sunday was not my Sabbath, I had been brought up to respect the traditions and convenances of those who worshiped on the first day of the week instead of the Biblical seventh day. I was surprised, therefore, to find all the German women with their embroidery and knitting, and they asked me where my work bag was. I had not until then become acquainted with the continental Sabbath—so different from the Puritan Sabbath. Today, the contrast would not appear so great.

The little village of Elgersburg is not far from Cassel and Hohenlohe, where the Kaiser's favorite Schloss was situated. As the Kaiser was elsewhere, we were enabled to visit the castle and were shown through the house and the spacious gardens.

On our European tour, we visited many cathedrals to

study the architecture and the many works of arts they contained. We were also naturally interested in the synagogues. Everywhere we went we made it a point to visit the old buildings. They were invariably situated in or near the Jewish quarters and while they contained no pictures, there were specimens of old hand-wrought seven-branched candlesticks, silver tops for the scrolls of law, large brass, copper or silver ewers and basins. There were no statues, no pictures, no pictorial windows because of the literal interpretation of the second commandment.

When we attended the services of the synagogue in London, it was the service of the Sephardic Jews and we found ourselves quite at home.

In the highest circles of London and Paris, we found Jews and Christians meeting on perfectly equal terms. This was the case in 1880 and this has been my experience during my many visits abroad. In the membership of the most exclusive clubs are found Jewish names. Aristocratic London is too old to be snobbish. Democratic New York is too young to be otherwise.

A special Providence seemed to guide us in planning our tour, else how could it have happened that quite by accident we found all the capitals of Europe decorated and illuminated for us! We had been in London for Queen Victoria's birthday. We were in Vienna for Emperor Franz Josef's birthday and were enabled to attend a gala night at the opera. The King of Bavaria was obliging enough to celebrate his birthday while we were in Munich, so again we had the joyous sight of a city gay with flags and banners—bright with lights at night. In Dresden, the King of Saxony had a birthday. In Brussels, an International Exposition was being held and the city was *en fête*. In the various cantons of Switzerland, we seemed to arrive in time to see the folk dances and hear the folk songs which were part of the canton fête celebrations. During these fêtes, the peasants were dressed in the costumes of the canton, thus lending vivid color and picturesque quality to the scene.

We went to Italy in the late autumn and remained until after the beginning of the new year. This, my first visit to that land of poetry and art, of blue skies and golden sunsets, made such a deep impression upon me that when I revisited it forty-two years afterward it was all as familiar as though I had seen it but a few months before. The spell that Italy casts over those who love her is never lost and revisiting the country only deepens first impressions. The courier who had piloted my husband's family through Italy, when he was a young boy, was available. So for the sake of "auld lang syne" he was engaged to make the trip with us. My French maid completed the "partie carrée." My husband and I were like two children off on a holiday. The courier and maid attended to all details and left us free to enjoy every minute of the trip.

When we took a diligence over some famous pass, my husband and I sat on the front seat with the "cocchière" and put the maid and courier in the carriage. Consequently, all the beggars and vendors of wares pursued them and left us in peace. I climbed to the top of the Milan cathedral. I visited every museum, every picture gallery, every church, every fountain, conscientiously, religiously, devotedly. But what I enjoyed most was a drive or a dinner or some function where I could study the life of the people. We went to the opera, to the theater, to concerts. We were eager to see, to hear everything.

In Venice, I felt as though we were royalty. The gondolier stood outside the door of our box all evening—during an operatic performance—so as to escort us to our gondola when we were ready to leave. On my second visit to Venice, more than forty years later, I actually did go around the canals in the royal gondola with the gondoliers dressed in the royal livery. It had been placed at our disposal by the Minister of Fine Arts, who was staying at the Royal Palace and was a friend of my niece who was in my party.[1] When we returned to our room at the hotel after a day's outing, the gondoliers serenaded us. We threw open our casement windows, the moonlight shed a radiance over the Grand Canal, the sweet Italian melodies floated up to us. I was indeed in fairyland with my Prince.

In Rome we found an American friend who had married an Italian—a nephew of one of the Cardinals. Through them we secured an invitation to the first reception given that season by the Pope, Leo XIII. The Pope had been in poor health and on that account had not held any of his usual levées. I was quite excited at the thought of being presented to his Holiness. I armed myself with several rosaries to be blessed by him and to serve later as gifts to faithful maids at home. We went to the Vatican early in the morning—about ten o'clock. I wore the conventional black silk dress with a black Spanish lace scarf over my head, and white kid gloves. We were given seats without backs on long benches in an anteroom. There we all remained a very long time while his Holiness was making up his mind whether he would receive his guests "en masse" or give us what was termed a private reception. The time would have passed more slowly had I not engaged in conversation one of the chamberlains who spoke French fluently and who was very entertaining and gallant. At last, after a wait of about two hours, we were informed that his Holiness was going to grant us a private audience in "Raphael's Loggie." We were told that we were very fortunate, as few people had the opportunity of being presented individually and of being permitted to converse with him. We all formed in line—two by two. There must have been about two hundred in the party.

[1] My niece was taken for the Princess Yolande, who had been recently married, and pedestrians rushed to the various bridges to watch our gondola.

We walked slowly, very slowly, with many delays, toward the famous loggie. The chamberlain who had been so kind and attentive walked along with me, explaining many forms and ceremonies, and giving me much information. When we arrived within a few feet of the Pope, who was seated at the farthest end of the loggie, I noticed that some of the devout visitors were kneeling and kissing his slipper. I saw a couple bow and then I saw the head chamberlain, who was standing near the Pope, point to the outstretched slipper of his Holiness and they were constrained to kneel and kiss his foot. At once I turned and said to my husband, "I won't kiss any man's foot, not even the Pope's!" My husband and his sister, whom we had met in Rome, suggested that we leave at once rather than have any disagreeable scene or scandal and thus embarrass our friends through whom we had secured our invitation cards. I asked my cavalier, the chamberlain, who stood near me, whether I was obliged to kiss his Holiness' slipper and he replied in an injured tone: "Comment? Ne pas vouloir bien reçevoir la benédiction de Sa Sainteté?" Whereupon I replied breathlessly, "Je ne peux pas me baisser, du reste je me sens prête à m'évanouir, il n'y a pas assez d'air ici—il faut que je m'en aille tout-de-suite," and bestowing the rosaries upon the French maid, I rushed out, followed by my husband and sister-in-law. I learned afterwards that some of our American acquaintances had only kissed the ring on the Pope's finger, and had not been asked to kiss his slipper. But after the little pantomime I had observed, I was unwilling to take any chances. When my maid approached the "throne," the chief chamberlain called out: "Monsieur et Madame Nathan de New York." Marie explained that Madame Nathan had been obliged to leave, not having felt well, so she and the rosaries received the papal blessing in our place. Many years later I attended a second reception at the Vatican and received the blessing of Pope Pius XI. The Pope on this occasion walked around the rooms greeting the guests and presenting his ring to be kissed.

However, far more interesting and spectacular was the consistory I attended in 1923 when two cardinals were invested and received their red hats. I was invited by a Princess of the church, Princess Spottiswood-Mackin, who had choice seats. So I was able to have an unintercepted view of the entire ceremony. This ceremony was held in the Vatican Chapel. The brilliant coloring of the costumes of the various groups of guards and henchmen, of members of different orders of Catholic societies, made a pageant that was medieval and picturesque. One gallery was filled with ambassadors and ministers plenipotentiary, the other gallery with prominent women, garbed in somber black, veils thrown over their heads. The Pope was carried in on his red and gold chair, on the shoulders of four stalwart men, his gold-embroidered cape streaming behind. The Choir of the Sistine Chapel assisted at the ceremony.

In 1880 only foreigners were enabled to be received both at the Vatican and the Quirinal, owing to the friction between church and state. Italians were obliged to choose between the two. If an Italian nobleman visited the Quirinal to salute his King, he was *persona non grata* at the Vatican. Such was the warlike status at that time between the Church of Rome and the state. But foreigners had open sesame to both palaces. It was through the courtesy of our American Minister, Mr. Story, that we received invitations to attend the royal ball at the Quirinal and for a luncheon given by Her Majesty, Queen Margherita.

We had the delightful experience of attending a gala operatic performance on New Year's night. The Opera House was lavishly decorated, their Majesties, the King and Queen, walking through a bower of flowers to reach the royal box. We were indeed fortunate to have secured, through our Italian friends, two good seats, for on such an occasion every seat was held at a premium. The boxes were filled with the élite of Rome, the women in beautiful gowns and wearing rare jewels. All the ambassadors and ministers were present, many of them wearing their brilliant sashes and decorations. The prima donna was singing an aria in the second act when the royal party appeared. At once she stopped singing. The orchestra played the national anthem, the entire audience rose to its feet, cheering and calling out, "vive il re, viva la regina!" Their Majesties bowed their acknowledgments from the box. It was several minutes before the prima donna could again begin her aria and the opera proceeded.

About ten years later, this whole scene flashed vividly before me in democratic America. The setting was the ballroom at the Grand Union Hotel, Saratoga, New York. I was the prima donna of the occasion—singing at a concert for the benefit of the New York Diet Kitchen. The President of the United States, Benjamin Harrison, was in Saratoga at the time and promised to attend the performance. This fact had been widely advertised and had greatly increased the sale of tickets. He was late in arriving. I was in the midst of singing my French chanson when I saw him and the committee enter the door. I turned to the accompanist and told him to play, "Hail to the Chief." At once the entire audience rose to its feet and applauded the President. After he was seated, I began my song again. The setting was different and the contrast was great between the brilliant Opera House at Rome and the bare simple ballroom of an American summer resort hotel. But the thrill of patriotism which animated both groups was the same—a love of country which found expression through homage to its leader.

After our tour through Italy, we went to Nice and settled down there for a brief season of gayety. My aunt—

my mother's older sister—had made Nice her home for some twenty-five years and she was, therefore, able to introduce us into the best circles of French society. In 1880 the Riviera was not the mecca of America tourists that it is today. My aunt took an apartment for us, engaged a valet, and I had my first experience of quasi-housekeeping with French servants. I say "quasi-housekeeping" because, although we entertained, no cooking was done in our kitchen. All meals were sent piping hot, ready-to-serve, from a caterer, whose delivery clerks—dressed in the white apron and cap of the chef—walked through the streets, balancing huge covered tin receptacles—resembling boilers—on their heads. My French maid kept the dishes hot on the little kitchen stove and gave them in proper sequence to the valet to serve. All I had to do was to let the caterer know how many "couverts" to send daily. Another equipment—which is part of every American household—had to be sent to us daily from outside. It was the cause of great excitement to the neighbors and their children. This was the bath tub, sent with attachment and curtains for shower bath and with the boiler of hot water. No doubt the groups of curious and bewildered children watching this strange apparatus wondered—like Svengali in *Trilby*—how we ever got dirty!

Those were full days in Nice—with yacht races to watch from the club house, *matinées dansantes* at the Messina and Mediterrannée Clubs, balls at the Préfecture where Le Comte et la Comtesse de Brançion dispensed hospitality so graciously. At the club dances I usually had as partners officers from our men-of-war stationed near Nice. But it was also customary to be invited to dance by those who had not been formally introduced. Thus I often found myself being whirled about by a French or Italian cavalier who was a complete stranger and it was not until later in the season that I learned that while it was permissible to dance with the unintroduced, conversation was interdicted. In the meantime, I had had many a delightful *causerie* with them. What a ridiculous convention this seemed to me.

The carnival at Nice during *mi-carême* was a brilliant spectacle, providing as well a jolly good time. The battle of flowers was the occasion for many a coquettish combat. The torchlight procession was held on Moccalotti Eve when the spectators endeavor to keep their own candles or torches lit, while trying to extinguish their neighbors'. We had seats on the grand stand, but my husband forgot to provide himself with matches, so when our candles were blown out, we would have remained in darkness had my neighbor not have chivalrously offered to keep them lit for us. He had heard me asking frantically for *des allumettes* and he gallantly turned to me and in his best American-French said he had his pockets full of matches and would keep our candles lit for us. Two ladies were with my cavalier and they very obviously were Americans too. They were all laughing and talking English. My neighbor took great pains to translate all their jokes into atrocious French, so I might enjoy them too. My spirit of mischief was aroused and I whispered all sorts of threats to my husband if he dared to address me in English. Then the next day when Lieutenant Emery introduced the kind stranger of the previous evening to my husband at the Club, he asked whether I was French or Russian, or was I Swiss or Belgian? He was greatly astonished to find that I was a compatriot. This episode was the beginning of a warm friendship which led to many good times.

The season at Nice that year ended suddenly with a terrible calamity. The Opera House caught fire just after a performance had begun. The fashionable box-holders—always late—had not yet arrived, but the "Paradis" or "family circle" as we call it was packed with the usual throng of music lovers. My husband and I had accepted an invitation to attend the preceding evening with friends who had a box and on the evening in question we were at home, writing letters and knew nothing of the tragedy until the following morning. However, because of five hours difference in time, the news of the terrible fire, with its large loss of life, was published in the evening editions of the New York papers and my father, brothers, and sister had an anxious night. They cabled us, but could get no reply. The telegraph office at Nice was swamped by the number of messages every one was trying to send. The Government had the first rights, then the opera singers were given an opportunity to wire their friends of their safety, and by the time the rest of us had a chance there was a line of applicants three blocks long. Our valet stood in that line many long hours, awaiting his turn. In the meantime, my father—fearing the worst—had cabled again to my aunt for news of us. Many perished in that fire and the flowers that had been ordered for the second battle of flowers were sent instead to place on the graves of the victims of the holocaust.

As I recall those full months of travel, all sorts of memories crowd upon me in bewildering confusion. But here and there some few incidents stand out more clearly than the rest.

I do not know whether Americans had the reputation of having extraordinary capacity in regard to the drinking of champagne or whether the German nobility were accustomed to drink it in large quantity—I only know that I was surprised when my husband and I were the guests of the Duke of Saxe-Coburg-Gotha in his box at the opera, one evening at Hombourg, to see brought into the box during the entr'acte a basket of champagne. The Duke was spending the summer at the pretty little German watering place with his morganatic wife, Baroness Ruttenstein—a former Viennese opera singer—and their son. We were the recipients of their cordial hospitality—invited to dine with them, drive with them, and were also invited to be their guest later on at their Schloss in Gotha. We were specially urged to join them for the hunting season. The Duke—Prince Leopold, a cousin of Queen Victoria's and a brother of the Queen of Württemberg—was gracious enough to offer to have me introduced at Court in Berlin and Vienna if we would remain abroad for the following season. But my husband was obliged to return to New York to help his co-executor settle his mother's estate and I, naturally, was unwilling to remain abroad without him. So after sixteen months of wandering through enchanted lands, we turned our faces homeward.

This, too, had its thrill. For we were to have our own home in the familiar New York environment, where we could receive our friends at our own fireside.

# CHAPTER V

## NEW YORK LIFE IN THE 'EIGHTIES—
## A CHAPTER OF CONTRASTS

AFTER sixteen months of foreign travel, we came home. Those months had been so crowded with rich and varied experiences that I felt myself to be an old married woman. I was not yet nineteen. Therefore, I brought to the new experience of housekeeping the same exuberant enthusiasm and spirit of adventure that had filled me when we sailed away to tread new paths in the old world.

We stayed at the Buckingham Hotel—the present site of Saks Fifth Avenue store—until we found the new home. It was natural to look for a house in which to establish ourselves. The modern apartment with its labor-saving devices and luxurious equipment was unknown at that time. Only those who desired to live economically considered renting a "flat." These flats had been made from remodeled private houses and were usually small, dark, and uncomfortable. We rented a three-story house located in Sixty-fourth Street, near Park Avenue. It was the conventional brownstone front, twenty feet wide, built on a lot of about one hundred feet in depth, and having the usual back yard.

I had all the fun of furnishing this house. My husband had some of the furniture made to order and we were fortunate in having inherited some old family pieces. One of these pieces—a lowboy—is still in my possession. The telephone stands on it with all its paraphernalia of huge directories, writing pad and pencil. Little did the craftsman who designed its lovely curves dream of the ultimate use to which it would be put. This table belonged to my great-aunt. I never sit at it without thinking of a story connected with her and the life of old New York.

Here is the story as told to me by Alexander Hamilton, son of the famous jurist and statesman. He had been a well-known figure in New York social life and at the time of my marriage was quite an old man. I remember his spending an evening at my home when he related the following incident:

When a little boy of seven, he had been taken by his mother to call on her friend, Leah Seixas, from whom I inherited the aforementioned table. While the ladies were chatting, another visitor was announced and in walked "Mr. Aaron Burr." When Mrs. Hamilton saw the visitor and realized who it was, she fainted. (In those days a fainting spell was the only proper outlet for a lady's emotions.) Aaron Burr procured a glass of water from the dining-room sideboard and gallantly presented it to the lady. Then—in a chivalrous way—appreciating that his presence was *de trop,* bowed himself out. The little boy watched this scene in bewildered amazement—understanding nothing. Later when his mother had sufficiently recovered to leave her friend's home, and they were walking toward their house, little Alexander—his hand in his mother's—gained courage to ask the meaning of the extraordinary scene. He then learned that the visitor who had caused such overwhelming emotion was no other than his father's murderer. To the childish mind this explanation proved even more bewildering. He had always pictured a murderer as a blackleg, an outlaw, certainly not dressed as a gentleman. How then could he have been a murderer? What a natural question was this for the child to puzzle over. And how this bit of intimate family history serves to connect us with the past.

To return to my new home: the whole house had to be carpeted, stairs and halls included. How different from the delightful simplicity of today, when cleanly hardwood floors require but a few rugs which can be utilized however frequently the habitat be changed. Our house, although considered small, required three servants besides a man to attend to the furnace, sidewalks, and back yard. We paid the average wage for efficient service, yet the wages of these three servants, combined with those paid to the furnace man, did not equal the amount that a housekeeper is obliged to pay today for one inefficient, immigrant girl. Moreover, in the early 'eighties, maids did not demand the privileges they expect today. A weekly Thursday afternoon out was unknown. Every other Sunday afternoon and evening and one evening a week was the invariable rule. A maid's working day began at six A.M. and didn't close until she went to bed at night. If the mistress were entertaining guests, the maids were required to sit up until the guests left—even though it were midnight. Otherwise ten o'clock was the closing hour for the house and any maid who came home later than this was apt to be dismissed. I felt that even maids needed some recreation, so I established my household upon an entirely different footing. My maids were permitted to go out of an evening when their work was finished, the one stipulation being that one of the three must remain at home ready to render any necessary service. As I had no heavy or extra work done on my Sabbath, they were also permitted to take every second Saturday afternoon for recreation. I was lax in holding them to the ten o'clock closing hour. If one of them went to the theater, one of the other maids was expected to wait up to let her in. A latch key to a maid was too great an innovation—even for me. I might have considered it, but I never could have won over my husband to my point of view at that time. I had the front basement room fitted up comfortably with rockers and easy chairs, so that the maids could use it of an evening to receive their "male friends." I felt that it was far better to allow them this privilege than force them to meet their "beaux" in the park or in questionable resorts. I was considered—in family circles—most radical and unwise in setting up precedents that would prove hardships for other housekeepers. After all, with all our boasted progress, we were not so far removed from the provincialism of Mrs. Gaskell's *Cranford.* Miss Mattie's rule in regard to "followers" was very strict, although the time came even for her when she had to relax it. My friends had an equal objection to "followers" but they were admitted to the kitchens under the comprehensive phrase of "long-lost brothers."

I was very young. This was my first experience in leadership, my first opportunity for self-expression. Instinctively I set my feet in a new path and instead of following the traditions of my world, I was unconsciously one of the fore-runners of what came to be later on the established precedent in domestic service. All this didn't seem very important at the time. But I can see it now as the first expression of that interest in the working girl which was later to become one of the dominant motives of my life work.

While writing of this domestic service, I cannot resist the temptation to relate a few amusing incidents. On one occasion I was interviewing a cook—with the object of engaging her. She claimed to be competent in her profession, stating that she could make all kinds of entrées, desserts, and soups. I asked her to tell me how, for instance, she made mock turtle soup. Her answer was so vague that I insisted upon knowing her recipe. She said: "I makes a good strong stock, just like anyone else, and then when I'm ready to serve it, I gets the little mock turtles and throws them in!" On another occasion, before ordering the lighting of a fire in the dining room, I told the waitress to let me know what the thermometer registered. She brought me the thermometer from my husband's dressing room, saying, "I brought it to you, 'cause I don't know *exactly* how the thing wurrks!" "But, Bridget," I said, "that is not the thermometer from the dining room." "Sure, and aren't they all alike?" was her reply. It was the same maid who asked whether she should cut the oranges in two halves or in four halves, and who said when asked what number glove she wore, "Well, sometimes one number and sometimes another, that depends upon the size."

It seemed to me at first that housekeeping would take up a large share of my time, but by being systematic, I found that an hour or so in the morning completed my daily tasks, except during the season of pickling and preserving when I had the old-fashioned housekeeper's love of a storeroom stocked with jars and bottles of my own filling.

I remember even years later, when I was President of the Consumers' League, some one called to see me in regard to some committee work. The maid told the visitor that I could not be disturbed. The caller insisted upon the urgency of her business. The maid, however, was obdurate, finally saying, "It's no use, I know Mrs. Nathan won't see any one until she gets her preserves off the stove and into the jars."

Who, today, would put up tomato catsup when there are Heinz's "57 varieties" to choose from? And who would corn or spice beef when a tempting delicatessen shop is at the corner? In those days housekeepers went to market. No one gave orders over the telephone. There were but few telephones and those were in business houses, not in homes. For the lazy housekeeper the butcher's and grocer's daily calls for orders answered the purpose. But I enjoyed going to market. I liked to make my choice from the variety of fruits and vegetables. I wanted to make sure that the steak was cut the desired thickness and that the fish was of the freshest. This habit I have always kept up. When keeping house in Paris, I rather resented the custom of the country which gave this prerogative to the cook.

Today we hear a great deal about the high cost of living. Prices of staple articles are undoubtedly double the price they were when I was a young housekeeper. But we forget the contributing causes. We, the public, demand more. Our standards have changed.

I can remember when my cook went to the basement door—at the ringing of the milkman's bell—with her pitcher in her hand, to have dipped out to her from the can her daily quart of milk, for which we paid six cents. The milkman's cart was a picturesque affair with its bright copper and tin cans and pint and quart dippers. And the patient horses, who needed no guiding, but stopped automatically at each customer's door. We drank this milk—so carelessly handled—without any qualms, with no thought of possible germs. Today we demand state-inspected dairies, milk delivered in sterilized bottles, every process from the source of supply to final delivery carefully guarded from contamination. The knowledge that both milk and water are important factors in spreading disease has practically eliminated epidemics of typhoid fever in our large cities. We pay for this immunity from disease in the added cost of a quart of milk and by a higher rate for water tax. In the same way, our demand for cleanliness and freedom from tubercular germs leads to state inspection of cattle and packing houses, and we pay more for our steaks. Our so-called dry groceries—flour, sugar, rice, crackers, tea—which used to be kept in bulk in open bins, are now put up in sealed packages and we pay for this extra cost of production. After all, if looked at from an intelligent point of view, it is less costly than the former lack of protection.

In the old days the larder had to be kept well filled, as members of the family circle were apt to call before lunch or before dinner and would expect to be invited to remain for a "pot-luck" meal. Yet no housekeeper wished to be considered extravagant, so between my endeavors to have sufficient for the possible guest who might "drop in" and the desire to keep housekeeping accounts pruned down to "family standards" I often felt myself to be between Scylla and Charybdis!

There were no women's club activities in the 'eighties. We had no civic duties, no public meetings to distract us from our homes and social duties. After my housekeeping duties were attended to, I spent my mornings practicing my singing and embroidering buffet scarfs, doilies, bureau covers, etc. Only the other day, while looking over my linen press, I came across an elaborately embroidered buffet scarf that I had worked in those long ago days of comparative leisure. And I marveled that I ever had the time and patience to spend my mornings at such work. In the afternoon I went out in a coupé to do shopping or to pay visits. Shopping took up more time in those days than at present, when "ready-to-wear" gowns and articles of underwear are to be found in all the shops. In those days goods for dresses had to be carefully selected; linings, whalebones, crinoline, belt tapes, ruches, trimmings, buttons, passementeries, etc., bought and all sent to the dressmaker's or to one's home where a dressmaker was engaged to work by the day. Underwear, too, was made at home—and usually a dozen or at least half a dozen of each article at a time. Sheets, pillow cases, and mattress covers were also made at home.

Visiting took up a great deal of time. Nearly every one had a day at home and it was not considered courteous to call on any other day. It might necessitate going to the same neighborhood several afternoons in one week, for it was rare to find neighbors receiving on the same day.

Upon our homecoming from Europe, we found a large circle of relatives and friends eager to greet us and give us welcome as part of their group. At first the joy of the reunion and the éclat that surrounded me after a year and a half's traveling abroad—a more unusual occurrence then than now—gave me the greatest pleasure. It was not long before we found this circle widening. Many of the acquaintances we had made abroad stretched their hands across the sea to us in friendly greeting. Many foreigners came to us with letters of introduction.

My Wednesday afternoons at home were very pleasant. At first only women called. Men were not supposed to have the leisure or inclination to make calls of an afternoon. But later on, after I had met many artists and musicians, as well as foreigners who were visiting New York, I often not only had representatives of the fair sex, but also many of the "unfair sex," as I jocosely called the men. Once, I remember, the Chinese Consul called with his guest, a secretary of the Chinese Legation at Washington. They were in oriental dress, their brilliant mandarin coats and jeweled headdresses making a picturesque bit of gleaming color in my drawing room. Bridget, my maid, confided to me later that she had nearly shut the front door in their faces when she saw those "Chinee men" with their pigtails down their backs. She thought at first they were Chinese laundrymen!

I began housekeeping under the most favorable circumstances. It was a joy to get our wedding presents out of storage and have them fit into our milieu.

My husband gave me—as a birthday gift—a Steinway grand piano, with an exceptionally sweet tone, which proved to be a source of the greatest pleasure to the many musicians who later played on it or sang to its accompaniments.

We gave many a "soirée musicale." These often had quite a cosmopolitan aspect. To our house came the Lord of the famous Muckross Abbey, Sonnenthal, the well-known German tragedian, Comte de Lafayette, descendant of the famous Lafayette, beloved of all Americans, Ole Bull's son, a violinist of distinction, but alas! greatly handicapped by his father's world-wide reputation, Ovide Musin, the celebrated Belgian violinist, Godowski, the Russian pianist, Henri Marteau, the young French virtuoso, and Gabrilowitsch, the renowned pianist and conductor. To meet these foreigners of distinction, we naturally invited some of our own distinguished Americans—Edmund Clarence Stedman, the banker-poet, Mr. and Mrs. Richard Watson Gilder, Brignoli, the sweet-voiced Italian tenor who made his home in New York, Mrs. McClellan, widow of the renowned General, Governor and Mrs. Hoffman, Mrs. Courtland Palmer, Baron and Baroness Neftel, Julia Marlowe, Mr. and Mrs. Carl Strakosh (Clara Louise Kellogg, the prima donna), David Bispham, and Mr. Samuel Clemens, better known as Mark Twain.

As I look back to those days, the distinguishing feature of our receptions—which contrast so strongly with the receptions of today—is the fact that we entertained our friends in our own home. Today, clubs and hotels take the place of home entertainments. This is largely due to the present custom of living in apartments, the increasing problem of efficient domestic service, and the modern habit of thought—to accomplish results with a minimum of responsibility. I wonder whether the modern hostess derives the same thrill and joy from her vicarious methods of hospitality as did the hostess of forty years ago, who planned with care and foresight every detail of the entertainment. It may not have been as "grand" or so "smart" as a modern function given at Sherry's, but at least in its fruition it was the expression of the hostess' own individuality. Herein lay its charm.

In the 'eighties there were no *"thé dansants"* of an afternoon. There were no cabarets, no dancing clubs. When we went to the theater of an evening, it was to see a comedy, a drama, or a Shakesperian tragedy. There was little or no vaudeville in first-class theaters, no "revues," no moving pictures or continuous performances. There was occasionally an "opera bouffe" or a musical comedy. The Gilbert and Sullivan operettas were popular at that time. Grand opera was given at the Academy of Music in Irving Place. It took us about half an hour to drive down in a coupé. There was no congestion of traffic as there is today. It would take longer today with an automobile, because of the traffic and the necessary regulations.

Adelina Patti was the favorite operatic star in those days. On the evening that she was advertised to sing, the Opera House was packed. It was common gossip that she received five thousand dollars a night—considered a large sum in those days. There was a current story that an impresario cabled to her to ask her terms and she replied: "Five thousand dollars a night, with Nicolini" (her husband, a tenor). The impresario wired: "How much without Nicolini?" Patti promptly cabled: "$5,000." The diva was fêted to such an extent that she was quite spoiled. I remember meeting her on one occasion on board the French steamer, *La Normandie*. The steamer was to sail from New York shortly. I was one of the guests at a breakfast given by Captain Frangeuil. After the noon breakfast, Madame Patti, Monsieur Nicolini, and a party of friends arrived to make arrangements to sail on the *Normandie's* next trip. One of Madame Patti's cavaliers asked the Captain to open some champagne for the party. This annoyed Captain Frangeuil, as he had intended doing so, but as host on board his own ship, he felt that no such request or suggestion should have come from a guest. However, he was very gracious and hospitable and ordered champagne for us all. The two groups were introduced and we had a pleasant half hour together. Then the tactless cavalier who accompanied Madame Patti suggested to the Captain that he offer his cabin to the diva for her proposed voyage, adding that she always expected this compliment to be paid her. But Captain Frangeuil had reached the limit of his patience. He responded that he was not in a position to do so. His remark to the rest of us—after Madame Patti had left the ship—was: "Quoique Patti qu'elle soit, je ne lui céderai point ma cabine!" We read in the papers shortly afterwards that Madame Patti and Monsieur Nicolini had sailed for France on another steamer.

Our summers were often spent at one of the typical large American country hotels. Our conception of summer life was entirely different then to what it is now. It seemed perfectly natural to me to form one of a group of women rocking on the piazza, embroidering and joining in the idle chat. Today a young woman would flee in horror from a three months' vacation spent in such a fashion. Our standard of what constitutes a vacation has changed. Today we plan to spend the summer either in our own villas or camps, or else travel abroad or go touring in our own country. Perhaps the most striking difference is that the American business man of today is learning how to play. In the 'eighties, he remained in the hot city all summer, earning the money that gave his wife and children the holiday. Today he appreciates that he needs the holiday quite as much as the rest of the family, and the summer cottage is selected with a view to providing him with his favorite pastime—golf, sailing, fishing, or motoring.

We spent several summers at the then fashionable watering place, Saratoga. The United States Hotel—that huge caravansary—was the mecca of many prominent New Yorkers. Many came for a short time—merely to attend the races. Our amusements were limited to an occasional game of croquet, or a bowling party, and dancing of an evening. Tennis was just beginning to be fashionable for young people. I was young enough to play, but I was a married woman. A sharp line was drawn in the old days between young girls and married women. The latter were supposed to be too dignified to join in such youthful sports. There were no golf links, so if a matron desired more exercise than a game of croquet or bowls afforded, she could take a long walk. Had I been at the seashore, I could have gone swimming. But there was not much freedom in swimming, in a bathing suit that extended from the collar bone to the wrists and ankles, and was further modestly covered by an extra skirt over the long pantalettes. The chief distraction was driving. Those who didn't drive sat on the front piazza of the hotel at Saratoga to see the well-groomed horses and stylish equipages go by. In those days even a wealthy man, who today would have a large country estate, often preferred to have a suite of rooms at a commodious hotel. Among the regular summer visitors at the United States Hotel was William H. Vanderbilt, who could be seen of an afternoon driving his famous horse, Maud S. One day he allowed me to pass him on the road. I was driving a horse hired from the local livery stable. I gleefully twitted him, saying that Maud N. could go at a more rapid pace than Maud S! I was considered rather sporty because I was fond of driving, and when my husband didn't hire a phaeton and pair of horses for me, I sometimes drove the horses that belonged to our friends.

The favorite drive was to the lake, where delicious fish and game dinners were served by an Indian named Crum, who lived in a small cottage with his two wives. He cooked the meals and his two wives served them. They were all apparently on the most harmonious terms. One well-known bachelor, whose sister had married the Governor of Rhode Island, gave a dinner there, which formed the topic of conversation for many a long day. He sent to New York for a huge box of American beauties to decorate the table, and also sent to Newport for large bunches of purple and white grapes from his hothouse. But this epicurean dinner did not taste better to me than did a picnic luncheon which we had one day under the trees. A friend of ours was in Saratoga with his coach and four horses. He asked me to make up a party to drive with him to Troy, where he intended sending his drag and horses to New York on the boat. I had the box seat and was delighted to have the opportunity to drive four horses—my host handing the reins over to me for part of the way. We were keeping house that summer, so we provided the lunch, while our host ordered the iced champagne. One of the party said she preferred ginger ale, but she was punished for her lack of good taste, for the two bottles we procured at a wayside inn, although marked ginger ale, had inadvertently been filled with kerosene oil. After she had taken one gulp from the bottle, the horrible taste remained with her for the rest of the day.

It was at Saratoga that a sensation was created by the action of the proprietor of the Grand Union Hotel. He refused accommodations to some members of a wealthy Jewish family, and afterward issued a statement to the effect that no Jews, except the members of two Jewish families who had for many years been their patrons, would in future be welcomed. I speak of this incident as "sensational" because it was the first time that any public discrimination had been made. This incident happened nearly fifty years ago. It proved to be an entering wedge. What is the situation today? Proprietors of fashionable resort hotels and of New York apartment houses frankly advertise that they exclude all Jewish patrons, using no discernment between Jewish families who have had generations of culture and refinement and those who lack such a background.

What is to be the outcome of this social discrimination? Are we of the cultured Jewish class to accept such a situation? Are we to acquiesce to segregation which amounts to forcing us into a social ghetto, or should we not make a protest?

To return to the summers of the 'eighties. Cozzen's Hotel, afterwards Cranston's, at West Point was a favorite resort of the young women of the day. The gray uniforms and brass buttons of the cadets added to the natural attractions of the place. It was a pretty sight to see the light organdie, beruffled dresses and gayly colored parasols about at dress parade. The Saturday evening dances and cotillions were the more brilliant because of the visiting cadets and officers. My husband often led these cotillions and I usually was chairman of a small committee to select the favors.

Mrs. John Bigelow, one of New York's best known society leaders, had her summer home not far from the hotel. Her husband had been Ambassador at the Court of St. James's, and she was prominent not only because of his position, but also because of her striking individuality. She had the reputation of giving cordial invitations and then frequently forgetting to remain at home to receive her guests. Mrs. Ulysses S. Grant told me of a dinner invitation extended to her and General Grant. When they arrived at her home, the house was in darkness and their hostess dining out.

When Oscar Wilde came to the United States to lecture, he was a guest at Mrs. Bigelow's West Point home. Mrs. Bigelow stopped at the hotel on her way to the station to announce his approaching arrival. She told us that she would bring him to the hotel, before taking him to her cottage, and she asked a group of us to remain on the piazza so she could introduce him to us. Mrs. Mackin (afterwards Princess Spottiswood-Mackin) wanted to make an impression on the apostle of aestheticism, so she went up to her room to make an elaborate toilet. When she returned, she found that Mrs. Bigelow and Oscar Wilde had already come and gone. Those of us who had been content to receive him in our simple gingham frocks had been presented to him and had been invited by Mrs. Bigelow to come to her cottage the following afternoon for tea. On that occasion, we all donned our best frocks and sallied forth to attend the "tea." Mrs. Bigelow and Mr. Wilde were out driving, we were told by the stately butler. We all left our cards and the next day Mrs. Bigelow called at the hotel, profuse with apologies—she had entirely forgotten about her invitation.

I recall another amusing incident connected with Oscar Wilde and Mrs. Mackin. Later in the same season at Saratoga, Oscar Wilde, who had been giving a lecture, joined us one evening as we sat on the piazza of the United States Hotel—James G. Blaine being one of our group. Mr. Wilde, whose unusual appearance always attracted a curious crowd, was followed by quite a mob. Mrs. Mackin, eager to save Wilde from further embarrassment and very much flustered and excited because he was joining our group, turned to Mr. Blaine—the oldest, most distinguished, and most honored member of the party—and asked him to get up and give his chair to Oscar Wilde. There was a moment of suspense—Mr. Blaine looked at the overwrought little woman, and with an amused expression, calmly kept his seat, while Oscar Wilde, followed by the gaping crowd, vainly tried to find a chair. It was a never-to-be-forgotten scene.

What few outdoor sports we had were carried on during the summer. Few people in New York went in for winter sports. If we had snow and ice, of course, some people went sleighing or skating, but it was only the exceptional few who went to Montreal for the tobogganing and other winter sports. No hotels in our country featured winter sports. There were few, if any, country clubs. Today when it is the usual custom to spend the week-end in the country, it seems difficult to picture the family life of nearly fifty years ago. Fifty years ago only invalids tried to escape the rigors of our New York winters. What a contrast to our present winter exodus to Florida, to California, to the West Indies, to the Riviera, to Egypt.

Only those who couldn't afford to live in the city remained in the country longer than two or three months. Today the situation is reversed. The larger the income the shorter the time spent in town.

Today in the cities, there is little or no visiting as we used to understand it. Club functions, civic meetings, committee meetings of various activities crowd the days to such an extent that there is little opportunity for the old-time form of friendly intercourse. We, today, depend upon greeting our friends at these meetings and our mutual interests form the bond which draws us together. In this way our circle becomes much wider and our interests broader than in the old days, but by some strange freak of chance, we often fail to touch those close by. Large cities are unneighborly. In this connection the following story is apposite: I was sitting on the deck of a steamer in far-off Alaska when a fellow passenger, hearing me called by name, came up to me, asking, "Can this be *the* Mrs. Nathan of New York?" I acknowledged being from New York, but it was only when she asked me whether I was President of the Consumers' League that I was sure I was the one she was seeking. It seemed that she had wanted to meet me for some time, to discuss a matter in connection with the work of the League, and although she lived in New York, and her home was one block distant from mine, she found her first opportunity for the desired interview when many thousand miles away from our own firesides.

In relating this incident, I have run ahead of my story. I have spoken of my mornings spent in embroidering and attending to my household duties, my afternoons taken up with shopping and social duties. But I have said nothing as yet of my restless spirit which reached out for broader contacts. Limited as my early activities were, they laid the foundation for more important work later. I had a natural pride in my city—the city in which nine generations of our family have been born. I must have felt the beginnings of an eagerness to help toward the uplifting of civic ideals—to be a vital part and influence in the great metropolitan life. These ideas were vague in my mind, and found no expression in words, for I was conscious that they would have met with ridicule, rather than sympathy. For women to dream of such ideals was not in harmony with the thought of the times. A friend of my own generation, when she was twenty-one, wrote these lines. They express the mid-Victorian sentiment to which I refer:

To sit behind the gilded lattice pane,
With perfumed toys idly play,
Whilst watching with a beating heart and kindling eye
The stream of life that passeth by.
To burn, to live our life out for ourselves,
Free and untrammeled from the social skirt
That holds us back, if we are fain to run too quickly.

It must have been about this time that I met the woman who was destined to have such a great influence over my life. My husband and I were invited to a friend's house to hear a paper read on Prison Reform. I was not specially interested in this subject. In fact, I had never thought about it. But I was beginning to be interested in wider social movements. Mrs. Josephine Shaw Lowell, who had been active in bettering the conditions of women prisoners, gave a poignant account of their hardships. She told of many injustices and of much unnecessary suffering they were forced to endure. I was deeply affected by the story of their wrongs. Before the evening was over, I was presented to Mrs. Lowell and, with evident emotion, I asked what could be done to change conditions. Mrs.

Lowell was impressed by my earnestness, and she said: "I am glad you realize the horror of the situation. One of my auditors has just said to me, 'I *enjoyed* your *charming* paper so much!' "

From that time, Mrs. Lowell took me under her wing and there grew between us a real friendship, despite the difference in our years. I admired her intensely and was only too glad to follow her lead in whatever direction she chose to take me.

A time came when I laid aside the embroidery of buffet scarfs and took up instead the scalloping of little flannel petticoats, the featherstitching of little flannel barrows, the fashioning of little nainsook night dresses. It may be far easier today for a young prospective mother to sit at a counter of a department store and order a complete layette for her baby, but she certainly loses the joy of making the garments herself, and with every stitch, sewing in her thoughts and hopes. This joy was mine. The deep, quiet happiness of coming motherhood enfolded me.

## An Interlude

We had waited nearly six long years for our baby, but when at last she came, oh, the joy! It seemed as though all the love during those years of waiting had been slowly growing, until at last it welled up and overflowed, embracing not only the tiny creature lying in the hollow of my arm, but the whole world besides. The six years that we longed for her seemed very, very long, but oh, how brief, how pitifully brief seemed the nine short years that we held her.

I could not at first grow accustomed to the wonder of motherhood. The marvelous happiness, the fulfillment of our love, almost frightened me. I would hang over the crib watching the sleeping child and exclaim to my husband, "It is too perfect. It cannot last!" Was this a

Annette Florance Nathan

My daughter.

Born January 28, 1886. Died January 17, 1895.

prophetic cry from the mother heart, feeling subconsciously the shadow that was creeping nearer and still nearer until at last Death himself stood by that precious crib and laid his quieting hand upon our darling little girl?

Before that shadow fell, our lives had been warmed by the sunshine of her presence. We had listened to the music of the child's laughter, to the patter of the little feet running to give us welcome. We had watched the unfolding of her mind that seemed to hold promise of noble, fine things. We had gained courage and strength ourselves from watching the development of these qualities in the child.

Such full happy years of planning for her future, training the awakening mind, so quick to take in new impressions! She seemed to inherit my facility for languages and at seven could express herself in French as easily as in English. Her little neighbors—two playmates—spoke German with their father, so she wished to learn that language too. She said, "I know every word in French now, why can't I have a German nursery governess and learn German, talking to her?" And we had the German governess for her. She had marked musical ability, and her great ambition was to be able to play so well that she could play my accompaniments when I sang. She memorized quickly and was able to play some simple compositions of Beethoven and Mozart without her notes.

Memories crowd upon me, and even at the distance of forty years, the wound is torn open. Such wounds never heal. Friends were kind. My husband's devotion in the sorrow that we shared together helped me to live during those first months. But it was the wisdom and sympathy of my very dear friend, Josephine Shaw Lowell, that gave me the strength to take up my life again. Richard Watson Gilder called her, "The lady of the lamp." Surely it was the lamp of hope that she held before my despairing eyes. Her days were full. There were many demands made upon her time. Yet she came to me at once, and sat an entire morning with me, making me see that I held within my hands the power of choice. It was for me to decide whether I was to allow my sorrow to spoil my life through selfish indulgence of grief, or enrich it through service to others. It was a hard path that Mrs. Lowell pointed out to me to tread, but I knew that she too had climbed it and had reached serene heights.

Was it providential that in the midst of a struggle not to succumb to this overwhelming sense of emptiness, the obliteration of all bright hopes that the opportunity to cast all this grief aside suddenly arose? I was the only one who could give certain sworn testimony before a Commission of Investigation looking toward the betterment of conditions for the working girls of the State. I made my choice. My crêpe veil was thrown aside, I faced the Commission in an effort to give whole-hearted testimony that would eventually lead to the protection that was to make the lives of many thousand girls less sordid and less gray.

## TO A. F. N.

Cease thy beating, Oh my heart!
    Canst thou then endure—pulse on?
Wilt thou verily not break
    Without her for whom do mourn
My eyes, my lips and my poor arms
    From which she has been torn!

Yea! Eyes that might as well be sightless
    Since her they no more now can see
Must still endure to gaze upon
    The flowers, the grass and every tree
She used to love to play among,
    So happy and so free!

And lips that should be mute and cold
    Since her to life they cannot kiss
Must still endure to speak and smile
    When told, The world is not amiss,
And Life is really worth the living
    Without that precious bliss!

Aye! Arms that feel so limp and empty
    Since she lies not in their embrace
Must still endure to bear Life's burden
    Sent to scourge our souls apace.
The coming years hold but the memory
    Of her sweet, joyous face!

March 30, 1895.

# CHAPTER VI

## WIDENING INTERESTS

In a preceding chapter I tried to give a picture of the normal everyday life of the average New York woman of my "set." This life did not satisfy me, nor fill my days. It left me restless, with a desire to use my energies in broader ways.

My husband's father—my uncle—had been one of the founders of Mt. Sinai Hospital. It was, therefore, natural that members of the family should take a deep interest in its growth and development. When the hospital established its training school for nurses, my cousin was asked to serve as its first president. On my return from our wedding trip, I was invited to become a member of the Board of Directors. It was unusual to place such a young woman—I was still in my teens—in positions which required good judgment and experience in reaching decisions. But no doubt the president felt the need of new material and the enthusiasm and energy of youth. This, my first experience as one of a Board of Directors, stands out in my mind as my initiation into work outside of my home. All my co-directors were women of more mature age than I. It is very likely that I felt an exaggerated sense of the importance of my position. I felt it incumbent upon me to attend every meeting, to give close attention to the proceedings, and to make myself familiar with the work of the organization. This spirit of earnestness and interest brought to this, my first directorship, I have brought to every succeeding organization of which I have been a part. It may have been an exaggerated sense of responsibility which overpowered me in this first experience; be that as it may, it served to impress upon me the actual duty of a Board Director. I have always felt that my name on a list of directors was of no value without my work, and because of this I have declined many an invitation to serve on a directorate. Not for any lack of interest in the various causes, but merely because I had not sufficient time to attend so many board meetings.

My next experience led me down to the East Side, where the Hebrew Free School Association was establishing schools for the purpose of teaching English to the recently arrived immigrants—and giving religious instruction to their children. At that time the kindergarten was not a part of the public school system. The association, recognizing, however, the advantages of this early training, opened a kindergarten and asked me to serve as chairman of the subcommittee in charge.

It was about this period that the outrageous persecutions in eastern Europe brought the enormous influx of Jews from Russia, Poland, and Roumania which poured into New York. Up to this time I may say that I had never heard the phrase, "The Jewish Problem." I have shown that our social life was an integral part of the social life of the community. My husband was one of the oldest members of the exclusive Union Club, as well as of several other of New York's exclusive clubs, and belonged to the Sons of the American Revolution. The members of these clubs and their families were entertained in our home and we were invited to theirs. Certainly such experiences did not tend to make for self-consciousness or gave any sense of social discrimination. We never felt that our religious background and outlook on life made a social barrier between ourselves and the best that New York offered. My husband was a faithful attendant at the synagogue. I usually accompanied him there on the Sabbath and Holy days. Notwithstanding my ever-widening interests, I never discarded my Jewish affiliations. When the sisterhood of the synagogue (analogous to a woman's auxiliary) was organized, I was its first president. Nevertheless, I was a pioneer among Jewish women in going outside of Jewish philanthropy and communal work.

Years later, when the National Council of Jewish Women was seeking a candidate for a new president, I was asked to allow my name to be brought forward. All this emphasizes the fact that it was recognized that I stood for Jewish interests, Jewish thought, Jewish feeling, quite as much as I stood for the broader and more universal outlook on life. Because of my recognized position as a Jewess, I was often invited to serve as a director in organizations, so that I might represent the ever-increasing Jewish interests. My cousins, Sarah Lazarus and her sisters, were acclaimed as leaders in the social and literary life of their day. Emma was doubtless the most brilliant of the group. Her strong Jewish feeling had lain dormant, until awakened by the persecutions of her people in eastern Europe. Her feeling that America was to be their place of refuge, their home, inspired her to write the poem which has been immortalized on the bronze tablet of the Statue of Liberty, standing at the gateway of New York harbor.[1]

It was this sudden avalanche of hitherto ghetto-imprisoned people that made it necessary for the Jews of New York to form committees at once in order to devise means of distributing these foreigners over the country and of endeavoring to Americanize them as rapidly as possible. My husband was one of the committee to help distribute the immigrants. It was often difficult to persuade them to leave New York. Many of them had relatives or friends who had preceded them long enough to have gained a foothold in the new land and it was only natural that

[1] See Appendix IV for poem, "The New Colossus."

these wretched, persecuted, terror-stricken people should long for the solace of companionship and friendship expressed through their mother-tongue.

I recall a vivid impression made upon me on one occasion when I was at the dock waiting to greet a member of the family returning from a trip abroad. I noticed a Polish immigrant on the deck of the incoming steamer, looking toward the new city. The impression made upon me was unforgetable. Were I an artist I could, today, many years later, depict the pathetic, haunting wistfulness, wonder, longing, loneliness, and bewilderment, even terror, that lay in his eyes. He had left behind him centuries of traditional habits of life, habits of thought. What was he to find in the new world? The expression in this man's eyes has always haunted me. It typified the attitude of our foreign immigrant toward his new home. It was the children of these immigrants that flocked to our kindergarten. These little ones were eager to learn, were tractable and many of them were most attractive, with blue eyes and light hair—a type often seen among the Russian Jews. From the kindergarten these children went to the public schools, and later to the City College. Today they are among those who form the strong commercial and financial backbone of our city.

I was not satisfied, however, to be identified only with Jewish organizations, and was glad to accept an invitation to become a member of the Board of Managers of the New York Exchange for Women's Work. I did not want to confine my work to a narrow communal circle. I must have had in me a strain of the spirit of my early ancestors who wished to take an active part in the civic life of the community, for I, too, felt the urge to be a part of the fabric—not merely a tiny thread weaving its way along the edge of the great pattern. The Exchange for Women's Work endeavored to solve the problem of the impoverished gentlewoman who felt she could not go out by the day to sew or to cook, but who needed to have her wares sold in order to eke out a small income. The Exchange not only provided a market for the product, it also helped consignors to become experts, to specialize, to become better craftswomen and artisans.

Again I was the youngest member of the Board. Mrs. William G. Choate, the President, was a woman of mature age and among the women grouped about her on the Board were such well-known New Yorkers as Mrs. Russell Sage, Mrs. William Perry, Mrs. Charles Terry, Mrs. Lowry, Mrs. Higginson.

Some of the committees met once a week, but the Board of Managers only met once a month and I did not find my duties onerous. Mrs. Choate always welcomed new members of the Board by calling upon them in their homes and she thus established social ties which made for a spirit of sympathy and friendliness at our Board meetings.

The final meeting of the season of the Exchange for Women's Work—the one in June—was held in Wallingford, Conn., at the country home of the President. The expedition to Wallingford for the June meeting was in a sense a gala occasion. We looked forward to spending the day at the old homestead, under the spreading elms of the sleepy picturesque village. The house had been the home of the Choate family for generations. The old rafters in the low-ceilinged living room were black and rough. A mirror was placed in this room so that the shady avenue leading to the door of the house was reflected in it and one felt that even sitting indoors, one could feel the waving branches of the wide-spreading trees. The spirit of friendliness shown by Mrs. Choate toward her directorate gave me a standard for action. When I became the President of the Consumers' League of New York, I am sure that the cordial coöperation and sympathetic understanding which always existed between me and my Board of forty members were aided by the social ties thus formed.

While serving on the Board of the Exchange for Women's Work, our attention was called to the fact that many of the consignors—gentlewomen in reduced circumstances, who earned a livelihood making beaded passementeries in their homes—would be seriously affected if a certain proposed new tariff bill became a law.

This bill (the Dingley Tariff Bill) contained a clause placing as high a tariff on beads in the bulk as on the finished beaded passementerie trimmings. Labor being so much cheaper in France, the importer would naturally buy the finished product rather than the raw material. Thus, if the bill passed, women in our country would be deprived of this work which was not only well paid, but was home work which could be done during leisure hours.

I was impressed by the statement of these facts and my interest was further aroused when a well-known manufacturer of trimmings gave me more details and showed me the injustice which would result from this tariff, if the bill were passed. He, seeing my interest, suggested that I take up the matter through correspondence with the New York Senators at Washington, with the New York members of the House of Representatives, as well as with the members of the committee who had the tariff bill under consideration.

The proposition at first seemed ludicrous to me. But when I found that he was serious, I was overwhelmed by the burden of responsibility that had suddenly been placed upon me. It was a new idea to me. Could one inexperienced, insignificant woman, through a written plea, swerve the minds of the men who were making the laws of our country? Yet I realized that my plea would be a disinterested one, while a plea from the manufacturers of passementeries would naturally be deemed one of self-interest and, therefore, might not carry as much weight.

I found no sympathy at home. My husband chaffed me good-naturedly, and was amused at my undertaking the serious correspondence which involved the presentation of facts with which I had first to make myself thoroughly acquainted. This only strengthened my determination to put the matter through. I warned him that if I didn't succeed through correspondence in getting the bill amended, I would make a journey to Washington in order to obtain personal interviews with the sponsors of the measure. However, this was not necessary. Much to my surprise and gratification, I was informed that my statements had been given due consideration and the tariff on the raw material (the beads) had been very appreciably lowered, in order that the working women of our own country might be given the work of making the finished product (the passementerie trimmings).

This was my first experience in the game of politics. I was flushed with triumph. The manufacturer who had told me about the tariff bill was so delighted at my success that he gave me a theater party, followed by a supper at Delmonico's.

This incident of getting the tariff changed was the first political work I ever did. There was a certain amount of elation and excitement in feeling that I had the power to help in big constructive work, national in scope. So, when Mrs. Josephine Shaw Lowell, at Dr. Charles Parkhurst's urgent request, formed the Women's Municipal League and consented to be the President, inviting me to serve as Vice President, I accepted with glee and enthusiasm. It was because of the glaring corruption in some of the city departments of government that Dr. Parkhurst felt that it was time that women should take a stand and come forward to assist the Citizens' Union in exposing the evils and in bringing about an era of higher standards. This was considered a most radical step.

Up to this time, women had not been expected to take

an active part in the political life of the city. Dr. Parkhurst blazed the way. He realized that here was an extraordinary opportunity for women to use their power and influence for the good of the city, even though they did not possess the ballot.

There was much scoffing among certain groups of men, who asked what mere women, with no political status, could possibly accomplish to change conditions. This movement meant for me the opening of prison doors. Women had been kept behind bars, their hands manacled, their feet tied by the ball and chain of conventionality. At last, we were summoned to go out in the open and do our share of human uplift work.

The spirit of my childhood days which had rebelled at the gift of my father's old tarnished cup when my brother had been presented with a bright, shiny new one, the spirit which had resented the fact that my brother was given more pin money than I, because he was a boy, the spirit that failed to understand why girls should wait for boys to invite them to dance—this latent feminism was now about to come into its own!

Men were not the only scoffers. There were women, too, who thought that these civic duties would take too much of a housekeeper's time. Some of the members of my family circle expressed this fear. Therefore, as a rebuke to such half-formulated criticism, I was more diligent than ever in carrying on my household duties. During preserving and pickling season, the usual allotment of jars was placed on the shelves, nor were social duties ignored. Dinner calls had to be made, afternoon teas had to be attended, whether graft or corruption were to be exposed in city departments or not.

Realizing that the best way to secure competent, efficient officials in the various branches of city government was to secure them through civil service examinations, I was glad to accept an invitation from Mrs. William Schieffelin, President of the Woman's Auxiliary to the Civil Service Reform Association, to become a member of that organization. Mrs. Schieffelin was a beautiful woman, and one of New York's social leaders. Her son, William Jay Schieffelin, inherited much from his mother, and his interest in civic affairs has led to his being the Chairman of the Citizens' Union for many years.

While writing of the Woman's Auxiliary, I cannot refrain from telling an amusing anecdote in connection with an annual dinner and meeting held by the Civil Service Reform Association. Carl Schurz, a leading citizen, who had come from Germany to escape militarism and autocracy, was the President of the Association. I had met him at a wedding reception a short time previously, when he and General Sherman having kissed the bride, attempted to kiss me, too, having been playfully introduced to them as "another bride." I protested with all the dignity I could muster that I was an old married woman of four or five years standing. My youthful appearance, however, seemed to bear testimony against me, and the last Mr. Schurz saw of me was when I was being carried off by General Sherman—to supper—he still urging his prerogative. When I met Mr. Schurz at the above-mentioned association dinner, his first question was, "Did General Sherman get his kiss?" "For," he added, "if so, I am entitled to one, too, since I was a claimant at the same time. It would not be fair,'" he argued, "to have allowed the General the privilege unless you grant me the same." At that moment Oswald Villard—who was at that time one of the editors of the New York *Evening Post*—came up to greet us and said he hoped he was not interrupting a conversation which apparently was an absorbing one. I offered to repeat to Mr. Villard what Mr. Schurz had just been saying to me, so that he could judge for himself how serious the topic of conversation had been! Whereupon the dignified, almost austere Carl Schurz dropped on his knees, placed his hands together in supplicating gesture and said to me in an appealing and comical way, "You wouldn't be so cruel as to expose me in the New York *Evening Post?*" We all had a hearty laugh, and as dinner was announced, Mr. Schurz gallantly offered me his arm and asked me whether he might have the honor of placing me next to him at the table. On our way into the banquet hall, I explained that I could not accept the honor of being seated next to him at the platform table, because I had learned that no women, not even Mrs. Schieffelin, the President of the Woman's Auxiliary, were to be thus distinguished. I had suggested to Mrs. Schieffelin that she insist upon this courtesy which I felt was due her, but she replied that she didn't care to be the only woman at the dais table, so she did not protest. Mr. Schurz grasped the situation at once and said, "She shall certainly sit at the platform table, and in order to make her feel comfortable, you shall sit there, too." So he quickly arranged that Mrs. Schieffelin should sit on his right and I on his left. No doubt the two men who had expected to sit at the end seats were relegated unceremoniously to another table.

It was in 1891 that Mrs. Josephine Shaw Lowell asked me to help her in investigating conditions in retail mercantile establishments. That was the beginning of a work which was later to absorb so large a part of my time that I was obliged to resign from several positions which had previously occupied my time and attention.

I have recently published a history of the Consumers' League movement,[1] but it seems fitting to speak here of the inception of the movement and what it meant. The condition of employees in department stores was brought to the attention of Mrs. Josephine Shaw Lowell. Her sympathies were aroused and she investigated and then called a meeting to discuss the matter. The subject was reviewed

1 *The Story of An Epoch-making Movement,* published by Doubleday, Page & Company.

from the points of view of both employer and employee and it was decided that the best way to change conditions was for the consumers—the purchasing public—to use their power and take the matter in hand. Thus the Consumers' League was organized.

I became absorbed in the work and accompanied Mrs. Lowell on all her early investigations. After Mrs. Lowell had served as President for nearly seven years, she resigned, and I was elected her successor. I became so closely identified with the work that thirty-five years later, after I had ceased all active participation in the organization, I was recognized by a saleswoman at one of our leading department stores. It is an interesting incident:

After making some purchases, I gave my name and address to a rather middle-aged saleswoman. She at once looked searchingly into my face and said, "Are you the Mrs. Nathan who did so much for the saleswomen in the stores?" I admitted that I had been for many years the President of the Consumers' League. She dropped her pencil saying, "Excuse me just a minute. I want the other girls to meet you." She returned from the other side of the counter with three other clerks in the department and introduced them to me, saying proudly, "This is the lady who got seats behind counters for us, got hours of work shortened, got the Saturday half-holiday for us in summer, got vacations with pay, and got better conditions generally for us." "Good Lord!" exclaimed one of the younger clerks, "you don't mean to say that conditions were ever worse than they are now?" "You don't know what you're talking about," said the older woman with conviction. Then she proceeded to tell the young woman of the conditions under which the women worked in that same store thirty-five years earlier.

It will not be necessary to repeat any detailed account of the work of the League, but it may not be amiss to express here my conviction that the Consumers' League was responsible to a great degree for my growth and development. I have told in *The Story of An Epoch-Making Movement* how my social conscience was awakened and how I learned to view facts from the point of view of the working girl. The great seething, hustling drab life of the submerged tenth had been hitherto a closed door to me. This work made me an articulate being.

The first time that Mrs. Lowell asked me to give an account of our investigation and tell of the principles and aims of the Consumers' League, I was frightened and self-conscious as a timid schoolgirl. It was at a meeting held in the Vestry rooms of St. Bartholomew's Church. Had the years stood still? Was I once again about to read my "graduation composition"? Certainly I was no more terror-stricken then than now. My hands trembled so that I could scarcely hold the paper. My knees were shaking beneath my skirts. Today their quaking would not have been invisible! My throat was parched and I gave a sigh of relief when at last the ordeal was over. I turned to Mrs. Lowell who sat at my side and I said, "Never ask me to read a report again. I'll sing for you with pleasure. I'll tramp the streets with you to make investigations. I'll contribute money, time, strength to the cause, but never again can I put in such a *mauvais quart d'heure* as the last." Mrs. Lowell smiled sympathetically and said, with a wise nod, "Oh, yes, you'll soon conquer that nervousness and make many more speeches." Her prophecy came true. Since then I have given addresses not only in various parts of our own country, but also in England, France, Germany, Austria, Hungary, Holland, Belgium, Sweden, Switzerland, and even in the Philippines, China, and Japan.

In connection with this statement, I am reminded of an amusing incident which occurred in Japan. After giving an address to a group of Japanese women who had gathered to hear me at Mrs. Asano's beautiful home in Tokyo, the reporter of one of the leading Japanese papers asked me to pose in the garden for a photograph, and he asked me whether I had spoken many times previously, and if so, where. In a vein of humor, I replied mischievously, "Oh, yes. I've spoken before." And then I glibly enumerated some of the many meetings I had addressed all over the world. He jotted this down—I presume in shorthand—and the next day my picture was published in the newspaper with an account in the Japanese language of my activities. I sent a copy of the paper to my niece who lived in San Francisco and who happened to have a Japanese cook at that time. She asked him to translate the text of the article for her. He read it and, shaking his head, said, "Oh, she make a lot of talk!" "Why, what do you mean?" replied my niece, fearing that I had unwittingly been involved in some scandal. "Oh," he retorted, "she talk a lot!" This phrase has become a classic in the family circle. However, I may state that although I may have "talked a lot" I have never accepted an invitation to speak unless I felt sure that I had a message to give.

I have spoken on industrial conditions, the ethics of domestic service, responsibilities of consumers, equal rights for women, the position of women throughout the centuries, the points of contact and agreement between Judaism and Christianity. I have spoken at International Congresses, before Committees of Congress and of State legislatures, in churches, colleges, schools, at political gatherings in large halls and in parlors. I have given addresses in English, French and German, but I have always made it a rule to decline any invitation to speak on subjects which did not lie close to my heart.

It was through my work in the Consumers' League, in endeavoring to secure better legislation for regulating hours and conditions in industry, that I became convinced that legislators would never give consideration to the women's point of view, so long as we women had no politi-

Medals bestowed in recognition of the author's work in helping to ameliorate conditions for women and children in industry, and for work in connection with the Woman's Roosevelt Memorial Association.

1: Presented by the Woman's Roosevelt Memorial Association, 1924.
2: Presented by the National Institute of Social Sciences, 1913.
3: Presented by the jury of the Liege Exposition, 1905.

cal status. Thus I became more and more interested in the Equal Suffrage Movement. My mind, in a way, had been prepared for this idea. There was nothing new or startling about it, since during my four years life in Wisconsin, I often heard accounts of what women were accomplishing in the western State of Wyoming, where they already had the vote. Moreover, I had sat at the feet of Elizabeth Cady Stanton in her home and had listened to her tell of her experiences as a pioneer in the cause. Her daughter, Harriot Stanton Blatch, and I were warm friends, and with her my husband and I had more than once sat at her mother's hospitable board.

It was always a pleasure to meet Mrs. Stanton's handsome son, Theodore, who had married a Frenchwoman and made his home in Paris. He was invariably one of the first to welcome us whenever we reached the French capital. He, too, was an apostle of the gospel of equal rights and as a journalist often contributed a noteworthy article in favor of the cause. Mrs. Stanton had raised and educated a family of five sons and two daughters and yet she had found time to write many articles and addresses, some of which her friend, Susan B. Anthony, delivered for her, because she did not wish to leave her growing babies.

It may not be amiss here for me to pay a well-deserved tribute to the modern woman who is able to combine so happily her household and social duties with her wide philanthropic and civic responsibilities. I have in mind several leading women in New York who are at the head of well-known philanthropic organizations. They are called upon constantly to give public addresses and to attend committee meetings, yet they have time to supervise their city and country homes, give entertainments for their daughters budding into womanhood, and far from becoming nervous wrecks, they are seen at all metropolitan functions, smiling and gracious, witty and winsome. These women—women like Mrs. John Henry Hammond, Mrs.

James Lees Laidlaw, and Mrs. Edgerton Parsons—have been able to accomplish much, because they were encouraged by the spirit of the age. The women who did pioneer work in New York were hampered by criticism and a spirit of antagonism. They were called "strong-minded women" and were scoffed at. That expression is not heard today.

I owe a debt of gratitude to the strong-minded women under whose influence I came. Their minds were strong, their natures sweet. It was a wonderful privilege for a young woman, just starting out in life, eager for self-expression, to have the guidance and example of such women as Julia Ward Howe, Josephine Shaw Lowell, Grace Dodge, Susan B. Anthony, Mrs. William Choate, Mrs. William Schieffelin, Miss Louisa Schuyler, Dr. Mary Putnam Jacobi, and Alice Stone Blackwell.

I cannot close this chapter without acknowledgment of the greatest help I received in all my work—my husband's unfailing encouragement and faith in me. It was his sympathy that gave me strength and confidence. He, too, had his outside interests along philanthropic lines. He was Honorary Secretary of the Hudson District of the Charity Organization Society and served as a director in more than one Jewish institution. For more than twenty-five years he was Treasurer of the Home for Aged and Infirm Hebrews.

He evinced his whole-hearted interest in all my work. When it was necessary for me to leave home to attend conventions or to give an address, he was as eager and keen as I was and he invariably accompanied me. It sometimes meant a probable monetary loss when the Stock Exchange was active, but he never considered a money loss equivalent to a loss of companionship, or a loss of spiritual values.

## CHAPTER VII

### CROWDED DAYS

THESE were indeed crowded days. Looking over my scrapbooks, I am amazed to find so many evidences of ever-widening interests. It was all so wonderful, so exciting, so thrilling.

To think, for instance, that Edward Everett Hale—one of my heroes, whom I had heard preach and had met in Boston—should write to me and beg me to serve on a committee he had formed with such people as Mrs. James T. Fields, Mrs. Mary Lowe Dickinson, Mrs. Francis Barlow, and Dr. William Rainsford, for the purpose of sending books to the Southern mountaineers.

The title of my essay on graduation day was, "Awake, 'tis day!" And I often thought, Ah, I'm awake now, awake to a day full of possibilities, never dreamed of in that long ago. I was delighted when I was asked to help in civic betterment. To do my bit for my beloved city stirred me to the depths. I was glad to be one of a committee formed to save Central Park from the encroachments of business, and preserve it for its original purpose—a breathing spot for the people. Later a similar committee was formed for Riverside Drive and here, too, I had the privilege of helping to save that unique driveway for future generations. By this time, I was beginning to be identified with a variety of progressive work for the welfare of women and children. Because of this interest I was asked to be one of the Board of Directors of the Martha Washington Hotel, the first of a group of hotels established in New York for the exclusive use of women.

It is difficult, today when women of all ages are free to go and come as they choose, to understand the hampering complications which surrounded them forty years ago, the moment they left their fireside without the protection of a man. It was, for instance, impossible for a woman arriving alone at night in New York to secure accommodations at a first-class hotel, unless she were personally known to the management. A woman reporter, claiming that such an absurd rule could not possibly prevail, determined to ascertain the fact for herself. Carrying her bag in her hand, she wandered from one well-known hotel to another vainly seeking a room. She stated that her train had been delayed and that accounted for the late hour her quest was made—between eleven P.M. and two A.M. Nowhere was she given accommodations. The clerks often stating frankly that without a "male escort" she could not secure a room at that hour of the night. The reporter's write-up of this experience created a sensation and incidentally proved a stepping stone in her career. She is now a well-known journalist.

It was the publicity given this incident that aroused public opinion to the necessity of establishing hotels for women. Hotels where women could arrive at any hour of the night, alone, without their respectability being questioned.

In connection with the absurd tradition that a woman to be respectable must be accompanied by a "male escort" another story comes to my mind. One hot midsummer day, Mrs. Harriot Stanton Blatch returned to New York from a day's outing with a *female* friend. They were stopping at the Women's University Club, which was then on Madison Square. The dining room was in the basement and on this sultry day was unbearably hot. Mrs. Blatch suggested that they walk across the square to the Hoffman House. This hotel advertised that its dining room on the roof was cool and open to all the breezes.

It was still daylight as they sauntered through the park and the sun sufficiently high for them to put up their parasols. Mrs. Blatch, knowing the stern morality (!) of New York hotels, took the precaution to inquire at the desk whether two ladies, unaccompanied by a gentleman, could be served at the restaurant on the roof. The clerk, being evidently new to the peculiar customs of the metropolis, answered without hesitation in the affirmative. Mrs. Blatch and her companion, therefore, took the elevator to the roof. They were shown to a table by the unctuous head waiter, but after being seated for some time and receiving no further attention they became restless. They looked about and noticed that parties who had come in later than they were being served, while no waiter had been sent to take their order. They summoned the head waiter to make a complaint. He raised his eyebrows, inquiring: "Are you not waiting for the rest of your party?" Upon being assured that they expected no one to join them, he stated peremptorily and without apology that the rules of the hotel forbade the serving of ladies in the roof restaurant, unless accompanied by a male escort. In vain did Mrs. Blatch contend that she had taken pains to make inquiries at the desk and had been informed that such was not the case. The head waiter was obdurate. He insisted upon their leaving the restaurant. So, followed by the astonished glances of those who had been witness to this controversy, they were obliged to leave the restaurant—dinnerless. The sequel to this story is that Mrs. Blatch, wishing to make this a test case, brought suit against the management of the hotel. Of course, this suit was of intense interest to all of Mrs. Blatch's friends and co-workers in the feminist cause. I was in court when the Judge gave the charge to the jury. He warned the jury against considering the sex of the plaintiff in arriving at their verdict. As the whole contention was one of sex, this charge seemed to me extraordinary and illogical. Needless to say Mrs.

Blatch *lost her suit,* but the feminist movement gained in strength.

It was about this time that Mrs. Lowell resigned as President of the Consumers' League and I was elected to fill her place. I was overwhelmed with a sense of the great responsibility thrust upon me. I lay awake at night wondering how I could possibly wear the mantle of this great and noble woman. The mere detail of parliamentary procedure filled me with alarm. I bought Fox's Parliamentary Law and studied everything I could find on parliamentary ruling. The members of the large board were all much older than I in years and in experience. I was determined to be worthy of the honor they had bestowed upon me. As President, I was an ex-officio member of all the committees. The lesson I learned years before in my first experience as a board member of Mt. Sinai Training School for Nurses stood me in good stead now. There was no detail of the work too insignificant to engage my attention, and I kept myself in close touch with all the work of the organization.

Through all these activities, I was gradually growing to appreciate that I had a message to give, that in this great seething city of New York my personality counted. The vision that had brought my ancestors to this new land of opportunity many generations before was filling my soul, too.

I was asked to speak from the pulpits of many churches on the subjects with which I had now become closely identified—Bettering Conditions for Women and Children, Civic Reform, the Political Status of Women. The fact of my being a loyal Jewess never limited my opportunities. On two occasions I was asked by the League of Unitarian Women to present the points of contact and agreement between Judaism and Christianity from Unitarian pulpits. It is scarcely necessary to point out that this meant preparation in the way of study and research work. The sympathetic coöperation I received from the leading clergymen of the country was really wonderful. While in the midst of activity, one does not always appreciate the encouragement one receives, but in looking back I can see what an amazing thing it was for a young woman to have her hands held up by such men as Bishop Potter, Rev. Heber Newton, Dr. Henry van Dyke, Father Lavelle, Father Huntington, Dr. Thomas Slicer, Dr. John Haynes Holmes, Felix Adler.

Dr. Percy Grant was always generous in offering his church (the Church of the Ascension) for all progressive movements. I spoke there on the Consumers' League and later in the interest of Civic Reform. When the first suffrage parade was being arranged, it was Dr. Grant who offered us the use of his Parish House as a resting place during the formation of the section that was to gather in West Tenth Street. I always found Dr. Grant most sympathetic and broad in his point of view. If any matter required publicity and it was brought to his attention, he was generous in giving that publicity from his pulpit. His breadth of view was stimulating, but his desire to have both sides of a question presented in the forum which he conducted in connection with his church—even though these views might be opposed to the tenets of his Church—brought him into conflict with his higher ecclesiastical authorities. No one grieved more deeply than I did that his later years were clouded by turmoil and dissension, for I well knew the sincerity of his purpose.

When Dr. Mottet of the Church of the Holy Communion inaugurated his midday lenten services for the working people of his neighborhood, he conceived the idea of having the message of the Consumers' League brought to these workers. He asked me to address one of those midday meetings. It is a source of great gratification to me that years afterward when Dr. Mottet was engaged in writing a history of the Church of the Holy Communion, he wrote, asking me to send him the gist of that address, adding that no history of the church would be complete without a chapter dealing with that occasion. Dr. Mottet's parish, situated in the heart of a district where many Russian Jewish workers earn their daily bread, had brought him into contact with many of their problems. His desire to minister to their needs with no thought of proselyting has shown me another beautiful side of his rare spiritual nature.

Bishop Potter gave me his cordial friendship. Once when addressing him, I called him "my bishop." His eyes twinkled with amused query. "Why not?" said I. "You are the Bishop of New York and I am a New Yorker." He was always ready to help in any cause brought to his attention, and while he was not *my* Bishop in the accepted sense of the term, his coöperation was given as freely as though I had been one of his flock. He was very broad and generous in his views, as the following incident will show:

A certain paragraph in an annual report of the Pro-Cathedral down on the East Side had been brought to my attention. This paragraph alluded in most derogatory language to the Russian Jews of that district. It was, from my point of view, most unjust and wholly offensive. Without hesitation I took the report to Bishop Potter and, laying the paragraph before him, asked whether the statements met with his approval. He read the paragraph carefully and agreed with me that the tone was offensive and the statements unfair. He also added that the young, inexperienced Vicar of the Pro-Cathedral had made a mistake in so expressing himself. The matter did not end here. Bishop Potter sent for the young Vicar and rebuked him. Later this Vicar called on me and frankly made an apology for the statement which had so aroused me. It was easy to see that his youth and zeal had led him to a disproportionate view. To prove to me that he had no desire to proselyte, that his one idea was to minister to the spiritual needs of a community that seemed to him without sufficient light, he then and there asked me to take charge of a class of children in religious instruction, putting a room of the Pro-Cathedral at my disposal. The idea appealed to me and I longed to be able to do it, but it was impossible. I simply did not have the time. The day had only twenty-four hours. However, rather than relinquish such an opportunity, I accepted tentatively and begged the wife of our Rabbi, Mrs. H. Pereira Mendes, to conduct such a class in my place. This she consented to do, and only discontinued it after two years or more when her health forced her to restrict her activities.

Years afterwards that young Vicar was made a Bishop of the Church and far from resenting my being the cause of his having been disciplined by his superior, he sent me an invitation to attend his ordination. I was glad to be present.

When I hear talk of prejudice and unkind feeling, I like to recall these evidences of true Christian spirit. After all what is the Christian spirit? The spirit of Christ, the spirit of the young Jew preaching the deeper spirituality of Judaism, his faith. This is seldom realized. The following story from my own experience will emphasize this point clearly. At a session of the Conference of the Federation of Churches of Christ, William E. Dodge, presiding, I was scheduled to speak on the relationship of religion and ethics to business life. I sat quietly on the platform—outwardly quiet, but inwardly with rising indignation—as one speaker after another stressed the importance of Christianizing the business world in order to raise standards. Finally I was introduced. Before giving my prepared address, I referred to the remarks of the previous speakers. I stated in no uncertain terms that it was obviously unnecessary to "Christianize" the business world, since three outstanding mercantile firms in our country, located respectively in New York, Boston, and Sacramento, had standards so high that they served as a measuring rod for others and these three department stores were owned and managed by Jews.

While it was undoubtedly interesting and gratifying to be invited to give addresses in various churches, not only in New York, but in other cities, I experienced an entirely different thrill when I was invited to deliver the sermon from the pulpit of Temple Beth-El during a Sabbath eve service. It happened that New Year's Day fell on a Friday that year, making this service a special occasion and bringing out an unusually large congregation. It was with a deep sense of satisfaction and delight that I mounted the pulpit where traditions had been discarded. I have been told that I was among the first women to be so recognized in any synagogue.

It may be a cause of wonder as to how I could have responded to all these varied demands without neglecting my home and my social duties. I don't know myself how I did it, for as I look back to those days of multiplicity of interests, there is also over them all the glamour and charm of a delightful social life. I am grateful to my ancestors who handed down to me a constitution that enabled me to work all day and play all evening without any sense of fatigue. I even managed to keep up my music and gathered around me quite a coterie of musical people. Ovide Musin, the well-known Belgian violinist, kept one of his violins under my piano, and Ole Bull, son of the famous violinist, made good use of it one day when he called.

Once when Nikisch had gone to Philadelphia, Baltimore, and Washington to conduct the Boston Symphony Orchestra, of which he was the leader, Mrs. Nikisch accepted my invitation to spend a few days with me. One morning after breakfast we sat down at the piano intending to run over a few German Lieder—we were still there when the butler announced luncheon! It was during this visit of Mrs. Nikisch that a most amusing incident occurred.

Timothy Adamowski had promised to send us tickets for a concert at Sherry's in which Paderewski and the Adamowski brothers were the stars. The tickets did not arrive, so I said to Mrs. Nikisch, "Never mind, we'll go to the concert and I'll get tickets at the door." "What!" protested Mrs. Nikisch, "pay three dollars a ticket? I never heard of such extravagance. I cannot permit it!" The wife of the conductor of the Boston Symphony Orchestra, accustomed to free access to all concerts, was horrified at the thought of my paying for her ticket. She asked for Mr. Adamowski at the door, but we were told that the concert had begun and the first trio was being played. When we reached the auditorium, Mr. Adamowski saw us and nearly dropped his cello. Until that moment his promise to send us tickets had entirely escaped his memory. I felt that my six dollars had been well expended, as not only did we enjoy a beautiful concert, but I met Paderewski afterward, and had a delightful chat with him in French. I had already met the Adamowski brothers, as they had frequently been guests at the suppers invariably given by Arthur Nikisch after the Symphony Concerts. To these, my husband and I were frequently invited. Indeed, I can still hear Mr. Nikisch's laughter as I told him on one of these occasions that when my younger brother had announced to me his approaching marriage and had asked me to officiate as our mother's representative, I had replied, "Certainly, provided the marriage does not take place on a Boston Symphony Concert date!"

Again glancing at my scrapbooks, I am reminded of still another activity. I was beginning to speak with my pen, as well as with my tongue. The scrapbooks are filled with letters signed by me on various timely subjects. These letters were published in the *Evening Post,* the

*Herald,* the *Tribune,* and the *Times.* Occasionally, I wrote an article for a magazine, and I am proud to remember that the first article I ever wrote appeared in the *North American Review,* at that time the leading serious magazine published in this country. It was a refutation of an article written by Prof. Goldwin Smith entitled, "The Old Testament: the Millstone around Christianity's Neck," which had been published in that magazine.

My days were crowded with scheduled engagements, and the unlooked-for incidents. As for instance the unexpected call at the end of a full day. One night when I came home late from the theater, I found on my desk a note from a protégée, urging me to come to her. Her eldest son—the apple of her eye—was critically ill. I went to her at once. The friendly human sympathy helped the lonely woman through the hard hours of the crisis.

There were many varied and amusing incidents connected with all this activity. Being in the limelight meant being besieged by reporters. They were constantly coming to the house for "stories." They would not be denied. One day I came home and found a man on a stepladder placed opposite my portrait in the drawing room, balancing a camera, just ready to take a snapshot. My indignant questions brought suave replies, while the bewildered maid explained that the gentleman had assured her that he had madam's permission to take the photograph. I never objected to supplying reporters with facts concerning the work in which I was interested—I felt that it was good publicity—but I did object to distorted facts and to intimate personal details with which they sometimes chose to embroider stories.

For instance, the Pope had just issued a manifesto against "Woman Suffrage." Late that night I was called on the telephone and asked my views. My husband, answering the telephone, stated that I was in bed and could not be disturbed. The insistent reporter asked for my husband's views. He replied that American women would no doubt continue to demand the vote with or without the Pope's sanction. The next morning on the front page of the *Times,* was the headline, "Mr. Nathan, speaking for Mrs. Nathan, says, 'The Pope may disapprove of Woman Suffrage, but God is on our side'!" My husband's indignation may be imagined.

One day about tea-time, a timid, girlish-looking reporter called at my home and appealingly asked me for an interview. She looked so frightened, seemed so at a loss as to how to begin, that I felt sorry for her. I had tea brought in and over the teacups I laughingly suggested what questions she should put to me. The poor child was delighted. She whipped out her notebook and between sips of tea and bites of cinnamon toast, she jotted down my answers to the questions I had myself propounded! She was quite charming and I had enjoyed the experience of interviewing myself. As she was leaving, she admitted that she was a cub reporter and that she had dreaded this interview as it was her first assignment. "However," she added, "if they are all going to be as delightful as this, I'm glad I decided upon journalism as a profession." Years later, "Beatrice Fairfax" and I had a good laugh over this, her first interview. She then told me of the experience of her second interview. She had been sent to the home of a certain social leader to get a special story. She called in the afternoon. The lady sent down word that she would see her that night between ten and eleven. The reporter sent back a message to the effect that being a stranger in New York she was timid about being out at night. The reply was: "Young woman, if you intend to earn your livelihood as a reporter, you'd better begin at once to get accustomed to night work."

Some reporters are not always interested in facts. What they want is a good story. Any incident which can be twisted or distorted into sensationalism will serve their purpose, as the following anecdote will show:

A certain young woman, a well-known author, socialistic in her tendencies, had been a speaker at a luncheon. We happened to leave the room together. Not agreeing with some of the statements she had made, we were discussing these points as we went down in the elevator together. We were still arguing as we left the hotel. As I was very much interested, I said to her, "If you are going uptown, jump into my car and we'll thrash this out as we go along." As she was about to get into the car, a young reporter who had been hovering around us interrupted, saying, "Oh, Miss Y., you promised to give me a story. Do walk uptown with me instead." The author admitted that the reporter had a prior claim, and politely thanking me for my proffered courtesy, she turned and joined the reporter. A couple of days later a friend showed me a clipping from a newspaper article. The article reported the luncheon, giving a résumé of the speaker's remarks, stressing the radical points. It then stated that Mrs. Frederick Nathan, one of the officers of the Association under whose auspices the luncheon had been given, had in a patronizing manner offered the speaker a seat in her car, which the young author, true to her socialistic views, had spurned with indignation! Some months later I met this reporter. She approached me sheepishly, saying: "I don't suppose you liked that story I got into the paper about you and Miss Y." To which I replied, "I certainly did not. It was a willful distortion of facts." The reporter airily answered: "Oh, you know, Mrs. Nathan, we reporters have to make a good story, or we lose our jobs!"

Writing of reporters and of women of socialistic views, Rose Pastor Stokes comes to my mind. Rose Pastor, an immigrant Russian Jewish girl, had first worked in a cigar factory and then, through native cleverness and ability, had become a reporter for a Jewish paper. She was sent to interview J. G. Phelps Stokes, who had shown an interest in socialism, although he was the son of a well-known millionaire, Anson Phelps Stokes, an ultra-conservative. He became interested in her, and the marriage which followed soon after attracted a great deal of attention. Rose Pastor Stokes always insisted that despite her becoming the wife of a wealthy man, whose social position was unquestioned, she still adhered to her socialistic doctrines. The fact that she enjoyed the luxury of both a country home as well as an apartment in the city, that she displayed handsome wedding gifts received from her husband's family, and that she lived on unearned increment, did not seem to clash with her widely expressed socialist doctrines.

Mrs. Stokes and I were on the program at a certain meeting held in Dr. Madison Peters' church. We were both speaking in the interest of the working girls. My speech came first. I was followed by Mrs. Stokes. She launched forth in denunciation of "society women" who wore expensive jewelry, while girls were working for "starvation wages." During her remarks, she turned and I fancied her eyes had a special glare as they fixed themselves on my amethyst watch chain. I grew very self-conscious and was sure that every woman in the church was mentally appraising that amethyst chain. As Mrs. Stokes resumed her seat, I turned to Dr. Peters who was conducting the meeting and asked for the privilege to say a few words more. Then I pointed out that the designers and makers of jewelry were among the highest paid workers in the country, whereas lacemakers (Mrs. Stokes was wearing a large exquisite handmade lace collar, fastened by a diamond pin) were among the most poorly paid. Moreover, in the making of lace, both eyesight and health were apt to be ruined. Although the meeting was held in the body of the church, those present could not restrain themselves—they burst into loud applause. They, too, had apparently resented Mrs. Stokes' implications.

Another tilt with Rose Pastor Stokes occurred in Philadelphia, the City of Brotherly Love! Again we were on the same program. This time it was at the Annual Meeting of the National Academy of Political and Social Science. The topic for discussion was, "The Condition of the Working Women in the United States." In the course of Mrs. Stokes' remarks, she stated that no one had a right to pay high prices for shelter, food, or clothing, so long as there were young girls working for starvation wages. She declared that any one stopping at a high-priced hotel was "particeps criminis" in keeping down wages. I could not follow her reasoning. I did not understand how I could have helped to increase working girls' wages had I gone to a third-class hotel. I was still more bewildered when I met Mrs. Stokes the following morning, breakfasting with her husband at the Bellevue-Stratford Hotel—the most luxurious in Philadelphia. I taxed her at once with inconsistency and she retorted that she had gone there purposely to learn just what prices were asked at such hotels. I pointed out that she could have easily gained this information from the desk clerk, without making herself "particeps criminis" in reducing working girls' wages!

In Philadelphia, addressing the National Academy of Social and Political Science; in Boston taking part in a National Religious Conference; in Chicago to speak at the Lincoln Center; trips to Albany, to Washington, to appeal for protective legislation for women and children—crowded days indeed! But crowded not only with interests and activities, but filled to overflowing with all that makes life beautiful: music, flowers, laughter, dancing, family reunions, friendship, sympathy, and love.

# CHAPTER VIII

## RECOLLECTIONS OF THEODORE ROOSEVELT

MEMORIES are part of our spiritual wealth. Land, houses, gold, and jewels are our material wealth. These we bequeath to our heirs. Our memories die with us unless we record them and thus leave them as a rich legacy to those who follow. I feel this so strongly that I take this opportunity to bind together a sheaf of memories regarding my contacts with Theodore Roosevelt, one of the most interesting and remarkable figures of his time.

My first recollection of Colonel Roosevelt centers in a gathering of the Nineteenth Century Club. This club was composed of well-known men and women interested in art and letters. At the meetings, it was usual to have one or two prominent speakers. Then came a general discussion, followed by a buffet supper. I remember that Mr. Roosevelt had but recently returned from his ranch-life in the West and that we were all eager to hear him. I cannot recall the exact subject of his address, but my impression is that he did not speak of his western experiences. He spoke on some phase of civic reform. It has been nearly fifty years since this meeting at which I first saw him, but I can close my eyes now and see him clearly as though he stood before me, a somewhat youthful figure, speaking in his characteristically emphatic manner, emphasizing his points with an outstretched index finger. Brander Matthews was the presiding officer that evening, and later, in response to my eager appreciation, he brought Mr. Roosevelt up and presented him. I cannot remember our topic of conversation, but I do remember my pleasure in that he lingered at my side and joined us at supper. This first meeting with Theodore Roosevelt amounted to nothing more than the usual social amenities, but his personality was so strong that the impression he left with me was indelible.

My next distinct recollection of Mr. Roosevelt was when I saw him seated at his desk at Police Headquarters, filling the office of Police Commissioner of New York City—the climax for me of an annoying incident. I had been caught downtown without an umbrella in a very heavy rain and went to the nearest cab stand and jumped into a hansom. This was long before the days of taxis. The driver, taking advantage of my apparent predicament, refused to take me anywhere unless I promised to pay double fare. I retorted that I would pay him the regular rate. He was not satisfied and felt that he could bully me into paying the extra fare. A policeman hearing the controversy came up to ask the cause of the trouble. I stated my case. The policeman replied, "I have no power to force the driver to take you at a lower price than he demands." "How about this legal rate card?" I asked, pointing to one conspicuously posted in the cab. The policeman merely shrugged his shoulders. "Very well," I said, "I shall take your number as well as that of the cabman." Taking out my notebook and pencil, I deliberately wrote down both numbers and then got out of the cab into the pouring rain. The thorough soaking that I got did not dampen my ardor, rather did it serve to inflame my indignation. When I reached home I wrote a letter to the Police Commissioner, Theodore Roosevelt, relating the incident.

In the letter I stated that I did not know to whom I was to complain about the cabman, but I was quite sure that he was the proper official to cope with the delinquency of the policeman. The next morning a police sergeant called, bringing me a letter from the Police Commissioner, asking when it would be convenient for me to call at Police Headquarters to prefer charges against the policeman. The sergeant was sent to serve as my escort. Realizing that there was no time like the present, I kept the sergeant waiting only long enough to don my hat and coat and accompanied him to Police Headquarters.

Police Commissioner Roosevelt received me in his private office. Here was the same youthful figure of the Nineteenth Century Club, but the responsibility, dignity, and authority of office gave him a power which made him seem years older.

I thanked him for his prompt attention to my letter and he thanked me for calling his attention to the dereliction of one of the police force. Then he directed the sergeant to take me to the Chief Inspector. The sergeant also went with me to the Mayor's office, where I was told I must lodge my complaint against the cabman.

The cabman was fined five dollars and warned that a second complaint would result in the loss of his license. The policeman was sent to a district in the Bronx, where, the cabbies being strangers to him, there would be no temptation to wink at violation of the law. The story seems trivial, but its value lies in the fact that unimportant as was the incident, the Police Commissioner at once recognized the responsibility of his office and the duty he owed to the citizens to make the police force as efficient as possible. Therefore, even the smallest infraction received his prompt and personal attention.

When Mr. Roosevelt was Governor of New York I had quite a correspondence with him in regard to various measures in which, as President of the Consumers' League, I was interested. I also had several interviews with him. In the discussion of these matters he did not always agree with my point of view, but I never failed to be impressed with his sense of justice and his desire for a "square deal." At that time the Consumers' League was trying to abolish the sweatshop system of work which was being carried on in the worst tenement house hovels on the East Side.

As President of the League, I presented the facts to Governor Roosevelt and asked him to suggest in his message the necessity of enacting laws to do away with these evil conditions. Governor Roosevelt had already endorsed the work of the Consumers' League and had said that he considered that we were doing one of the most important pieces of work in the country. Nevertheless, he never took any one's dictum without looking into the matter personally and becoming acquainted with all phases of the subject. Therefore, before writing his message, he came to New York to make a tour of the worst type of sweatshops, and he came right from the railroad station to the office of the Consumers' League to ask me to accompany him on this investigation. After this tour of inspection and after studying the problem from all sides, he incorporated in his message the following paragraph, a strong protest against the sweatshop system, saying: "It is everywhere agreed that this tenement house sweatshop system is degrading to the unfortunate individuals engaged in it, and to the social and moral life of the community in which it exists. I recommend that the Legislature provide for additional factory inspectors, so as to bring the total number up to fifty, and also that the Governor be empowered to appoint unsalaried deputies."

He was always interested in labor problems and during the short time (two years) that he was Governor of the State of New York, he signed seventeen labor bills, passed for the purpose of providing better protection for the workers of the State.

At the time of the Buffalo Pan-American Exposition, the Consumers' League made an application for space, in order to have a contrasting exhibit of sweatshop goods and goods made in model factories. This application was denied. I appealed to Mr. Roosevelt, who was then Vice President, to use his influence to secure the desired space. Mr. Roosevelt's interest was at once aroused. He felt that here was a case where fair play was not being shown. An opportunity was in danger of being lost to educate the public through the demonstration of the contrast between the product of sweatshops and goods made under wholesome conditions. I had considerable correspondence with him about the matter. The last letters on this subject received from him were written from Sagamore Hill, his summer home in Oyster Bay, an evidence it was vacation time. Nevertheless his interest did not flag. These letters were confidential in character, but showed that he had gone over the situation from all angles. His judgment was that in view of the facts, the Consumers' League would be ill advised to press the point. How many men, overwhelmed with affairs of state, with innumerable demands made upon their time and encroaching on a vacation, would have devoted real thought and study to such a question as I had brought to his attention?

One of my most treasured mementoes is my own visiting card with a penciled line in Governor Roosevelt's handwriting—"Admit to me at any time. Theodore Roosevelt." This has an interesting and amusing story attached to it. The New York State Federation of Women's Clubs met in Albany for its annual convention during Governor Roosevelt's administration. A brilliant reception was tendered the delegates one evening at the Executive Mansion by Governor and Mrs. Roosevelt. I was to be one of the speakers, so I was in line with the delegates at the reception. When I reached the Governor, he shook hands cordially with me and said: "Oh, Mrs. Nathan, you are just the woman I want to see. Can you come to my room at the Executive Chambers tomorrow morning at ten?" "I would be delighted to obey this summons, your Excellency," I replied, "were it not for the fact that I must give my address in the Assembly Chamber at that hour."

"Then can you come at eleven?" he asked. "I leave for Syracuse about that hour," I said in a dejected tone, "to give an address there later." With his usual tenacity of purpose, he asked, "How about nine o'clock? Would that be too early for you?" I expressed my readiness to go at that hour. His military secretary, Mr. Treadwell, who was standing next to him, reminded the Governor that he already had an engagement for that hour. In his impetuous manner he waved aside the interruption and said, "That makes no difference. Mrs. Nathan must be admitted to me as soon as she arrives." To clinch the matter, the Governor said to me, "Have you a card with you?" I at once drew a card from my case and the Governor wrote on it the line quoted above, "Admit to me at any time."

As may be imagined, this rather lengthy conversation was holding up the line—the reporters were staring wide-eyed and showing signs of suppressed excitement. One of them was bold enough, in her eagerness to be first with her story, to ask me to show her the penciled card. I gladly complied. This reporter made good use of her story. The next day one of the New York papers had flaming headlines stating that Governor Roosevelt had held up the long line of delegates while he talked with Mrs. Frederick Nathan and had written on her card, "Admit to me at any time." The other reporters had made their own interpretation of the incident and I read with amusement that I had asked Governor Roosevelt for his *autograph* and he had graciously given it to me!

Governor Roosevelt's urgent desire to talk to me on this occasion was in connection with the appointment of a State Factory Inspector. The Labor Unions and the Consumers' League had been urging him to appoint a certain experienced woman for the position. Her splendid qualifications for the post were recognized on all sides. Governor Roosevelt himself admitted that she was an expert in this field, and would no doubt fill the position admirably. However, he explained, his *constituents would expect him to appoint a man.* Progressive and independent as he was, he never lost his keen political sense. So long as his constituency was composed only of men, he appreciated that he had to consider their wishes.

Roosevelt had often been criticized for "political expediency." I never felt this to be a just criticism. Rather, I was impressed by the broad general view that he always took, looking at a problem from all sides, not allowing any detail to escape him—then would come the decision. It seems to me that his independence was shown by his utter indifference to criticism following a decision which had political significance.

A story comes to my mind when I actually had the temerity to ask Mr. Roosevelt—then recently elected Vice President—to be my mouthpiece. Here is the story:

The newly elected Vice President was to be the chief speaker at the opening exercises of a country home for tubercular patients. I was among the specially invited guests, but had not been asked to speak. I felt very strongly in regard to certain conditions which made such an institution necessary and was genuinely sorry that I was not to have the opportunity to voice my views. Mr. Roosevelt stood near me during the buffet luncheon that preceded the meeting. I spoke to him of the conditions which made necessary this institution about to be dedicated. I reminded him of "Lung Block" on the East Side —so called because all the workers bent over their heavy foot-power driven machines, and, living in the midst of squalor and unsanitary conditions, became afflicted with tuberculosis. I was emphatic in bringing to his attention the fact that the treasurer of the institution which was about to be opened derived a great part of his wealth from the sale of these very same sweatshop-made garments. I asked Mr. Roosevelt if he didn't consider that it would be wiser to change working conditions so as to obliterate a "Lung Block" rather than build an institution for the victims of it. I added, "I wish I had been asked to speak today, for these are the views I would have expressed." Mr. Roosevelt looked at me searchingly and asked, "Would you like me to say it for you?" I assented without hesitation. He did not forget. Later in his speech he stressed those very points which we had discussed, looking me straight in the eye as if to remind me that he was keeping his word. I was well satisfied. These statements, coming from the Vice President, carried far more weight than if I had voiced them. Later on when we were all preparing to leave, Mr. Roosevelt, who was being escorted to the train by the president of the institution, turned and asked whether I would drive to the station with them. That was a thrilling drive. Never before and never since have I felt so much like "the first lady of the land." Mr. Roosevelt always attracted a great crowd. His popularity was immense, and in his native State of New York this popularity reached a climax. Great crowds had gathered to cheer the former Governor of the State—now Vice President of the Union. He bowed right and left, acknowledging the acclamation of the crowd; their welcome evidently gave him genuine pleasure. Suddenly I realized that I—sitting in the carriage—was unconsciously also bowing right and left, as though the plaudits included me. The whole situation was spontaneous and infectious. While we were waiting at the station for the train to arrive which was to take us back to New York, many persons came up to shake hands and congratulate him upon his accession to the Vice Presidency. I made use of the opportunity to get in a little suffrage work, and said, "I did what I could to help elect you, Mr. Roosevelt, I campaigned for you and I would have voted for you, had I had the privilege of the franchise." Whereupon, a woman who had overheard my remark turned and said, "Mr. Roosevelt, I am from Colorado and I *voted* for you." Mr. Roosevelt grasped her by the hand, saying, "Ah, that's what counts." At this time, Mr. Roosevelt was not at all convinced of the value of equal suffrage, which gave his remark significance.

Some years later, on his return from the Middle West, he told me what had finally won him over to the cause. He had noticed that in the States where women had the vote, the political situation was intelligently discussed around the dinner table, the men and women of the family exchanging their views, whereas in the East it was after the ladies had withdrawn from the dining room that the men felt at liberty to discuss politics. He felt that in the enfranchised States of the West an entirely different attitude was held on the subject and he recognized the value of the youthful voter getting the woman's point of view as well as the man's.

It was during his period of vacillation—after he had left the White House—when the suffrage leaders were endeavoring to get him to commit himself to the cause, that the following headlines appeared in the papers, "Roosevelt a Laodicean. He believes in Votes for Women, but he says he does not consider it one of the most important matters of the moment." Shortly afterward I gave a luncheon at the National Arts Club in honor of the ex-President, Theodore Roosevelt. Fred Terry, the English actor (brother of Dame Ellen Terry), had told me that he would rather meet Roosevelt than any one else in our country. As Mr. and Mrs. Terry had entertained me in their delightful home at Primrose Hill, London, I was glad to be able to show them some hospitality in return when they came to New York, so I built the luncheon around Mr. Roosevelt, who at that time was one of the editors of the *Outlook.* I had some interesting people at the table. I remember that I placed Ida Tarbell next to Mr. Roosevelt—who as guest of honor naturally sat next to me.

The club chef, having heard for whom the luncheon was

to be given, had made a miniature White House in spun sugar. It was lighted by electricity and formed the centerpiece on the table. During the course of the luncheon, I referred to the headlines I have quoted and teased Mr. Roosevelt about his being called a Laodicean. He—so positive in all his views to be so lukewarm on any subject. I told him I was going to quote his words in my suffrage speeches. "I don't see how that will help the cause," he exclaimed in a puzzled tone of voice. "Because," I retorted, "if we women were *red men, brown men, yellow men, black men,* demanding justice you would be the first to say, 'There is nothing of greater importance than that these men should have a square deal'." He pushed back his chair, turned squarely around in his seat so as to face me, and bringing his hand down on the table said, "By George, Mrs. Nathan, you are right!"

I have in my scrapbook three impressive looking cards of invitation, two from the White House and one from Theodore Roosevelt for the McKinley inaugural ball—the time that Roosevelt was elected Vice President. Mr. Roosevelt had written us, regretting that he could not send us tickets for the inauguration ceremonies at the Capitol as he didn't even have enough to go around his large family circle, but he sent us the tickets with his compliments for the inaugural ball and hoped that we would think it worth while to go to Washington for the event. Did we think it worth while? There was no doubt in my mind as to the potential pleasure on such an occasion, and it did not require much persuasion to bring my husband to my point of view. It was a most brilliant occasion and came quite up to our expectations. President and Mrs. McKinley were, of course, in the large center box, Vice President and Mrs. Roosevelt in the box adjoining. Mrs. McKinley, not being strong, remained seated in the box the greater part of the evening, the President remaining by her side. Vice President and Mrs. Roosevelt mingled more generally with the crowd. I have a delightful and unfading impression of their charm and graciousness of manner in making every effort to present their friends to the President and his wife. It was but natural that the Roosevelt coterie should outnumber the McKinley coterie two to one. Mr. McKinley's "home town" was in the Middle West, Mr. Roosevelt's was but a five-hour journey to Washington. Now these inaugural balls have faded into memories—they belong to the past. With Mr. Wilson's idea of Jeffersonian simplicity, the inaugural ball was dispensed with at his first inauguration. His second inauguration took place in 1917, during the war, when, of course, any such festivity would have been out of place. The succeeding presidents, Mr. Harding and Mr. Coolidge, did not revive the former custom.[1] Yet these balls given once in four years added unquestionably to the gayety and brilliancy of Washington. The Army, the Navy, the Diplomatic Corps, were always in evidence, the uniforms and decorations giving a cosmopolitan air, which gave them somewhat the character of a foreign court ball.

The two White House invitations of which I have spoken came to us during President Roosevelt's administration. I was in Washington to speak at a meeting of the National Woman Suffrage Association. I wanted to see President Roosevelt, so I wrote jocosely, asking whether my participation in the Woman Suffrage Convention would bar me from the White House. His reply came promptly in the form of two invitations—one to the Army and Navy reception at the White House, considered the most brilliant of all the official receptions; the other to the supper which was to follow the reception. These small suppers after a reception were a feature of the Roosevelt administration. The guests were limited to their personal friends, and those whom they were pleased to honor.

The memory of this brilliant reception has never been

1 President Franklin D. Roosevelt is reviving the old custom.

effaced. Like all my sex, brass buttons and epaulettes have their fascination for me. It was wonderful to be piloted through the historic rooms by our old friend, General Gillespie, then in command in Washington, who presented every one of note to us. It was still more wonderful to have Admiral Dewey recall me from former Saratoga days. It was most wonderful of all to have been greeted by Mrs. Roosevelt with even more than her usual gracious charm and to have our hands clasped warmly by the President, while his characteristic "delighted" seemed to convey a specially personal note. The reception was an official function and showed the President as the head of the nation and Mrs. Roosevelt as truly the first lady of the land. At the supper which was held in one of the smaller upstairs rooms, the President and his wife appeared in a different aspect. Here they were the gracious and graceful host and hostess, dispensing hospitality to their friends.

Another reception comes to my mind, when Mr. Roosevelt was not host. This was after he had left the White House and was in London on his return from his famous hunting expedition in Africa. Whitelaw Reid was then our Ambassador to the Court of St. James's, and tendered a reception to Roosevelt, at his beautiful home, Dorchester House. My husband and I happened to be in London at the time, and Mr. Reid honored us with an invitation. Mr. Roosevelt stood with Mr. Reid, at the head of the beautiful broad stairs, greeting the guests as they arrived. As I came up and held out my hand, Mr. Roosevelt said, "Why what are *you* doing here among all these Londoners?" I made some laughing rejoinder and then asked him, "Which do you enjoy more, being a lion in London, or shooting lions in Africa?" He showed his teeth, with his well-known smile, and whispered, "Shooting lions in Africa."

Among the letters received from President Roosevelt while he was in the White House, is one that has a very special interest for me. But first I must tell the incident which led to the writing of it. Professor E. R. A. Seligman of Columbia University and Morris Hilquit agreed to debate the question of "Competition versus Coöperation" at Cooper Union. The topic was one of great interest at that time, and drew a characteristic Cooper Union crowd. I was among the group of Professor Seligman's supporters, invited to sit on the platform. Mr. Hilquit was extremely radical and denunciatory in his remarks. When he came to speak of Mr. Roosevelt—our President—his language was more than denunciatory. It was abusive and offensive. It was not only because of my warm personal feeling for President Roosevelt that I resented these remarks, but also because as a loyal citizen I could not sit quietly by and hear such epithets applied to the President of the United States. I have always felt that the highest official elected to represent the American people should have his office respected by those whom he served. Without giving thought to my conspicuous position—I was seated on the stage in the front row—I jumped to my feet and said in a voice loud enough to be heard in the farthest corner of the large hall: "Mr. Hilquit, you have no right to insult the President of the United States. Personally, I do not consider your statements true, but whether true or not, the office of our President must be respected, even if you don't respect the man." I sat down, trembling with indignation. There was an uproar of mingled cheers and hisses. Mr. Hilquit turned white with anger and facing me said, "Yes, Mrs. Nathan, I have a right to say what I said, and now I shall repeat it more emphatically." Thereupon, he continued in the same strain. I jumped to my feet again, saying, "Then I for one refuse to listen to you." I turned and left the platform. Several of those sitting near me followed my example. By the time we reached the exit we had quite a little following. The reporters seized upon this incident and the next morning's papers had flaming headlines. When President Roosevelt's attention was called to this sensational account, he wrote thanking me for taking the public stand I had, adding that statements such as Mr. Hilquit was reported to have made caused people to become ultra conservative, just as ultra conservative statements caused many to become ultra radicals.

I have another letter from Theodore Roosevelt which I prize very highly. It was in the summer of 1912 that Roosevelt, dissatisfied with the policies of the Republican Party, headed the Progressive Movement. Women were interested in this new party, because in its platform it had declared boldly for equal suffrage. Mr. Roosevelt, knowing my active interest in the Woman Suffrage Movement, wrote me a personal letter asking me to serve as a Chairman of the Woman Suffrage Committee of the National Progressive Party. The letter follows:

"My dear Mrs. Nathan:

"May I ask very warmly that you head the Suffrage Committee in the Progressive Service? It is, in my judgment, essential that we have at the head of that committee a woman who is known as much more than only an agitator for suffrage for women. She must be a convinced suffragist eager for the cause, but she must also be identified in the public mind with other movements—that is, she must embody our principle, that we are for suffrage because women are not merely entitled to it as a right, but are entitled to it as a means of rendering more efficient service to the community as a whole. Now, my dear Mrs. Nathan, you embody this principle.

"I earnestly ask that you will accept the head of this committee. The chairmanship of this committee if accepted by you will make you one of four people who are directing the policy of the popular government department of the Progressive Party. I need hardly say to you that there are few if any positions of leadership in our party so important as this, and I am tempted to say that there are none more important.

"Earnestly hoping that you can accept, even at the cost of considerable personal inconvenience, I am,

"Very sincerely yours,

(*Signed*) "THEODORE ROOSEVELT."

Having accepted this position, all communications sent to Mr. Roosevelt in regard to the subject of Woman Suffrage were passed on to me. It would have added enormously to my already crowded days, had it not been for the efficient help given me by the secretary of my committee, Alice Carpenter. It was a stimulus to feel that I was a co-worker with Theodore Roosevelt. Indeed *he* felt that I was more than a co-worker. He called me in regard to all matters pertaining to equal suffrage his "boss." But as Kipling said, "This is another story."

The suffragists were planning their great parade, which was to be preceded by a mass meeting at the Metropolitan Opera House. They looked around for the biggest drawing card and felt that the success of the evening would be assured if Theodore Roosevelt could be prevailed upon to make this the occasion of his maiden speech for suffrage. He was then one of the editors of the *Outlook,* which, under the editorship of Lyman Abbott, had strongly opposed the equal suffrage movement. A committee was delegated to wait upon Roosevelt and invite him to be the chief speaker at this meeting. At first he declined. After listening to the pleadings of the committee, he said, "I made up my mind not to make any speech on suffrage unless ordered to do so by my boss." The women exclaimed in amazement, *"You* taking orders from a *boss!* Impossible." "Well," he retorted, "Mrs. Frederick Nathan is the Chairman of the Woman Suffrage Committee of the National Progressive Party. All matters relating to suffrage come under her direction. Therefore, she is the boss! If she says I must make this speech, I suppose I'll have to do it, but unless she does, I must decline." The committee left, feeling that the object of their visit had been accomplished and that they had secured the prize for the evening. For well they knew it would require no persuasion on their part to induce me to use my *authority* to *order* Mr. Roosevelt to accept the invitation! It was a red letter night for me. I escorted Colonel Roosevelt to the stage where he sat between Anna Shaw (who presided) and me. The Opera House was packed to the ceiling. He received a tumultuous ovation, and a thrill ran through me as I heard our greatest American speaking in defense of a cause which lay so close to my heart. Theodore Roosevelt could no longer call himself a "Laodicean" in regard to Woman Suffrage. It was characteristic of him that once he was convinced of the value of a cause, he gave no half-hearted sympathy.

I distinctly remember a meeting held in Utica. We were both on the program as speakers, and I sat immediately behind him. He was campaigning for Davenport, who was the candidate of the Progressive Party for the Governorship of New York. In the midst of his speech these words rang out: "I want Davenport for Governor of my State, because I want my State to be a better governed State. I want my grandchildren when they vote–" and swinging around suddenly and facing me with that emphatic forefinger almost shaking in my face, he continued, "Mrs. Nathan, did you hear me say my grand*children?* I did not say my grand*sons* because I hope that by the time they vote, my grand*daughters,* as well as my grandsons, will exercise the franchise." I doubt if there were many in that large gathering who had ever given a thought to the question of woman suffrage, but Colonel Roosevelt's strong personality and his impassioned speech brought out a wave of spontaneous enthusiasm. It was a fine bit of propaganda. Even Colonel Roosevelt's sister, Mrs. Douglas Robinson, who sat next to me and who had been an avowed anti-suffragist, joined in the general applause.

The last time I saw Theodore Roosevelt was in the early autumn of 1918 not long after the death of his son, Quentin. It was Lafayette-Marne Day and he was to be the principal speaker at the exercises held at City Hall. As chairman of the Women's Committee, I was in the Governor's room to receive the guests of honor. Colonel Roosevelt greeted me with his usual cordiality, adding, "This seems like old times!" I was shocked at the great change in him. His face showed the terrible strain under which he had endeavored to keep a calm exterior. He had seen four sons go to the war. He was wearing a crêpe band on his arm, the gold star was in his window. Those were dark days under which we were all living, but for a virile man of action, of dominant power, to be forced into comparative inactivity, must have seared his very soul. Scarcely more than three months later—he was gone.

One of the greatest characters in American history had passed away. During those early post-war months how we missed him! We longed for his ability to see through the fog of circumstance, the truths of a problem. We missed his grasp of a situation and his fearlessness in judgment, his defiance of criticism when upholding the right. As time wore on, however, I felt a sense of gladness that Theodore Roosevelt had passed away in the zenith of his strength, rather than to have lived on until the feebleness of old age overcame him.

No one had more genuine admirers than Theodore Roosevelt. Soon after his death, his followers began to discuss a fitting memorial for him. My friend, Mrs. William Curtis Demorest, felt that the women of the country would want to do their share to perpetuate his memory. She asked a small group of us to meet at her home in order to discuss various suggestions and decide upon the most appropriate as an offering from American womanhood. It was decided to purchase the site of Roosevelt's birthplace, 28 East 20th Street, New York City, have the house reconstructed and furnished as it had been in the days of his early boyhood, and keep the house next door to it (his uncle's home) [1] as a museum for the varied mementoes of his full life, a library for the books he had written, and build an auditorium where lectures could be given, meetings held, moving pictures shown, all in the interest of patriotic education, emphasizing Roosevelt's ideals.

The Woman's Roosevelt Memorial Association was organized, and I was elected to the Board of Directors. I was also Chairman of a Woman's Roosevelt Memorial Association Committee in the National Arts Club, formed for the purpose of securing the interest of members of the club in the memorial. To further this end, a dinner was given at the club at which I presided, and among the speakers were the architect who reconstructed the house, Theodate Pope; the sculptor who made the Roosevelt medal for us, Anna Hyatt; the Reverend William D. Manning—not yet Bishop; Harold Howland, formerly on the staff of the *Outlook;* Carl Akeley, the explorer and one of Roosevelt's biographers, and Mrs. Douglas Robinson, Roosevelt's sister. Theodore Roosevelt had been a member of the National Arts Club and his fellow-members turned out in force to pay tribute to his memory.

Some years later, a fête champêtre was given at Claremont to raise money for the Woman's Roosevelt Memorial Association. I was asked to take charge of the bookstall. A member of the Authors' League, I am fortunate in knowing many authors and poets. I asked some of them to help the cause by sending me an autographed copy of one or more of their publications. They responded generously. It occurred to me to ask Bishop Manning for an auto-

[1] This property was owned by my paternal grandfather before it came into the possession of Silas Weir Roosevelt.

graphed copy of the Bible. I wrote him that while I knew he was not the author of the book, I felt that the autograph of the Bishop of New York on the flyleaf would add to the value of the book and would bring a higher price. He at once sent me a beautifully bound Testament with the following inscription:

> The life of Theodore Roosevelt should inspire us all to higher ideals, and to truer following of the teachings of this holy Book.
>
> WILLIAM T. MANNING,
> *Bishop of New York.*
>
> May 26, 1925.

I felt that this Bible with its fine tribute to Theodore Roosevelt should belong to the Roosevelt family, to be handed down from generation to generation. I, therefore, communicated with Mrs. Roosevelt and she at once expressed great delight at the opportunity I had given her to purchase it for her eldest grandson. Bishop Manning was greatly pleased to learn from me who had been the purchaser of the book.

I have had many pleasant things said to me during my life, I have had the encouragement that comes from praise and appreciation, but perhaps the most valued piece of commendation I ever received were those words of Theodore Roosevelt: "Mrs. Nathan, I consider your work in the Consumers' League is as valuable a piece of work as any being done in the country."

In my copy of Mrs. Douglas Robinson's book, *My Brother, Theodore Roosevelt,* she has written the following on the flyleaf:

> Inscribed for Maud Nathan whose splendid service to her country in various capacities was much admired by my brother, Theodore Roosevelt,

with all good wishes from Corinne Roosevelt Robinson.
October 27, 1921.

When Mrs. Douglas Robinson was presenting one of her granddaughters to society at a reception she gave at the Colony Club, it was very sweet to me to hear Mrs. Robinson say, as I greeted the young debutante: "Helen, I want you to know Mrs. Nathan, she was an old friend of Uncle Ted's—he was a great admirer of hers."

In looking back down the long vista of years, it is associations, contacts, memories such as these that stand out like high mountain peaks, above the shadowed valleys.[1]

[1] See Appendix V for letter from Mrs. Corinne Roosevelt Robinson after reading this chapter.

# CHAPTER IX

## A SECOND VISIT TO LONDON

When I was married in 1880, there were no women's clubs in New York, with the exception of Sorosis, which was literary and cultural, the characteristics of the early clubs. Women were beginning to feel the advantage of forming themselves into small groups for study and self-expression. Or, as Agnes Repplier once expressed it, where "they could hurl papers at each other's heads!" The literary or cultural aspect was the nucleus of the woman's club idea all over the country. Later women began to realize what a power they could be in the community for welfare work and civic reform. It wasn't long before there were committees formed within these clubs for more altruistic work. Moreover, conditions were changing. The social coterie was widening. It was no longer possible to walk down Fifth Avenue, bowing right and left to one's friends. The Avenue was now crowded with people whom one didn't recognize. Not only were there strangers from all parts of our country, but also from all parts of the world. New York was rapidly becoming cosmopolitan. As it became more and more cosmopolitan, habits of thought and of living changed and life quickly adapted itself to the new conditions. There was a need for clubs more definitely social in character, where one could entertain friends from other cities, free from the embarrassment of possible domestic complications. A radical development was the forming of clubs to have a membership consisting of both men and women.

The National Arts Club and Barnard Club were among

the first to initiate this new movement. It appealed to me strongly; it was reminiscent of the co-educational experience of the Middle West. I joined the two clubs.

It is almost impossible now to realize the conservative attitude held once upon a time in regard to women's clubs. A club woman was supposed to neglect her husband, her children, her household. She was depicted in the comic papers lounging ungracefully in a chair reading a dime novel, smoking a cigarette, with a highball on a table beside her. The contrasting picture showed her husband trying to wash the dishes or darn stockings, while the frowsy, unkempt children sprawled on the floor, quarreling among themselves. The theaters, reflecting the sentiment of the time, produced laughable skits where the positions of husband and wife were reversed. The wife kept her engagement at the club of an evening and the husband stayed home in solitude, to watch over the sleeping baby. How archaic all this seems today! Today a woman's social rating is as much determined by her club membership as is her husband's or her son's.

Have the gloomy prophecies of the conservatives been fulfilled? Has the advent of the club woman meant the disintegration of the home? Has the development of new interests weakened the more homely ones? On the contrary, the broader contacts have helped the individual woman to solve her problems. By hearing discussed problems common to all households, she has acquired new ideas, has gained a sense of fellowship, and has been eager to add her mite to the solving of these mutual problems.

It was largely through the medium of these clubs that I was able to give the message of the Consumers' League. Through work in and for the League, I was becoming an authority on welfare work for women and children.

It was in 1899 that I was appointed for the first time a delegate to a convention of the International Congress of Women. It was held that year in London. In addition to being a delegate, I was on the program to give an address on "The Ethics of Money-Making and Money-spending." At Milwaukee the previous year, I had addressed a convention of the General Federation of Women's Clubs. But it seemed of far wider importance to be a member of an International Congress, meeting in historic London. The idea of the Congress was the development of the desire of women in all countries to gain force and power through organization. The congress was composed of delegates from the different National Councils of Women, these councils being made up of many women's organizations, all national in character. The delegates to these congresses were women of intellect and of progressive ideas and I felt a pardonable pride in having been appointed a delegate and a speaker.

It was to be our first trip abroad since that thrilling, epoch-making one in 1880—our wedding trip. The excitement and anticipation that filled me were quite as great as in those long-ago days, but of an entirely different nature. The first time I could think only of all the pleasure I was to receive from new experiences. Now mingled with this was the thought that I had a message to give. On that first trip I was an onlooker. This time I was to be a participant. Even the crossing was different. The *Lucania* was large and palatial compared with the little *Scythia,* just as the *Majestic* today would dwarf the *Lucania.*

As we expected to be in London during the entire month of June, we had been advised to take lodgings, rather than engage rooms at a hotel. My husband, with his New York standards of the comfort and luxuries of a New York hotel, at first demurred at the suggestion of lodgings. But I was eager for the new experience and prevailed upon him to engage a suite at Number 2 Granville Place, Portman Square. This address is indelibly fixed in my memory because of the following incident. When we arrived at Euston Station, London, we found that all of our luggage had not arrived. Through inadvertence, some of our "boxes" had been put on the second section of the train. We had been met at the station by a friend, and my husband thought it would be wiser for me to go at once to the lodgings, while he waited to recover the missing pieces. The second section was to follow within half an hour, and he said he would be delayed only a short time. I asked him whether he remembered the address of the lodging and he waved me away somewhat impatiently, assuring me that there was no danger of his being lost in London. I had my misgivings, but I drove off with my friend in a four-wheeler. I found the rooms fairly comfortable and began unpacking at once. This so engrossed me that I did not realize how the time was passing. I glanced at the clock—nearly two hours had gone by. My husband had not arrived. I was somewhat uneasy, but reminded myself of the many amusing anecdotes related of the slowness of English trains. Another hour passed. There was a balcony outside our window. I hung one of our steamer rugs over it, that it might attract the wanderer's attention, in case he had forgotten the number. Another hour passed and no sign of the missing husband. By this time I was really anxious and decided to take a hansom and return to Euston Station, to find out for myself what had happened. My friend accompanied me. As we drove into the station, I met a four-wheeler, its roof laden with luggage, and I could discern my husband sitting inside. The traffic had to be held up while I hailed the outgoing cab and called to my husband to know the cause of the delay. He looked somewhat sheepish and his answer was vague. I sternly asked, "Do you know where you are going?" In a tone of injured innocence, mingled with self-confidence, he retorted, "Of course, I do!" With a jerk of his arm he pulled down his cuff and showed me the address plainly written on it.

My friend taxed me with undue anxiety and lack of confidence in my husband's exactitude, which he had evinced by having written the address on his cuff. I was both mystified and skeptical and knew there was more in this than met the eye. My friend and I went to a club for tea and it was not until my husband and I were alone, dressing for dinner, that the full story was unfolded. When the train section came in—on time—he found the missing luggage, had it piled up on the four-wheeler and jumping into the cab told the driver to drive to Number 2 Portman Square.

The cab drew up before an elegant residence. My husband was surprised and changed his views on the spot in regard to London lodgings. He rang the bell. An obsequious flunkey in imposing livery threw open the door, while two other flunkeys appeared as if by magic on either side of the hall, to relieve him of his hat and coat. My husband beamed. This was better than any New York hotel.

He turned to one of the flunkeys, asking, "Shall I find Mrs. Nathan upstairs?" Over the expressionless face of the dignified, impassive butler, there passed a swift look of amazement. "I beg pardon, sir, I don't understand." In the meantime the cabby had been unloading the luggage and was trying to deposit it in the spacious hall, while waiting impatiently for his fare. My husband began to be suspicious. He said, "This is Number 2 Portman Square, isn't there a suite of rooms engaged here for Mr. Frederick Nathan of New York, and didn't Mrs. Nathan arrive a short while ago?" "You are right, sir, this is Number 2 Portman Square, the residence of the Duke of Fife." My husband turned, without a word, and telling the cabby to replace the luggage, he sank back into the cushions—he was lost—alone in London!

The cabman turned and asked, "Where shall I take you, sir? Shall I try Number 2 Granville Place—right around the corner? There are lodgings there, sir." "No, no," said my husband peevishly, "I never heard of such a street. Take me back to Euston Station." When he told me the story, I could hear him say this in the hopeless voice in which he might have said, "Take me back to New York."

He thought he could recognize the cabman who had driven me away from the station and by going back he might find him and get the correct address from him. He had to wait a long time, but finally the man drove in. My husband pounced on him and when the address was given him, he did not this time trust to his memory, but wrote the full address on his cuff! My wifely instinct had been right. It was so funny that even as I write it, I have to laugh. At the time, however, I threatened to tag him, "If lost, strayed, or stolen, return to Number 2 Granville Place, Portman Square, London." I kept a diary of this visit to London, and as I glance through it today, I live over again a very wonderful experience.

We arrived in London about two weeks before the opening of the Convention, so I had plenty of opportunity to enjoy the great city at its most attractive season. Our cousins who had entertained us on our first visit nearly twenty years before had passed away. Their children, now grown, accepted their heritage of affection for the American cousins and did all in their power to make our stay a pleasant one. We had brought letters of introduction to many notables, and we enjoyed the most cordial hospitality. One afternoon we were invited to take tea at Fulham Palace with the Bishop of London and Mrs. Creighton. Tea was served in the lovely garden. It was all so characteristically English, the beautiful lawns, the wide-spreading trees, the tea-table laden with scones and crumpets, toast and marmalade and a variety of cakes, the old silver service brought out by the pompous-looking butlers. The Bishop wore his gaiters, his apron, and wide shovel hat. He added to the picturesqueness of the scene and gave the foreign touch to our American eyes. Mrs. Creighton was more than ordinarily keen and alert. She had a vivid interest in all welfare work. I found it quite unnecessary to explain the Consumers' League to her. What she wanted to know was about the details of its working. The Bishop was very solemn looking, but had a quiet fund of humor. Some of the stories that he told me I remember to this day. Here is one of them: When making a speech, he was accustomed to place his watch on the table in front of him, where he could glance at it occasionally. One evening as he stood on the platform to address a large gathering, he noticed a watch on the table. It had been left there by the chairman. At the close of the speech, he mechanically took up the watch as usual and dropped it into his vest pocket. As the Bishop was about to return to his seat, the chairman smiled and said, "No, my Lord Bishop! That won't do. There were too many witnesses, hand back my watch!" "Your watch?" said the Bishop. Putting his hand in his pocket he drew forth two watches. His bewilderment aroused the merriment of the audience.

We had brought letters of introduction to Lord and Lady Battersea. Their cordial hospitality is among my pleasantest memories. Lady Battersea was a daughter of Lord and Lady de Rothschild, members of the famous de Rothschild family and a great-niece of Sir Moses Montefiore. She was very handsome, and her beautiful home, Surrey House, at Marble Arch, made a stately background for her charming, gracious hospitality. Cyril Flower, Lord Battersea, was a distinguished looking man with the keenest sense of humor of any Englishman I ever met. His blue eyes fairly twinkled over any expression of our American humor and he showed his appreciation by his ever-ready and apt retort. He was related to the well-known Flower family of Stratford-on-Avon, to whom we also brought letters and who entertained us at tea, when bicycling through that picturesque and historic town.

Our acquaintance with Lord and Lady Battersea, which later developed into a warm friendship, lasting through many years, held a peculiar interest for me. Lord Battersea was a member of the Church of England. Lady Battersea had never renounced the faith of her fathers. This apparently made no difference in the happiness of their married life. She often attended services with him on Sunday and identified herself with his church interests. This did not in the least seem to weaken her zeal for the communal work in connection with the synagogue, and Lord Battersea frequently attended the Saturday Sabbath services with his wife. Lady Battersea observed the Jewish holidays, and in their home Christmas and Easter were seasons of festivity. I remember once when visiting Lady Battersea at her country home, Overstrand, I was attracted to the binding of a book on her library shelf. On opening it, I found it to be a Jewish prayer book, printed in Hebrew and English. It made me feel at home to read the familiar text, and yet there was no jar, and I felt no inconsistency when a few minutes later Lady Battersea took me upstairs to a tower suite, which she called the Bishop's suite, because it was always specially reserved for the annual visit of the Bishop of the Diocese. I recall one of the rooms of this suite with special vividness because on its walls were hung autographed photographs of the Prime Ministers of England from the time of Lord Russell. Years before when I was in London, I noted the lack of prejudice against the Jewish people. Upon this visit, this impression was deepened. I had a wider opportunity to note that at the exclusive clubs where I was taken, at the various social functions, receptions, dinners, teas, cultured Jewish people mingled as a matter of course and with no evidence of discrimination. Perhaps I was quick to notice this because of the new conditions of racial prejudice which were gradually developing in my own city of New York. Yet where is society more delightful, more cultured, more distinguished, more recherché than in London? In the quarter of a century that has passed since these impressions were formed, racial prejudice in New York has developed to such a degree and with such bitter feeling that a real vital problem has arisen.

Lord and Lady Battersea invited us to spend a weekend with them at their beautiful estate, Overstrand, in Norfolk. There we met some distinguished people—a celebrated author whose recently published book was creating a furor, a well-known violinist whose marriage into the English peerage caused her to retire from the concert platform, and a descendant of that Earl whose name is literally in everybody's mouth: Sandwich. She told us the story. The old Earl of Sandwich was so engrossed in his writing that he refused to answer a summons to dinner. He told the servant to bring him some bread and meat. This was done. He put the two together and ate his "sandwich" while continuing to write. A very amusing incident comes to my mind connected with a dinner at Surrey House—Lord and Lady Battersea's London residence. It was in the days when women wore long gloves to the dinner table. We took them off after we sat down and then there was no place to put them. We had no pockets and evening bags were small. There was nothing to do but put them on the lap, under the napkin, and invariably they were forgotten when one rose from the table. On this occasion, as we sat down and I drew off my gloves, I turned to my neighbor, a Colonel in the Royal Guards, and said, "Which would you rather do, put these gloves in your pocket for me until after dinner, or get under the table and pick them up for me when I drop them upon rising?" He laughed and said, "Give me the gloves," and he put them in his pocket. We had a great deal of banter when he declared that the only way I could recover my gloves was by coming to Barracks the following day to get them. I protested that as they were the only pair of long gloves I had, and as I couldn't go out to dinner without them, I would have to go dinnerless until I reached Paris to purchase another pair! He was obdurate and after dinner he brought his wife to introduce us, saying to her, "My dear, I've invited Mrs. Nathan to take tea with us tomorrow at Barracks," and then, seeing her surprise, he hastily added, "I want her to see our new American rocking chair." She was a tall, angular woman, stiff and unbending, and wore dangling from a chain a monocle. As he finished speaking, she slowly adjusted her monocle in her right eye and, looking me over from the tip of my slipper to the very last puff and curl in my hair, said, "Awh, awh!" She turned and rejoined the group with whom she had been chatting. The Colonel showed signs of embarrassment and it was impossible for me to resist saying, "You had better give me back those gloves. Your wife was not sufficiently cordial." Without further controversy, he meekly handed them back to me and I never saw the new American rocking chair!

My friend, Dr. John Graham Brooks of Cambridge, Massachusetts, was anxious for me to meet Claude Montefiore, the Oxford scholar for whom he had great admiration. Dr. Brooks gave us a letter of introduction to Mr. Montefiore and within a few hours after receiving it, he called and invited us to dinner. I mention this to show that contrary to the generally accepted opinion, the English are neither cold nor inhospitable. They may be cautious and rightly so, but when approached with proper introductions, they open to you their hearts and their homes. Later we were invited by Mr. Montefiore and his mother to spend a week-end at their country home at Cold East, near Southampton. Here we met many distinguished people, among them Mrs. Montefiore's son-in-law and daughter, Sir Lewis and Lady McKiver. This acquaintance with the Montefiore family also ripened into friendship and each new year invariably brought a card of greeting from Mr. Montefiore as well as from his cousin, Lady Battersea.

Lady Battersea and her cousins, Mr. and Mrs. Leopold Rothschild, were interested in the National Council of Jewish Women, which had recently been organized in the United States. A meeting was held at Mrs. Leopold Rothschild's beautiful London home and I was among those invited to speak.

Many distinguished social functions were tendered the delegates to the International Convention. Mrs. Rothschild threw open her famous country estate, Gunnersbury Park, giving a garden party in honor of the delegates. This was an unusually brilliant affair, attended by many distinguished men and women. On this occasion, Lady Battersea showed a special interest in me, keeping me by her side and presenting me to all the notables. The Bishop of London and Mrs. Creighton also gave the delegates a garden party. Indeed, the delegates were fêted on all sides. The Duchess of Sutherland entertained us at Stafford House, considered at that time the most beautiful private residence in London. This was an evening reception and stands out in my mind as a magnificent spectacle. Lady Aberdeen, the President of the International Council, the Duchess of Sutherland, and the Countess of Warwick received us at the foot of the picturesque staircase. This staircase divided at the broad landing and went up on either side to the historic picture galleries which were thrown open for the occasion. The beautiful evening gowns, the superb jewels—tiaras of pearls and diamonds worn by the women against the wonderful setting of this beautiful house—made a picture that is unforgetable.

Lord and Lady Battersea's reception at Surrey House was equally brilliant. This reception held a special note of pleasure for me, because of Lady Battersea's gracious friendliness. She seemed to consider me her protegée. She made me remain close to her so as to enable her to present all the distinguished visitors to me. I met Lecky, the historian, the two Balfours, Arthur and Gerald, Herbert Asquith and his wife, Margot (he was not then thought of as Prime Minister), Lady Randolph Churchill and Mrs. de Navarro (Jennie Jerome and Mary Anderson, both my compatriots), Lady Lyndsay, Mrs. Whittridge and Mrs. Humphry Ward (daughter and niece of Matthew Arnold), the Marchioness of Dufferin, Sir Michael Bannerman, leader of the Irish, Morley, the leader of the opposition, Mrs. and Miss Bryce, mother and sister of the former British Ambassador to Washington, later Viscount Brice, Lady Ribblesdale, Sarah Grand, Liza Lehman, Mrs. Craigie, Mrs. Henschel, Miss Toynbee, sister of Arnold Toynbee, and many others. The climax of all the public functions was being received at Windsor Castle by Queen Victoria. She was quite aged at this time and her health was feeble. Lord Aberdeen, who had made all the arrangements, including a special train to Windsor, had assured her Majesty that no formal reception would be expected of her. She consented to receive us if it would involve no interference with her daily routine. We assembled in the courtyard of the castle and as the Queen came out of the door to enter her carriage for her usual afternoon drive, she stopped for a moment and bowed. The delegates all curtseyed and Lady Aberdeen stepped forward, curtseyed, and kissed her Majesty's hand. After the exchange of courtesies between the Queen and Lady Aberdeen, her Majesty extended an invitation to the delegates through Lady Aberdeen for us to visit the castle and partake of the collation prepared for us in St. George's banquet hall. Her Majesty was then assisted into her victoria by her faithful Indian servant, dressed in picturesque native costume, and then driven away. The august occasion was over. The impression left on my mind was that of a tiny old lady, very feeble, dressed in simple black, with the characteristic Victorian bonnet. I marveled at the power held by this frail little woman—Queen of England, Sovereign of all the British Dominions, Empress of India.

The Countess of Warwick gave a garden party at Reading, where she had established a school of agriculture and horticulture for girls. Lady Warwick was a pioneer in this work. At that time agriculture, landscape gardening, horticulture, were not considered suitable occupations for women. Today many women are ranked as authorities on these subjects. Later during the same season, my husband and I were guests at Warwick Castle—the most beautiful castle in England—and Lady Warwick, receiving us in her private apartments, showed us special attention.

There was much private hospitality extended to my husband and myself. Is there any wonder that I find a note in my diary to this effect: "I sit up half the night answering invitations"? One day we lunched with Sir Samuel and Lady Montague—afterward Lord and Lady Swaythling. Sir Samuel showed us one of his most treasured possessions, the original salver sent to Cromwell by Israel Mannassah. This gift caused Cromwell to allow Jews to return to England to live.

One day we were specially invited to evensong at St. Paul's Cathedral. After the service we were taken up to the organ loft to meet the organist, Sir George Martin. He showed us the mechanism of the wonderful organ—tremendous in size and volume. He played a fugue with variations to show us its tonal quality and power. Then he took us into the Cathedral Close for tea, where Lady Martin was waiting to receive us. Had I starred my diary, à la Baedeker, this occasion would show three stars. We passed through an arch, through an alley past Pater Noster Row, and through Amen Corner, thus called because one came to a full stop after Pater Noster. The Close was in a secluded corner, walled in on one side by a part of the original Roman wall covered by ivy. Here, in this quiet bit of green, hidden away in the heart of the great throbbing bustling city, tea was served. This charming modern English social function set in a background of ancient English history.

We also found ourselves in a setting of Jewish background and tradition. The chief Rabbi of England, Rabbi Adler, was most cordial in welcoming us to both his town and country home. And I may say here that whenever we were in London during the Jewish Holy days, we were urged to join the family party at such celebrations. Rabbi Adler's daughter was one of the first women to be elected to the London County Council. She was greatly interested in all educational and welfare work and in civic reform.

We were entertained at Parliament House, at teas and dinners, on the beautiful terrace overlooking the Thames. I was impressed with the social side of British political life, with its leisure for the graceful amenities. My thoughts reverted to the time when I visited the Capitol in Washington to hear an important debate. There was a hurried luncheon in a subterranean room of the building with confusion amid the clattering of dishes and the hurrying and scurrying of waiters and members of Congress.

It might be supposed from all I have written of London festivities that the delegates to the International Convention spent all their time wining and dining and that the sessions of the Congress were of secondary importance. But indeed this was not the case. The high light for me of this London experience was the evening I gave my address before the Convention. It was my first experience as a speaker outside my own country. Members of my family circle had teasingly warned me that my American intonation and inflection would not be understood by a British audience. So when Lady Aberdeen introduced me, I confess to a little nervousness. Westminster Town Hall was so big, its history so overwhelming, the crowd so huge, the faces so unfamiliar. But I had not spoken many sentences before these unfamiliar faces became friendly, became familiar, lighted by the same warmth of response and appreciation that I had found in the upturned faces at home. There was one face in that vast audience that stood out clearly and distinctly among the rest—my husband's face, turned toward me with pride and encouragement. He was proud of the fact that I stood there, one of the youngest of the delegates, that my fluency in French and German had made me sought after by the foreign delegates as interpreter, and that the vocal training I had received had given my voice such resonance that it now carried to the farthest corner of the hall. This fact was proven by the following incident which occurred on our homeward voyage. My husband was approached by a fellow passenger who asked him whether he were any relation to the Mrs. Nathan who had given an address at Westminster Town Hall. The questioner said that he was in the last row of the long, crowded hall and could not see the speaker plainly, but he had heard every word of the address. My husband turned, and bringing the gentleman to me, introduced him to the speaker whom he had heard but had not seen.

I felt that evening, as I sat on the stage, the great contrast between this meeting and the meetings I had addressed at home. Titles do add a certain glamour, just as gilt buttons and gold lace appeal to the imagination. I had in my own democratic country sat on the platform with noble women, great women, women who had been pioneers in blazing the trail for those who were to follow;

these were simple women, the very bone and sinew of our democracy. Now I was sitting on the platform with titled women, women of wealth, of power, of historic ancestry, of a breeding that carried back through the centuries which had produced the bone and sinew of English nobility—synonymous with English democracy. I acknowledge that this had its effect upon me. My reaction to it was a glow of satisfaction, that our family traditions and home training had been a preparation for such diversified contacts in life. My mother had always insisted upon a high standard for courtesies and customs, however different might be the standards of our neighbors.

My address at the Convention was so well received that I was asked to repeat it at an overflow meeting in the small hall in the same building. At other sessions I read papers confided to me by delegates who were unable to attend the Convention. The whole experience was wonderfully stimulating. The delegates sent to this International Congress were among the most prominent women of their countries, distinguished in various walks of life. I formed many friendships and when as a delegate I attended succeeding congresses, one of the greatest pleasures was the renewal of these ties.

At the close of the Convention, my husband and I were joined by a friend—a professor from Johns Hopkins University, and we three made a bicycle trip through lovely, rural, historic England. On our first trip to England, we had seen the landscape from the top of a coach, this time we were trying to peep over the hedges from a bicycle saddle. A few years later, we rolled swiftly in a luxurious motor car through the Cathedral towns, the Lake Country, Devonshire, Surrey, Cornwall—compassing in three weeks what would have taken us twice as long had we traveled the country in the old way.

Which of these three touring methods is best? There is something in the atmosphere of England that inclines one to leisure. There is a quiet restfulness that saps our American rush and hurry. We become willing to go slowly and enjoy as we go. Bicycling gives the zest of physical exercise. Motor travel is delightful, but for England give me a coach. It is only from its elevated seat that glimpses can be caught of the glories that lie behind the high, sheltering hedges and walls.

From England we crossed the Channel to Paris, and then, after a short stay, we went to Vichy, where my husband took the cure. We returned home in September with a firm determination on my part not to let another nineteen years go by without revisiting the old world.

# CHAPTER X

## CAMPAIGNING FOR CIVIC REFORM

ONE morning all New York was laughing over a story which appeared in all the newspapers. A policeman had been found asleep, off his beat, at midnight. The person who found him peremptorily asked him why he wasn't on duty. The policeman replied: "That's none of your business, and who the H—— are you, anyway?" He received no reply at the time, but to his discomfiture his question was answered the next morning when he was summoned to police headquarters and faced the Police Commissioner, Theodore Roosevelt. It was the first time that a New York Police Commissioner had been known to make his rounds at night, indicative of a new standard of duty for both Police Commissioner and policeman. Was this the beginning of the awakening of civic conscience which was stirring New York? New York City had been for years in the grip of a political ring whose campaign motto was: "To the victors belong the spoils." Theodore Roosevelt was the first Police Commissioner to defy this ring. Under his administration, promotion for the policeman was not a question of "pull" and "graft" but was the reward of good conduct.

This defiance of the Police Commissioner's began to be reflected in the attitude of the citizens. If a public officer could strike defiance at the ring, surely high-minded citizens could do likewise. It wasn't long before a wave of "civic reform" was sweeping over New York City. I have already spoken of the Women's Municipal League. As one of its Vice Presidents, I was pressed into this campaign for good government. I was only too glad to throw myself into this work, because for some time, Consumers' League work had been hampered and thwarted by political conditions which had made it difficult to get laws enforced. It was self-evident that we could gain desired results more quickly through coöperation with government officials. It was equally self-evident that these government officials must be of the proper kind, men of singleness of purpose and high standards. Here seemed an opportunity for women to prove their ability and originality and to contribute a new element to the political game. Besides being a Vice President of the Women's Municipal League, I was also a Vice President of the Social Reform Club, a club composed of both men and women. This club, too, became an active factor in the campaign. The newspapers were quick to seize upon the new picturesque quality of having society women enter the field of politics. They made the most of it in their stories and cartoons. One of these cartoons showed a powerful woman sweeping away the tiger and all his accessories from the city, and the caption was: "Now for a clean sweep!" In a corner of the cartoon, there was a list of the leaders, the women of Gotham, who were engaged in this political house cleaning:

| | |
|---|---|
| Mrs. Robert Fulton Cutting | Mrs. William E. Dodge |
| Mrs. Charles F. MacLean | Mrs. Prescott Hall Butler |
| Mrs. Willard Parker | Mrs. Arthur Brooks |
| Mrs. Wm. Jay Schieffelin | Mrs. Robert Abbé |
| Mrs. Richard Watson Gilder | Mrs. Richard Mortimer |
| Mrs. Frederick Nathan | Mrs. Charles Russell Lowell |
| Mrs. Henry D. Coppet | Mrs. Charles Duggin |
| Mrs. Wheeler H. Peckham | Miss Kate Bond |
| Dr. Emily Blackwell | Mrs. James A. Scrymser |
| Mrs. I. H. Morse | Mrs. A. C. Runkle |
| Mrs. Charles H. Russell | Mrs. E. L. Godkin |
| Mrs. Henry M. Saunders | Mrs. George Haven Putnam |
| Mrs. R. J. Cross | Mrs. Boudinot Keith |
| Mrs. R. S. MacArthur | Mrs. Merritt Trimble |

Mrs. William Rhinelander Stewart

Many of these women were among the social leaders of their day, and they gave a tremendous impetus to the movement to raise standards in local politics. For a long time the leading women in England had taken an important part in political campaigns, but it was a new step in our country. New York was on the eve of an exciting mayoralty election. The forces aligned against the corrupt political ring put forward a Fusion candidate for Mayor—Seth Low.

The amount of campaign work involved was enormous. There were not many women in our group who were accustomed to public speaking. Because of my experience, I was constantly called upon to address meetings and it was no unusual thing at the height of the campaign for me to speak twice a day. I spoke to small groups in fashionable parlors. I spoke at mass meetings at Carnegie Hall and Durland's Riding Academy. I was heckled by huge audiences at Cooper Union. I mounted soap boxes at street corners. I went down to the Russian Jewish quarters on the East Side and spoke to groups of women who had confidence in me as a co-religionist and were eager to receive any message I might bring them. This message had to be translated for them into their own tongue—Yiddish—before it could be comprehended. Little Minnie Rosen, a girl who worked in the sweatshops and who had brought to the Consumers' League her tales of woe and despair, was ready to give enthusiastic service as interpreter.

Day by day the excitement of the campaign grew more and more intense, as we neared that fateful Tuesday in November which was to decide the issue. Never before had an election day meant so much to me. I had always been sufficiently interested to be a part of the cheering crowd on Broadway election night, but this time I watched the bulletin boards with throbbing, personal interest. While I had not actually voted for the Fusion candidates,

I had done my bit to win votes for them. When finally the returns showed that our candidates were elected, I doubt whether Mrs. Seth Low was any happier than I. The women's work in this campaign proved the value of our assistance. Certainly the Citizens' Union must have felt this, for at the beginning of the next political contest, they formally invited the Women's Municipal League to coöperate with them. This campaign was of unusual interest, because both the Republican and Democratic machine leaders had refused to place the name of William Travers Jerome on either ticket for reëlection as District Attorney. To those of us who had appreciated his good work, this fact spoke volumes. The independent Republicans and Democrats united in placing his name on an Independent ticket. It was an exciting issue and proved a glorious fight. There was widespread prophecy that Jerome could not possibly be elected, for two reasons: first, because both rings and the regulars of both parties were against him, and, secondly, because of the inherent difficulty of voting a split ballot. Few knew how to mark the ballot so that it would not be thrown out—a campaign of education was necessary.

Through my work in the Consumers' League, I was known to a large number of manufacturers and heads of industrial establishments. Therefore, when I was appointed by the President of the Women's Municipal League, Chairman of the Committee on Ballot-instruction Booths, I circulated the following letter:

"The Women's Municipal League is endeavoring to secure rooms in different localities all over the city where voters may be instructed as to the correct method to vote a split ticket. At every election many ballots are wasted because of ignorance or carelessness in this respect. It is hoped that in the interest of civic education, you will permit some one to explain the proper method to the voters who frequent your building. No politics will be discussed. If you consent, kindly fill out enclosed blank and send as soon as possible to

"MRS. FREDERICK NATHAN,
*"Chairman, Committee on Ballot-instruction Booths."*

. . . . . . . . . . . . . . . . . . . . . . . . . . . . . . . . . . . . . . . . . . . . .

Please send a man to instruct voters how to vote a split ballot. . . .
Address . . . . . . . . . . . . . . . . . . . . . .
On which days of the week . . . . . . . . . . . . . . . . . .
During what hours . . . . . . . . . . . . . . . . . .
Signature . . . . . . . . . . . . . . . . . . . . .

This was hailed as an original and effective method of reaching a large number of voters and stimulating their interest. In many of the stores and factories we were allowed to place a table and chair for the instructor near the door where the employees, going out at the noon hour and at closing hour, could stop and be shown how to vote for an independent candidate without invalidating the rest of the ballot.

Miss Margaret Chanler, the President of the Women's Municipal League ,wrote to me to express her gratification at the success of this undertaking, which she felt was one of the most important and interesting bits of pioneer work accomplished during the campaign. Royall Victor, a chairman of a Committee of the Citizens' Union, also wrote: "I indeed thank you for the ideas and assistance you have given. Excellent results are coming in from the men I have sent to the stores. The man who went to Siegel & Cooper's was especially enthusiastic regarding the effectiveness of the work you have done."

It was a unique method of educating the voters and proved so popular that the Citizens' Union could not provide a sufficient number of instructors, so the Women's

Municipal League undertook to supply some. This was productive of many amusing incidents. One appealed especially to my sense of humor. A colored voter—not as quick-witted as many of his race—had some difficulty in absorbing the instruction that a woman was endeavoring to make clear to him. After spending some time in explaining the matter and exercising much patience, he claimed that he understood and he thanked the lady cordially, saying he'd be glad to do a good turn for her some day. She at once said, "If you really want to prove your gratitude, you will have an opportunity, perhaps, before long, when the question comes before you of giving women the vote; you can then vote in favor of it." "Oh, no," replied the negro, "I'm sorry I can't do that, 'cause I don't think women is intelligent enough to vote."

I don't think I ever worked harder than during this intensive campaign. I was in it with my whole heart and soul. The Women's Municipal League asked me to represent them as the one woman speaker at one of the final mass meetings held at Carnegie Hall. This meeting was to be addressed by Seth Low, District Attorney Jerome, as well as by Jacob Riis, some of the other candidates on the Fusion ticket, and other distinguished people. It was indeed an honor to be on the program with such speakers —an honor, but also a tremendous responsibility. I felt the enormous importance of presenting the cause in a way that would appeal most strongly to the voters. Besides this, I wanted to prove worthy of the trust placed in me by the Women's Municipal League. I knew the facts by heart, but how were they to be presented in a picturesque manner—in a way that would capture the imagination of the crowd? This question was always at the back of my mind, during the activities of these crowded days.

As I lay awake one night, revolving the details of the campaign in my mind, suddenly, as in a flash, the answer came clearly to me. I recalled a conversation that I had

had with Frank Stockton, when I twitted him about his story, *The Lady or the Tiger.* Here was the topic of my address, these my symbols. The lady represented the emblem used by the Citizens' Union, a woman with outstretched arms protecting the home, the workers, the city. The tiger, the famous Tammany emblem. It was so obvious that I wondered that I hadn't thought of it before, and I lived in daily dread that some one would make use of the analogy before the meeting took place. Even as I sat on the stage the evening of the meeting, I trembled lest one of the speakers preceding me should steal my thunder.

I gave my address with all the dramatic force I could put into it. Then at the close I paused for a moment and put the question, asking: "The Lady or the Tiger—which will you choose?" There was a volley of applause and as it subsided, a small boy sitting near the center aisle, close to the stage, jumped up, waving his hands wildly, and yelled: "I choose the lady!" A policeman guarding the aisle was caught by the infectious spontaneity of the boy and he called out, too, "Give me the loidy!" The speech took like wildfire, not only according to the New York papers, but also according to accounts and editorials which appeared in papers all over the country. I think, however, that my greatest gratification was derived from the letter sent to me by the Women's Municipal League, stating that "at the annual meeting a very sincere vote of thanks was passed for your efficiency during the Jerome campaign."

What was the result of all this work and effort? Did the prophecies come true? *Jerome was elected.*

The final echo of the Jerome campaign was the dinner at the Astor Hotel, given by Mr. Fulton Cutting, chairman of the Citizens' Union, to celebrate the victory. The only women invited were the officers of the Women's Municipal League, and we were honored by being given seats at the platform table. It was a large gathering. There were probably three hundred or more men. Mr. Cutting had invited all the members of the Citizens' Union who had actively participated in the campaign. Mr. Cutting, as host, presided, seating Mr. Jerome at his right, and I was given the seat next to him. I had written to Mr. Cutting that Emma Lazarus' poem, "Victory," had a peculiar significance for this occasion and suggested that it be read at his dinner. Mr. Cutting agreed with me as to the appropriateness of the poem and wrote that he would call upon me to read it. The dinner was a brilliant one. There were no set speeches, but Mr. Cutting called on the chairmen of committees and of sub-committees to tell of the work which had helped to bring about victory.

As one chairman after another was called upon, I grew more and more amazed and more impatient. There had been no mention made of the Women's Municipal League. I whispered to Mr. Jerome, "I wish I could tell what the women workers in the campaign did." Mr. Jerome replied, "Why don't you?" "Because," I retorted, "Mr. Cutting hasn't called upon me." Just then Mr. Cutting turned and asked me to read my cousin's poem. As I rose, Mr. Jerome laughingly whispered, "Here's your opportunity to tell your story. I dare you to!" A dare! I never could resist one. The old wave of defiance surged through me. I turned to Mr. Cutting and asked, "May I speak for a few minutes before reading the verses?" "You may speak as long as you like," he replied. And I did. I ended by reading the verses and as I sat down I was greeted by a storm of applause and shouts of, "Don't stop. Go on!" I was obliged to rise twice in acknowledgment of the appreciation, and as the men apparently expected me to say more, I added in a deprecatory way, "I could have made a better speech, but for two reasons: first, it was so very extemporaneous; secondly, I had no trouser pockets into which to plunge my hands." This brought a gale of laughter, for every man who had spoken had kept his hands in his pockets—probably groping there for ideas!

The newspapers made much of this extemporaneous speech. One caption was, "Woman Captures Jerome Jubilee!" Another was, "A Woman After-dinner Orator at Last!" One of the leading papers devoted an entire page to the incident, publishing my photograph and dubbing me, "New York's feminine Simeon Ford, whose triumphs of postprandial wit mark the beginning of a new era in the public activities of women."

I took part in other campaigns. I remember one when we prevented a street railway company from laying two additional tracks on an avenue near which there were several public schools. Four tracks on this avenue would have jeopardized the lives of the many children who crossed the avenue several times daily. All this work was good training for the big campaign which was to come later—a campaign far-reaching and national in character—the most important campaign of all: the Equal Suffrage Campaign.

## CHAPTER XI

### SUFFRAGE

THE interest in the Equal Suffrage Movement had for many years been confined to a small group of women, pioneers in the movement. These women devoted all of their time and energy to the cause. Their efforts received but little attention unless scoffing and ridicule may be called attention. Nevertheless, they kept steadily on, blazing the trail for others to follow. The methods of these pioneers were neither militant nor dramatic. They talked and they wrote, but they made no spectacular effort to get a hearing. Later on, in conservative England, the militant wing of the suffrage party—the suffragettes, as they were called—were smashing windows, chaining themselves to the railing of the House of Parliament, going on hunger strikes, heckling all political speakers, and making themselves generally a nuisance. Their methods did not appeal to the leaders of the American Suffrage Association. But unquestionably these tactics brought the whole movement within the limelight and quickened a general interest. The world was beginning to realize that the whole question of the franchise for women was tied up with all educational and social work.

My experiences in endeavoring to get legislation enacted for the better protection of working girls had strengthened my convictions that until women obtained the franchise, their influence with members of the legislature would continue to be a negligible quantity. So more and more of my time was given to work which I felt would hasten the day when women would have, on equal terms with men, the privileges, the rights, and the burdens and responsibilities, too, of the franchise.

Dr. Mary Putnam Jacobi begged me to assume the Presidency of the New York State Suffrage Association. I declined, because I felt that I could not do justice to such an important piece of work and at the same time continue my work with the Consumers' League. However, when Miss Mary Garrett Hay, President of the Equal Suffrage League of New York City, asked me to be a candidate for the Vice-Presidency of this league, I accepted, feeling that this position would not involve so much responsibility and work. Also I was glad to have the opportunity of coming out boldly and identifying myself with the movement. In the Equal Suffrage League were many prominent representative women, but as yet none of the so-called "society women" had joined the ranks. The first of these women to show an active interest was Mrs. Clarence Mackay—later Mrs. Duer Blake—prominent socially. She was a member of the school board at Roslyn, Long Island, her summer home, and was a member of the Consumers' League.

When she expressed to me a desire to know more about the Suffrage Movement, I invited the leading suffragists to an afternoon tea at my home to meet Mrs. Mackay. To all of Mrs. Mackay's questions, intelligent and forceful replies were given with reliable data to reënforce the statements. This discussion convinced Mrs. Mackay of the value of the movement and she soon afterwards joined the ranks of the suffragists. She was the first of the so-called fashionable group in New York to become a convert to the cause. Largely through her efforts, a debate on the suffrage question was arranged to take place at the Colony Club, then at the corner of Madison Avenue and Thirtieth Street. Miss Margaret Chanler, now Mrs. Richard Aldrich, took the affirmative in the debate and Mrs.

Group of Suffragists

Seated, left to right: Mary Garrett Hay, Harriet May Mills, Mrs. Henry Villard, Mrs. Belle de Rivera. Standing: Mrs. Elder, Portia Willis, Mrs. Edwards, Mrs. Olive Scott Gabriel, Maud Nathan, Maude Ingersoll Probasco.

Caroline Hazard the negative on the question, "Should the Franchise be Bestowed on Women?"

Mrs. Mackay gave a luncheon of twenty-four covers at her home on the day of the debate, inviting Mrs. Carrie Chapman Catt, Mrs. Ida Husted Harper, Mrs. Harriot Stanton Blatch, and me, to meet her other guests who were all members of the club and were to attend the debate later. By asking each of us four suffragists to say a few words before leaving the luncheon table, Mrs. Mackay cleverly arranged that her guests should have their minds properly attuned before reaching the club.

I well remember the discussion and the suppressed excitement which seemed to animate all present. My nervousness was due not only to the intensity of the occasion, but also because of the fact that one of my husband's nieces had chosen that day for her marriage, at a later hour during the afternoon. I was very anxious to hear the entire debate, but I well knew that if I were to present myself at my sister-in-law's home too late for the marriage ceremony, not only would I be in disgrace, but the cause of equal suffrage would receive a mortal blow from the entire family circle. So, between my desire to hear just one more word of the argument and my fear that if I did I would be too late for the wedding, I was sitting on pins and needles. Finally, I tore myself away, only to find that the coupé I had ordered was not at the door. I rushed frantically to the corner and looked in every direction—not a coupé or any kind of vehicle in sight. No taxis cruising up and down in those days in search of passengers. There were a few private coupés with coachmen and footmen in livery and I was, in my desperation, wondering whether I could be audacious enough to commandeer one of these, when Mrs. James Speyer—always kind and gracious—stepped out of the doorway of the club and asked whether she could take me anywhere. I explained my predicament and she grasped the situation at once. Her coachman drove us quickly to my sister-in-law's home. My husband was on the steps of the house, looking anxiously for me. He rushed me indoors and we managed to take our places within the family circle just as the bride was coming down the stairs. Two minutes later, my reputation would have been lost, and the subject of equal suffrage would have been taboo forever in my husband's family. It was already taboo in my own intimate family circle. My sister, Annie Nathan Meyer, who had been instrumental in founding Barnard College, for the higher education of women, who had gone to Denver, Colorado, to attend a convention of the Association for the Advancement of Women, who had addressed the Parliament of Religions in Chicago, who was one of the first women in New York to ride a bicycle—at a time when it was considered most unwomanly to make herself so conspicuous—who, in brief, stood for everything that claimed to be progressive, took her stand on the opposite side and joined the group of anti-suffragists!

My two brothers also set their faces against the proposed reform. My older brother was so irascible when the subject was mentioned that he refused to discuss it. My younger brother, a lawyer, was quite willing to argue about it, but his denunciation was so vehement and seemed to me—an humble layman, not versed in legal lore—so illogical and absurd that I preferred not to carry on a discussion with him. Years later, after our battle had been won, it was interesting to me to hear the arguments used by two legal lights in explaining their votes. My lawyer brother said that he had voted against the suffrage amendment, because he could not conscientiously vote in favor of suffrage for women, but he was glad we had won because of our brilliant fight. My cousin, Judge Cardozo, said that he had voted in favor of the amendment because he could not conscientiously vote against it. Obviously it was common justice that the women should have the vote but he was sorry we had won, as he had sore doubts as to the result of the experiment. My retort was to declare that according to the fiat of a well-known Bishop, they were arguing like women. This Bishop said, "When women argue, either their premises are all right and their conclusions all wrong, or their premises are all wrong and their conclusions all right."

This incident in which Judge Cardozo figured brings to my mind another incident quite as amusing, which also centers around him. The Consumers' League was circulating a petition for signatures in order to help secure some special legislation at Albany. There were two forms of petitions. One headed, "We the undersigned citizens," the other, "We the undersigned women." Inadvertently the secretary sent Judge Cardozo the latter form. He signed it, returning it to me with the observation, "For *your* sake I have signed away my sex!"

Fortunately, my husband's views in regard to equal suffrage coincided with my own. He not only gave me every encouragement, but he gave tangible evidence of his support on all occasions. He was one of the small group of men to march with the women in their first suffrage parade. He was one of the leaders of the Men's League for Equal Suffrage. It was at his suggestion that the International Men's League was organized at Stockholm with representatives from England, France, Germany, Hungary, Holland, and the United States. In all the work that I did for the cause, my husband was at my side aiding and abetting me. When we took a motor trip through New York State, in order to attend the annual convention of the State Suffrage League, which was held that year at Cornell University, Ithaca, my husband always helped to secure a crowd of listeners whenever I stopped to make a speech. He helped to distribute the literature and whenever he was in the midst of a throng, he led the applause and cheering. At the time that the suffrage amendment was voted upon in New York, my husband was an invalid, but he insisted upon being wheeled in his chair to the polls so that he could have the gratification of voting in favor of it.

This has its peculiar significance for me. It was the last vote he ever cast.

It was at the convention at Ithaca that I was asked to substitute for Rev. Anna Howard Shaw who, because of freshets in the Middle West, had been detained on her railroad trip and was unable to reach the convention in time for the first evening's session. I had very little time for preparation and I was greatly disconcerted, for the Cornell students who had crowded the gallery of Goldwin Smith Hall to hear the famous orator started to leave when it was announced that I had been asked to take Rev. Anna Shaw's place on the program. I wanted those students to hear my plea for votes for women. I could not bear to see such good plowing material get away. So looking up at the boys as they were putting on their overcoats, I said, "I don't blame you, boys. You came to hear our most eloquent speaker. You are in the same situation as the sons of one of your well-known professors. He used to insist upon his sons attending his lectures. One cold, rainy evening when they were sitting reading cosily by the fire, their father said, 'Come, boys, it is time to go out to hear my lecture.' Thereupon, the younger son replied, 'Oh, Dad, couldn't you give us a licking instead this evening?' No doubt you, too, would rather have a licking than remain to listen to my speech!" They all laughed, took off their coats, and sat down again.

I have not yet given the sequel to the debate which took place at the Colony Club. Mrs. Mackay formed the Equal Franchise Society, with both men and women on the Board, and asked me to serve as one of the Vice Presidents. This new league conducted a vigorous and

Benjamin Nathan Cardozo

Justice of the United States Supreme Court, great-grandson of Simon and Grace Seixas Nathan.

picturesque educational campaign. Among the well-known men on the Board were:

| | |
|---|---|
| PROFESSOR JOHN DEWEY | COLONEL GEORGE HARVEY |
| MELVILLE STONE | RABBI STEPHEN WISE |

The league was influential in getting a hearing at Columbia University during its summer session. This was an innovation. I felt honored when I was selected to make the first suffrage speech within these sacred walls. This address was entitled: "The Working Woman and the Ballot." It was published later by the Equal Franchise Society and used by it as propaganda. Speaking from university platforms, addressing street corner crowds, making dashes to outlying districts, never flagging in my Consumers' League work, is it any wonder that I lost my voice and my physician ordered me to a sanitarium for a complete rest?

I went to a little sanitarium in Connecticut. I followed the doctor's orders strictly as to *physical* rest. But how can any one with an active brain rest mentally? Certainly I could not. I had left my secretary in New York in charge of my mail. She had instructions to forward only the most important letters. I had hardly been gone a week when she began to urge me to enter a contest which was being carried on in the New York *Herald.*

This newspaper was offering two prizes of one hundred dollars each for the best letters pro and con on the suffrage question. At first I paid no attention to these urgings, but one evening—having finished my book, and there being nothing special to do before the nurse came to see that the lights were out—I picked up a pad and scribbled a few hundred words of argument. The next day I enclosed it in a letter to my secretary, asking her to type it and send it to the *Herald,* if she thought the argument convincing. She at once replied that the letter had gone.

I had entered the competition. I thought no more about it. Many weeks later, in answer to a request, I gave an address for the Consumers' League from the pulpit of an Episcopal Church at Riverdale. After the service, the rector took my husband and me to the rectory for Sunday dinner. The rector's wife greeted me effusively and with warmest congratulations. Of course, I thought she was referring to the address I had just concluded. I was amazed, therefore, when she showed me the front page of the *Herald* with my picture and the announcement in huge headlines that I was the winner of the one hundred dollar prize for the best suffrage letter. I learned later that I had competed with twenty-five thousand contestants from every part of the world. The National Woman Suffrage Association got permission to republish the letter and it was widely circulated as propaganda.

There is a deep national psychological reason for the wide diversity between the methods used by the English women in their struggle to obtain the franchise and the methods used by the women of the United States. English history shows that any great change in its political life has always been preceded by an upheaval. Runymede, Charles the First, Cromwell, and later, in our own time, the long debated Irish question, are all proofs of this statement. The reasons seem to be the Englishman's love of tradition, dread of change, and willingness to muddle along until finally the explosion occurring forces radical change upon him.

A well-known Englishman told me that the aggressive, militant methods of the suffragettes had accomplished more for the cause than all the years of patient, dignified strivings of the older wing of the suffrage party. For our nation different methods were needed. The nation was hardly out of its swaddling clothes. It was just beginning to walk. Its voice was just beginning to be heard among the nations. It was not hidebound by tradition. Its youthful adventurous spirit, its sense of humor, its love of fair play, demanded a different stimulus. Instinctively and without reasoning about it, we knew this and we set to work to keep ourselves in the public eye in a fashion that would interest and not antagonize. We put our heads together and devised all sorts of original "stunts," anything that would give us publicity, without violating any existing law.

We inaugurated the novelty of giving twenty-four-hour speeches from automobiles stationed at various points in the city. Every quarter of an hour a new speaker relieved the preceding one, taking up the argument exactly where it had been left off. We chose our stations according to the trend of the crowds. The congested shopping districts, the factory neighborhoods, the theater zones, collected the largest number of people. Of course, these crowds thinned out in the "wee sma" hours, no matter where the automobile happened to be stationed. But the suffragists, undaunted, continued to plead their cause, even though their listeners might only be a belated night reveler, a policeman on his beat, a milkman making his early rounds, or a white-wing sweeping up the litter of the previous day's campaign. And always there was the reporter, ready to pounce upon a story, should the twenty-four-hour speech lag by as much as thirty seconds.

In contrast to the twenty-four hour speeches, we gave what we called silent speeches. For this purpose, we obtained permission to use some prominent window of a vacant store. Here we installed a mechanism that displayed at regular intervals large printed placards, stating woman's need of the franchise. These silent speeches drew crowds almost as great as the twenty-four-hour speeches, the police frequently dispersing the crowd on the plea that it was obstructing traffic. This always incensed me, because the huge crowds which gathered in front of baseball bulletins were always left unmolested.

Then we took a cue from the political methods of the men. The city being politically divided into senatorial, assembly, and election districts, we placed our own leaders and captains in each of these districts, just as the Republicans and Democrats did. I was appointed the leader of my assembly district and it became my duty to ascertain the convictions of every woman in my district in regard to the question of equal suffrage and to enroll them in our party if they were in favor of the cause.

In connection with this work, Mrs. Marie Jenny Howe, the leader of her assembly district, and I arranged a propaganda skit. It was a burlesque in the form of a debate between suffragists and anti-suffragists. Mrs. Howe posed as a modern, up-to-date anti-suffragist and I took the part of the anti-suffragist of a previous generation. Mrs. Howe was dressed in an exaggerated form of the fashion of the day. I wore hoop skirts, a cap on my white curls, a fichu pinned with a large cameo brooch, a camel's hair shawl draped over my shoulders, and I carried a funny little sunshade with a handle that folded in two.

Two well-known suffragists, using the conventional arguments, were always pitted against us. Our sallies were so amusing, so absurd, and yet so imitative of the arguments frequently heard from the lips of the suffrage antagonists, that our audiences were invariably convulsed with laughter. We were urged to repeat our skit on all occasions. Even the men's Republican Club of my district tendered us an invitation and the members crowded the auditorium to the doors. We fashioned our campaign along the lines laid down by the men in their political work. We held our first convention at Carnegie Hall. I was appointed the temporary chairman. I sat on the stage watching the delegates file in with their banners, district by district, until the vast auditorium was completely filled. I rose to open the meeting at eight P.M. precisely. My gavel fell, and the first genuine political mass meeting of women ever held in New York City was called to order. After my opening remarks, I turned the meeting over to the permanent chairman, Mrs. Carrie Chapman Catt.

Many, many times since then I have been one of a large audience at Carnegie Hall. I have seen the auditorium and galleries crowded, but it is a far different feeling to be one of an expectant, eager, listening throng, from experiencing the thrill that fills one when facing that throng from the stage. This mass meeting was a milestone in the long road which had been traveled since the pioneer meeting at Seneca Falls in 1848. The goal now did not seem so far distant. A few more turnings, a few more obstacles to overcome, and it would be won. Won not only for our generation, but won for all succeeding generations of women.

We left no stone unturned to get our propaganda over. I was often delegated to speak during the entr'actes of plays and moving pictures. This brings me to an original method of bringing our cause before the public. Jacques Copeau and his French company were producing some of the Brieux plays in New York. In one of these plays there was a scene between a candidate for election in the Chambre des Députés and several of his constituents. Each visitor urged the candidate to further some special measure in regard to his or her particular hobby. We had the brilliant idea to ask Monsieur Copeau to allow a suffragist to appear in this scene, to plead the cause of suffrage. He gracefully and sympathetically acquiesced. I was delegated to fill the rôle. I wrote my little speech in French, using all the most forceful arguments at my command. I memorized that speech so that I could have said it backwards. I practiced dramatic gestures before the mirror. Monsieur Copeau did not require me to rehearse. The night of my appearance I was stationed in the wings and was told what my cue would be. I knew that the front rows were filled with my friends. I was on my mettle, not only to do my best for the cause of suffrage, but also to justify the confidence placed in me by Monsieur Copeau. As the scene progressed, I grew more and more excited, fearing lest my cue be forgotten, or worse yet, lest I miss it. At last I heard it. I walked on the stage and was greeted not only by the candidate, Monsieur Copeau, but also by a burst of applause from my friends in the audience. It all came so naturally and worked in so well with the rest of the scene, that only those in the secret knew that it was an interpolation. At the end of the act, Monsieur Copeau expressed his willingness to have me appear in the scene every night that the play was produced.

Thirteen years later, I met Monsieur Copeau at a reception tendered him at Columbia University. As I was brought up to be presented to him, he gave me a quick glance of recognition and said, "Mais, nous avons joués ensemble!"

Sarah Bernhardt was another French thespian who showed her interest in suffrage. In recognition of this interest, the Woman Suffrage Party tendered her a reception at Headquarters when she was in New York. I was asked to make the speech of greeting in French, and present her with a bunch of yellow roses. This time it was a little more difficult to proceed with my speech. Each sentence was punctuated by Mme. Bernhardt's exclamations: "Ah. Mais c'est trop gentil." "Ah non, je ne mérite pas celà." "Que vous êtes aimable!" "Qu'elles sont belles, ces roses." And so on and so on. I thought my little speech would never be finished. The next day I received a gift from Sarah Bernhardt. It was her photograph and over her autograph were the following words:

"Avec mes remerciments et ma sympathie,
Sarah Bernhardt
à Madame F. Nathan qui a bien voulu m'accepter
comme collègue."

There was plenty of hard work connected with the suffrage campaign. Plenty of excitement. Plenty of interest. Plenty of amusing incidents. My work was not confined to the city and state of New York. I was personally asked to help in the campaign being conducted in Ohio and Wisconsin. My husband and I made this an occasion for a motor trip and I invited a friend to go with us. She was an avowed "anti," but was fond of motoring. We stopped at various places *en route*. Whenever a favorable opportunity presented itself, the car was halted and I would jump up on the seat and start an impromptu speech. It was amusing to see my "anti" friend's efforts to collect a large crowd. Although she did not approve of the cause I was espousing, she was fond of me and was interested in seeing me make a success. She would circulate among the listeners, distributing tracts. She would arrange my flags with which I illustrated my remarks. At the end of the trip some one asked her whether she had been converted to the cause. "Oh, no," she replied. "Maud Nathan would lose all interest in me were I no longer material for conversion."

Times change, fashions change, and with them comes a change in the association of ideas. Short hair, short skirts, knickers, are today associated with the youthful figure—flapper type, demanding no rights while calmly appropriating them. Short hair, short skirts, bloomers, used to be associated with the strong-minded, aggressive woman, insistently demanding her rights.

Because of this tradition, we suffragists were particular about wearing our best gowns when publicly pleading our cause. On one occasion, there was to be a joint hearing of suffragists and anti-suffragists in regard to the proposed amendment before Committees of the Senate and Assembly at the Capitol in Albany. The suffrage delegation was given one side of the Assembly Chamber, the anti-suffragists the opposite side. We sat glaring at each other.

I wore my most becoming gown and my most fetching hat. The doorkeeper gave me one look and directed me to the anti side of the chamber. I was amused to find that my carefully selected costume had landed me in the wrong camp. I at once recognized the mistake and joined my fellow delegates on the other side of the chamber. Presently the chair next to me was taken by Miss G., a well-known "anti." She was wearing her usual mannish tailor-made costume, high stiff collar, shirt front, four-in-hand tie, coat of masculine cut, and dark Derby hat. She looked about and saw herself surrounded by her antagonists, her friends sitting opposite. She jumped up, exclaiming, "That man at the door sent me to the wrong side of the hall," and turning to me, she said, "Why didn't you tell me?" I realized how the mistake had been made, but there was nothing for me to say, except, "I supposed you had been converted over night." I wonder whether that doorkeeper at the Capitol has progressed beyond such traditional association of ideas.

As I said before, through all this activity for suffrage, I never lost sight of the interests of the Consumers' League. The twenty-fifth anniversary of the Consumers' League was approaching. We wanted to make this a special occasion. Whom would we get as principal speaker? There was no man more prominently in the public eye at that time than President Wilson. A delegation was appointed to wait on the President and extend an invitation to be present at the proposed dinner and give the address of the evening. I was chairman of the committee of eight that went to Washington. Mr. Tumulty, President Wilson's secretary, had arranged a twenty-minute interview for us with the President. As we entered the President's office, we were all presented and then President Wilson courteously indicated the chair by his desk which I took, the others seating themselves in chairs ranged along the wall. The President gave me his fullest attention while

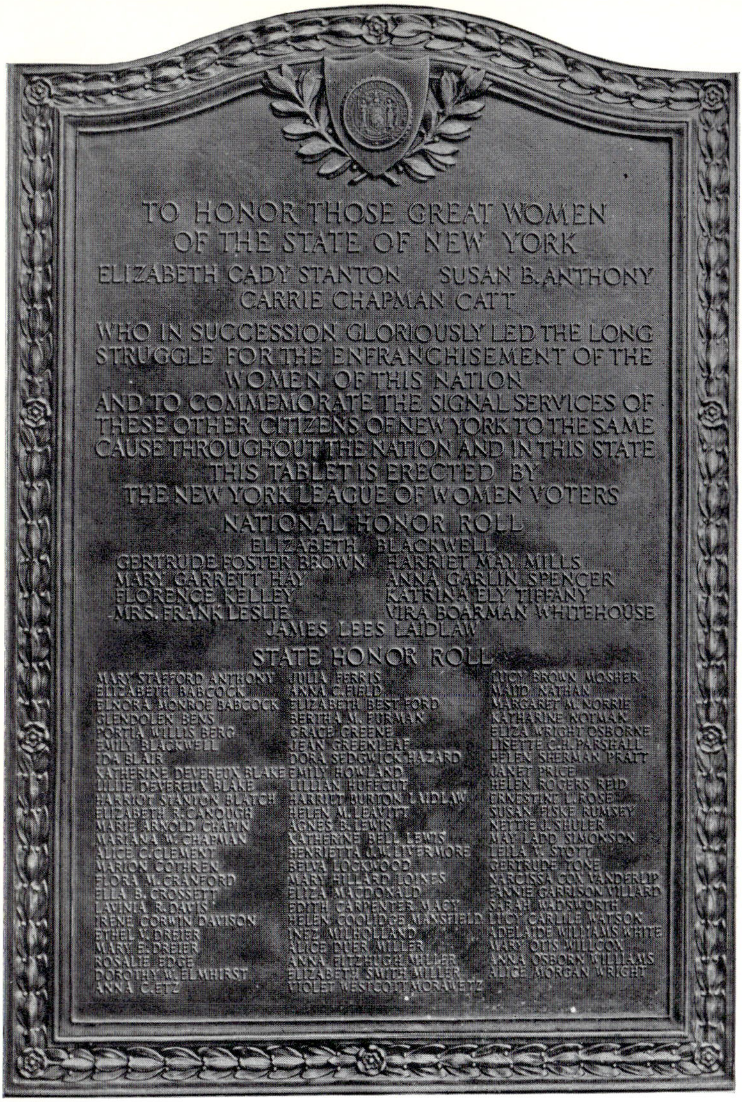


Bronze tablet erected by the Tenth Suffrage Anniversary Committee of the New York League of Women Voters, in the Capitol, Albany, November 22, 1931.

I made my request, as briefly and succinctly as possible. When I had finished the President said, "Mrs. Nathan, many men have come to me with similar invitations, and I only wish they could have presented their case as admirably and as forcefully as you have." I blushed like a schoolgirl, and for the first time during the interview I felt embarrassed. I could only stammer, "Oh, Mr. President, what a compliment!" "Madam, you deserved it," he replied. He accepted our invitation, provided that the foreign situation would permit of his absence from Washington. There is both a climax and an anticlimax to this interview. The foreign situation became so acute that it was impossible for President Wilson to leave his desk. My object in extending the invitation to President Wilson was to gain publicity for the Consumers' League and to honor its twenty-fifth anniversary. Incidentally, I won President Wilson to the cause of suffrage. Mr. Tumulty told a friend of mine that President Wilson had said after my interview with him: "Tumulty, that was a very fine speech Mrs. Nathan made today. When I hear a woman talk so well in the public interest, it almost makes me believe in woman suffrage." At the next election the newspapers announced that President Wilson had voted in favor of suffrage for women. I have made many converts for the suffrage cause, but of this bit of unconscious propaganda, resulting in President Wilson's conversion to the cause, I am especially proud. It has been many years now since the yellow banner with the legend "Votes for Women" has been seen fluttering everywhere. The younger generation has almost forgotten what it looked like. The unborn generation will never know it existed. But to us who waved it together with our beloved stars and stripes, who marched under it, who carried it with us across continents and oceans, who wore its emblem on our breasts, it has become associated in our minds with an undying loyalty to a cause. We knew we were working for the future, but we were living so intensively in the present that we scarcely realized how soon the tomorrow of our hopes was to become the today of our accomplishment. I remember with what anxiety we watched the bulletin board at the Women's City Club the election night that was to decide whether New York State had voted for or against the amendment. When at last the figures showed that in our State, at least, we had won a victory, we were almost staggered. We could hardly grasp the fact. It seemed too good to be true. Two of my cousins and their wives were with me, watching the returns at the club. One of them had voted for, the other against the amendment. When the final result was known and jubilation began, I took my party to the dining room and ordered drinks. The cousin who had contributed his vote to our success was given the privilege of ordering anything he wanted. The other cousin was allowed to drown his defeat in water.

When our final victory came and we had won our thirty-sixth State, I think the majority of the men were with us. They certainly showed their chivalry in their congratulations. I shall never forget my sensations when I went to the polls for the first time to vote. I was prepared to take my place and stand in line, but as I entered the door, two gentlemen ahead of me stepped out of the line and raising their hats, said, "Mrs. Nathan, we yield our places to you. You have earned a great victory. You deserve first place in the line." I thanked them cordially, but declined their offer, saying I had always worked for *equal rights,* not for *special privileges.*

We American suffragists did not confine our interests to our own country. We were eager to help women of other countries in their struggle for freedom. I was frequently appointed a delegate and speaker to international congresses.

In a former chapter, I spoke of my first International Congress. These conventions met about once in five years.

I was delighted to be elected a delegate to the one held in Berlin in 1904. We planned our summer with this in view. It made a very busy season—from the family point of view, a most hectic one, for I had attended a convention at St. Louis in the late spring of that same year. The Congress met in June. The preparations for the St. Louis convention included writing and printing a report, securing speakers for the two sessions for which I was responsible, besides all the details incident to taking two young girls with us. There were not many days between the return from St. Louis and the date of our sailing for Europe. The five-story house had to be closed and I would not have felt satisfied had I not supervised every detail. My husband's niece—his ward—was to be married from our home the following September. Certain preliminary arrangements had to be made for the wedding and breakfast before we left home. I was not only to be a delegate, but also a speaker at the Berlin Congress. Feeling that my message would carry more weight if I gave it in German, I wrote it and had it translated before we sailed. It can easily be imagined that when the *Kronprinz Wilhelm* sailed away, I sank exhausted into my deck chair. The voyage held no thought of discomfort for me as I looked forward to those seven days of absolute rest. We sailed directly to Germany, being transferred from the steamer to a small tender, which took us up the Weser River to Bremen harbor. This Congress held all of the old pleasures which I had so enjoyed in London, with the added pleasure of renewing the friendships I had made five years before. I also enjoyed the foreign setting and the foreign language. The three official languages of these Congresses were English, French, and German. All of the official business was conducted in one of these three languages and whenever translations were required, there were official interpreters present to undertake this. I was appointed one of the official interpreters and served in this capacity at three later conventions: Budapest, Geneva, and Rome.

The feminist movement was not popular in Berlin. Nevertheless the meetings of the Frauenkongress were crowded and the messages were well received. The result of my address on "Der Liga von Konsumenten" was the forming of a committee to establish a Consumers' League in Germany. Berlin vied with London in the hospitality shown the Congress. The Kaiserin tendered a small reception to the officers. The Chancellor and his wife, Count and Countess von Bülow, and the Minister of the Interior and his wife, Count and Countess Posodowski, opened their adjacent gardens and together gave us a brilliant garden party. The City Fathers, not to be outdone, arranged for a banquet in the Rathaus—a banquet for one thousand guests. The details were as elaborate and as beautiful as though a small fraction of the number had been expected. The flowers and table decorations were lavish and each guest was presented with a souvenir—a small bear holding a rose. The bear was the insignia of the city and was decorated with the national colors engraved in gilt letters, "Frauenkongress," and filled with chocolates.

In the midst of all this official recognition, the Kaiser made no sign. He may have been champing at the bit, but there was no protest until it was announced that Baronin von Suttner, the author of "Die Waffen Nieder" —"Lay Down Your Arms"—was to give an address on "Peace" at the Rathaus. Then the royal voice thundered and the War Lord laid down his now famous dictum: that women should confine their energies to the four K's—Kinder, Kirche, Kuchen, und Kleider—children, the church, cooking, and clothes.

This being published in the newspapers made a tremendous sensation. We of the Congress feared that the Kaiser —in his wrath—might use his authority to have the Rathaus closed to Baroness von Suttner. We were prepared for

Group of the Founders of the Men's International League for Equal Suffrage

Stockholm, 1911.

Standing, left to right: Frederick Nathan, New York; Dr. Ch. V. Drysdale, London; Herr Franz Lehnhoff, Bremen; Herr W. A. E. Mansfeldt, Utrecht. Seated, left to right: Mr. Alexander Pataj, Budapest; Mr. F. F. W. Vehrer, Holland; Mr. J. Dubreuil de St. Germain, Paris; Dr. F. A. Bather, England.

such a contingency and had engaged another hall in the event of her being refused admittance. When Baroness von Suttner arrived at the Rathaus to deliver her address, there was such an enormous crowd gathered outside the building that she took it for granted that the doors were locked. She was about to announce that she would give her lecture at the other hall, when to her surprise, she was informed that the huge mass of people represented an overflow from the large crowd that already packed the auditorium of the Rathaus. Baroness von Suttner told me herself that her hat and veil were almost torn off her head in making her way to the platform through this dense crowd. She was obliged to repeat her address later to the waiting crowd outside. The Kaiser's manifesto proved the best kind of an advertisement. The next day the *goose-step* of the Kaiser's military guard seemed more ludicrous than ever.

Besides the official functions, we were entertained widely by the distinguished citizens of Berlin. Lady Battersea, who attended the Congress as a delegate from the British Council of Women, holding up her hands in despair, said to me one day, "How do you ever get time to answer all the invitations? I sit up half the night attending to mine. I should have brought my secretary with me." I laughed and told her that I was only repeating my London experience of five years before.

Stockholm, the Venice of the North, was the setting for the Congress of 1911. The municipality tendered us a colorful greeting. Flagpoles had been specially erected on the quay in front of the Grand Hotel—our headquarters—and the twenty-three flags of the nations represented at the Congress were waving a welcome to us when we arrived. Pennants with the legend, "Röstratt för Kvinnor," were flying everywhere, and the phrase became as familiar to us as our own "Votes for Women." These Scandinavian countries were far ahead of us in the matter of equal suffrage. In Sweden, the women at that time had the municipal vote—now they are fully enfranchised. In Norway they had the full vote and the Norwegian Government sent an official delegate to the Congress, paying all her expenses. The delegates from Finland were two members of Parliament. The delegate from Iceland, Miss Laufig Asmundsson, was a picturesque figure in the bridal costume—with headdress—of her country. She reported that in Iceland the Lutheran Church—the State Church—had revised its prayer book so that anything that might affront women was omitted. It is interesting in connection with this to note that the Episcopal Church has revised its marriage service so that the word "obey" is omitted from the bride's marital vows. The orthodox Hebrew prayer book still clings to its Orientalism. These sentences are still repeated in the service: "Blessed art Thou, O Lord our God, who hast made me a man." The women say: "Blessed art Thou, O Lord our God, who hast made me according to Thy will."

Miss Asmundsson wrote her address in English, but owing to a severe cold was unable to deliver it. Mrs. Catt, the presiding officer, asked me to read it for her. This led to an amusing complication. At the close of the session, I was surrounded by a group of interested women plying me with questions in regard to the status of women in Iceland. These women had come in just after I had begun reading the paper and had not heard Mrs. Catt's apology for Miss Asmundsson and her introduction of me. It was impossible for me to give satisfactory replies to all these questions and finally I confessed my ignorance. Whereupon, one woman scornfully remarked: "Why does Iceland send a delegate who is so poorly informed?" They all enjoyed a hearty laugh after explanations ensued. It had been arranged that Dr. Anna Shaw was to preach the sermon at the Church of Gustaf Vasa on Sunday afternoon. The Women's Choir of Göteborg was to sing and Miss Elfrida Andrée was to preside at the organ. The church was so crowded that the aisles were choked with men and women who stood during the entire service. Dr. Shaw gave her sermon from the foot of the pulpit—the authorities of the church having decided at the last moment that it would be improper for a woman to ascend the pulpit. This is a striking illustration of the inconsistency which has always governed man's attitude toward women.

One of the Congress meetings was held at Skansen, the public park. The huge bowlders made admirable platforms from which speeches were made in English, German, and the Scandinavian languages. Afterwards there were folk songs and national dances in costume. The pages at the Congress were young university students, wearing their university caps and sashes of yellow and blue—the Swedish colors.

At the sessions of this Congress, some interesting facts were brought out. A Swedish woman, a physician, related that because women had only the municipal vote and not what was called the political vote, men through political influence grabbed all positions with good salaries. Women demanded that some of the overseers appointed to supervise homes where orphans had been placed should be women, especially to look after the little girls. The men in authority said that the work was too fatiguing for women, necessitating, as it did, much travel. The women replied that many women endured this fatigue without monetary compensation. Finally, after much pressure was brought to bear, the women succeeded in having the position of overseer thrown open to their sex. Two women then received appointments. However, they were paid lower salaries than the men and were allowed less for their expenses—food and lodging. The men appointees were permitted to travel second class—where cushioned chairs lessened their fatigue. The women were required to travel third class where uncushioned seats were the rule.

Miss Nina Boyle, the delegate from South Africa, related

that after the Boer War, some of the rights and privileges previously enjoyed by women were taken away from them. When the question came up of restricting these privileges in regard to the native men, the authorities said, "Oh, no, we cannot take away any rights which citizens have once had bestowed upon them, it's not constitutional." Yet these same rights had already been taken away from the women. Have men really a sense of humor?

Mademoiselle Belle, one of the French delegates, told of a novel campaign conducted in France. The authorities of that Republic—with its motto, "Égalité, Fraternité et Liberté" proclaimed that women could not stand as candidates for the Chamber of Deputies, although the law did not prohibit it. The authorities also decided it was perfectly legal for male idiots to vote, even those incarcerated in asylums were permitted to register and were led to the polls on election day, the authorities contending that there was very little difference, after all, between idiots and other men!

One woman, a strong suffragist, had a protégé who was an idiot. She registered him as a candidate to sit in the Chambre des Députés. She then introduced him to audiences, explaining that legally he was eligible for the office of deputy and could register and vote, but she—who was his guardian—could do neither, because she was a woman.

There were many interesting excursions planned for us. Visby, on the island of Gotland in the Baltic Sea, was the setting of a unique entertainment. We were transported to the middle ages. The ancient town wall which encircled the village was in excellent condition. Mrs. Benedicks-Bruce, a prominent Swedish woman, widow of an English artist, invited a group of delegates to visit her at her beautiful home at Visby. Mrs. Bruce arranged to have a choir of singers—all women—dressed in white vestments, march up the steps of a half-ruined, ivy-covered medieval church at sunset, singing old Swedish hymns. The effect was marvelously impressive.

We visited the university town of Upsala and were shown the old Gutenburg Bible, the oldest printed Bible known to exist. We drove to the mounds of the Scandinavian gods, Odin, Thor, Fricka, where they are supposed to be buried. We visited the old church and graveyard and then we were taken to a nearby cottage where we were served with "mjod"—mead—the alleged nectar of the gods. We drank the mead from old horns, just as the gods and goddesses were supposed to do centuries before. Thus we drank in wisdom and strength. Thus we imbibed courage and power, the attributes of the gods, qualities which led us on to the Valhalla of our hopes.

The Scandinavians have many customs which seem strange to western eyes. From a sheaf of these, I shall cull one, because it recalls the old Puritanism of our *Mayflower* ancestors. In Norway we were shown an ancient pole, not unlike the totem pole of the Alaskan Indians, to which was attached a ring and those who refused to attend church were placed in the ring and left to the obloquy of the passers-by.

Two years after the Stockholm Congress, I was again a delegate at Budapest. It always gave me the greatest pleasure to be appointed a delegate to these international congresses. My husband and I enjoyed the ocean voyage and foreign travel. The vacation had an added zest because of the combination of work and play.

I was by this time an old and seasoned traveler, and it might be supposed that my enthusiasm had weakened, the keenness of my impressions had been dulled. On the contrary, my appreciation was quickened by my varied experiences.

As we glided along the Danube at sunset, approaching Budapest, that first glimpse of the old world city was never to be forgotten. Buda with its magnificent buildings, its medieval Fisher Bastion, rising above the smiling Danube on one side—Pest with its turrets, its towers in the rising light of the moon, on the opposite side, made a profound impression.

As we stepped off the boat, we were greeted by the strains of Hungarian music. The quay was gay with men and women seated in front of cafés as in Paris, quaffing their drinks, amid gossip and laughter, typical of leisure-loving Continental Europe.

Budapest rivaled Stockholm in its picturesque and generous hospitality. The Hungarian Parliament appropriated ten thousand crowns for the entertainment of the visitors. The city of Budapest appropriated an equal amount, and the Hungarian women collected and spent almost one hundred thousand crowns additional.

The city officials, members of Parliament, the Minister of Education, and other dignitaries, entertained us, and although the opera season was over, a special performance was given in our honor. All the boxes were at the disposal of the delegates. Addresses of welcome were made by Dr. Bela de Jankovics, Minister of Education, and Dr. Stephen de Barczy, the Burgomaster. The Grand Duke and Duchess were present on this occasion. The Free Masons opened their club house for the first time in its history to women. They arranged a meeting and asked for a few speeches on the subject of suffrage. I was among those who gave addresses. This congress attracted more than usual attention. Twenty-six nations were represented. There were many visitors registered besides the large number of delegates and alternates. Among the distinguished visitors were the Duchess of Marlborough, from England, Frau Marianne Hainisch of Vienna, Mrs. May Wright Sewall from the United States.

Among the Hungarian delegates were women belonging to the nobility. They sat side by side with peasant delegates from the provinces, the first named wearing up-to-date Parisian gowns, the latter with their colorful Hungarian costumes and bright kerchiefs on their heads.

While the official languages of these congresses were invariably English, French, and German, an exception was made at Budapest out of consideration for the Hungarian peasant delegates, who only understood their own tongue. One of the leading Hungarian delegates made special translations for them. My own speech was given in the three official languages. That is, I divided the address into three parts, giving the first part in French, the second in English, and the third in German. Having learnt by heart a well-known Hungarian phrase of appreciation, I closed with that, in recognition of the gracious hospitality which had been extended to us in this beautiful Hungarian city. Notwithstanding that many of the Hungarian leaders spoke English very well, there were some ludicrous mistakes made when notices were given in our language. For instance, when we were asked to assemble outside to have a photograph taken, some one particularly requested that, "The most *renounced* foreign leaders of the cause" should be in the group. Again when we were asked to sign up for the banquet, so that the caterer would know how many he was to serve, we were requested to "send our names to the *undertaker* so he may know how many he is to prepare."

One of the most interesting personalities I met during my work for suffrage was the Anglo-American, Lady Astor. At an International Congress, held after the war, at which we had been fellow delegates, she graciously invited me to visit her at Cliveden. So when I was spending a week-end in that neighborhood, we drove over one afternoon, and I thus had an opportunity of seeing Lady Astor in her home setting. During the war, Cliveden had been used as a hospital for wounded Canadian and American soldiers, and those who had died there were interred in a secluded part of the grounds. We saw the sunken graves with their flat uniform tablets, of ten Canadian soldiers, four American soldiers, and the two trained nurses who had also sacrificed their lives. It was from this part of the grounds that the soldiers used to sit and watch the river while they were convalescing from their wounds.

At one end of the cemetery was a dripping well, symbolic of tears. At the bank opposite the entrance was a large bronze figure of a woman, with uplifted face and outstretched arms, dominating the quiet graveyard. On the pedestal were inspired words from the Book of Wisdom.

We saw the ornate chapel, the dome of which was beautiful and the frieze decorated with stories from the Old Testament. We wandered through the grounds and finally climbed the steps of the terrace to approach the house. Lady Astor, stepping out of a French window, made an attractive picture, with her girlish figure in a gray riding habit and her arm thrown around her young son, who was dressed as an American Boy Scout.

Lady Astor, always vivacious and animated, seemed more youthful and active in the environment of her own home than elsewhere. She ran down the steps of the terrace to pluck a fragrant gardenia for me. She led us indoors to meet Lady Geddes and two other friends. Lady Geddes was the American wife of the British Ambassador to the United States and I had the pleasure of seeing her in Washington the following winter on one of her days at home.

Lady Astor drew me to a bench in the garden, where we discussed the feasibility of having women appointed as secretaries in both British and American Embassies. She said she would try to get a woman Attaché for Washington and begged me to use my influence to get one appointed to serve in London. While I am on the subject, I may as well say here that the following winter I made an appointment with Secretary of State Bainbridge Colby, whom I knew personally, to talk the matter over with him. He

Corner of cemetery at Cliveden, home of Lord and Lady Astor. Cliveden was loaned as a hospital during the war. The statue was erected as a memorial to English and American soldiers who died here.

seemed favorably disposed toward the suggestion, but his tenure of office was nearing its close and he advised me to place the matter before his Republican successor. I followed his advice, but up to now nothing has developed.

To go back to Cliveden, Lady Astor took us through the beautiful house, even upstairs to see her bedroom, with its old carved ebony four-poster and its little secret panel for valuables. Jumping up lithely on the lace spread, she opened the panel and said, "But you see, it's empty. We English have no money to hide away now. It all goes in taxes!" We had a delightful visit. All the more delightful because we did not expect to find our hostess at home. We had been told that she was away.

Nashdom, where we were spending the week-end with my English cousins, was close to the Cliveden estate. The villa, with its eighteen master bedrooms and twelve servants' rooms, its charming terrace and its tennis court, had formerly belonged to the Princess Dolgorouki. It was an estate of fourteen acres, beautified by many noble oak trees.

For one coming from a so-called prohibition country, the wonderful array of beverages served at Nashdom seemed quite marvelous. For lunch, we had the choice of whisky, ginger ale, cider, beer, and cocktails. For dinner, cocktails were served first, then Madeira, red or white wine, champagne, port, liqueurs, and whisky and soda for those who wanted it. Yet there was no evidence of intoxication, no boisterous behavior, no excess drinking. How much better it all seemed than our stupid, so-called prohibition which only serves to whet the appetite for drink and leads to surreptitious violation of law.

One of the pleasant recollections of my visit to Nashdom was the opportunity I had to go over the golf links with the Misses Leitch and the Misses Wheeler. Each woman gave the man who played against her a handicap and yet not one of the four men won a game! I was feminist enough to chuckle over this for some time.

Before taking the Channel boat to Havre, we found time to spend a day at Cold East with that delightful scholar, Claude Montefiore, and his wife. Whenever I went to England, he always entertained me most hospitably. His outlook on life was so broadening, his spirituality so compelling, that I never liked to be in England without having an opportunity to be uplifted by a talk with him. I must have looked much younger when I left him, for when I reached Southampton, an inspector, wishing to fill out some necessary paper, asked my age. I replied, "Fifty-six." He repeated, "Thirty-six?" I retorted, "Well, if I look only thirty-six, let it go at that." We had an uneventful voyage. Four days after we arrived in New York, I marched in the suffrage parade to celebrate our victory. We had won our thirty-sixth State. The Federal Amendment to the Constitution had been ratified by a two-thirds vote.

"Les moyens employés par les Americaines pour obtenir le vote,"[1] "The methods employed by the American women to obtain the vote"—had met with success. After the parade, Mrs. Borden Harriman and I had a tête-à-tête celebration. We were so excited, so exhilarated, that we felt the need of a wind-up spree. But alas, we could think of nothing more wildly gay than a cup of tea in a quiet corner of the Waldorf!

1 The title of the address I gave at the Geneva International Congress in 1920.

# CHAPTER XII

## WORK AND PLAY

POLITICAL work did not interfere with other activities. These did not slacken in the least. Indeed, it rather stimulated them. I was learning new methods. My knowledge of human nature was being broadened and I was learning how to handle it. I could bring to committees and clubs a wider experience, a deeper thought, a fresher stimulus. The press was featuring me as "One of the busiest of American women." The old adage, "If you want anything done, go to the busiest person in the community," was evidently applied to me. My mail was filled with requests to address every conceivable kind of meeting, to speak on every subject under the sun. I was asked to serve on innumerable boards and every fanatic pleaded with me to support his cause.

Peace societies asked me to be their delegate and spread their propaganda. During the war I was bodily lifted to the stone coping in front of the Public Library to make an appeal for recruits. I was asked to serve on a committee to raise funds for the building of the Cathedral of St. John the Divine. I was urged to support the Zionist Movement. The societies opposed to unrestricted immigration asked my support for further measures to restrict immigation. The Jewish societies pleaded with me that I use my influence to modify restrictive immigration laws. The W.C.T.U. urged me to coöperate with them. The Association to Amend the Volstead Act asked me to preside at one of its luncheons. Editors of newspapers asked me to reply to articles and sermons concerning feminism. The

"New Savagery" was the form in which one preacher denounced the modern woman. My reply to this denunciation may have proved his point, for it was indeed savage. I did not always have a secretary. Sometimes it devolved upon me to open and sort this volume of mail. I made a rule then, which I have adhered to through all these years, to give personal attention to every request and appeal.

My husband and I were accustomed to spend four or five months away from New York, traveling and holiday-making. Our destination frequently depended upon my engagements to attend conventions and congresses. Twice we crossed the continent to California. The first time we took our bicycles—the second time we took our automobile. Our objective the first time was Los Angeles, where the General Federation of Clubs was to meet. On our second trip, San Francisco was our destination, and again the General Federation was the recipient of California hospitality. Many miles, many cities, lie between New York and Los Angeles, New York and San Francisco. The distance was bridged by friendship, cordiality, and mutual understanding. The new cities did not seem strange or unfamiliar, for club women everywhere threw open their homes to give me welcome. On those trips, we broke our journey at several of the large and important cities, where meetings had been arranged. I accepted invitations to speak in Jewish temples and from the pulpits of various churches. Wherever there was a local branch of the Council of Jewish Women, I was welcomed with flowers. Wherever there was a local branch of the Consumers' League or Suffrage Headquarters, I received greetings equally cordial. With such evidences of friendship, how could one feel a stranger? Sometimes I spoke on some phase of industrial, economic, or ethical questions. Sometimes on equal suffrage. On one of these trips, after attending the convention of the General Federation of

Frederick Nathan and Maud Nathan as Mephisto and Elsa, at a costume party given at their home.

Women's Clubs in Milwaukee, we specially arranged that I should revisit Green Bay, Wisconsin—the little town where I had spent four years of my early girlhood. Green Bay turned out en masse to welcome me. I was coming home! I was one of their own. I had left there an inexperienced girl of sixteen. I returned a woman of the world, whose name was known in the realms of welfare work throughout the country. I like to remember the wonderful welcome that was given me. The former principal of the High School, Professor Briggs, came from Oshkosh to greet me and to attend a reception tendered me. This was a great effort on his part, as it entailed a return trip by night, with no sleeping accommodations. How proud I felt that my old professor should have felt it worth while to have thus honored me. Some of my former schoolmates came from fifty miles distant. I recalled them all, calling them by their former nicknames, much to their amusement. I gave a speech from the platform of the schoolroom from which, as a girl of fourteen, I had been graduated. I occupied the pulpit of the church where I had gone in those early days to hear the singing and to listen to the sermon. I gave an address on equal suffrage in the very hall where—years before, with trembling knees and faltering voice—I had read my graduation essay. We were pursued by invitations for dinners, receptions, yachting parties. My pleasure was increased by the pride and joy that shone from my husband's face.

As I look back over these years, my mind becomes a kaleidoscope of memories, fragmentary, but always colorful and often amusing.

Once on our way to the Pacific Coast, our two nieces, who accompanied us had great fun secreting their rings and pins in extraordinary hiding places. There had been several hold-ups on the transcontinental trains just before we started. We had been warned to hide our jewelry. We reached our destination without any untoward incident, but the girls sent up a wail of disappointment. They had missed a thrill. They had not been searched. My husband, most modest of men, was featured in some of the California papers as a New York multi-millionaire, traveling with his wife and two nieces. The girls made the most of this and nicknamed him "Multi" on the spot. For the rest of the summer that was the endearing name by which they called him and he was expected to live up to its implication. Whenever they wanted to purchase some extravagant souvenir, they would exclaim, "Oh, Multi will get it for us!" These nieces were unusually beautiful and naturally attracted much attention. They took a mild interest in the varied and magnificent scenery through which we passed. But they felt that scenery was monotonous compared with an infinite variety of young men. Once, on the Columbia River, my husband suggested their moving to the other side of the deck where they could get a view of the gorgeous spectacle of five snow-capped mountains. The reply was: "All mountains look alike, but if you happen to see five nice looking young men, we'll change our seats!" All the fun, however, was not furnished by the young people. We were to visit Yellowstone Park and had been told of "Larry," an amusing character who was in charge of a tent where tourists usually stopped for lunch. He was famous for his wit and humor, and it was related that of the thousands of tourists he met each year, he never forgot a face. He had been so well described to us that my husband recognized him as we drew up. "Hullo, Larry!" he called out. "I'll bet you don't remember *me!*" Larry gave him one piercing glance and replied without a moment's hesitation, "Of course I do. You're the gentleman who left last season without paying me the ten dollars you owed me!" The laugh was on my husband. It was this same quick-witted Larry who had a bright retort for Miss Helen Gould—now Mrs. Finley Shepard. She, armed with a camera, said to him, "Come outside, Larry, and let me take you." To which he replied, "Oh, Miss Gould, I wish you'd take me for life."

Our summer holidays did not always have conventions and congresses as our objective. There were some interesting bicycle tours—one through the Evangeline country in Nova Scotia—one to Greenacre on the Piscataqua River, where Miss Sarah Farmer gathered people from the Orient as well as the Occident for her conferences. One of the most beautiful drives we ever took was in Nova Scotia around St. Mary's Bay from Yarmouth to Digby.

A most delightful experience was our trip as guests of Robert Ogden to visit Cincinnati College, Hampton University, and attend the annual conference of the Board of the Southern Educational Association of which Mr. Ogden was then President. Mr. Ogden was a veritable "Prince of Hosts." He chartered a private train for guests—about a hundred men and women who were interested in educational and sociological problems. I remember Walter Hines Page, later our ambassador to the Court of St. James's, and Mrs. Page, Albert Shaw, editor of the *Review of Reviews,* and Mrs. Shaw, ex-Governor Montague of Virginia and his wife, St. Clair McKelway, editor of the Brooklyn *Eagle,* and Mrs. McKelway. These names stand out among many others equally brilliant and well-known. Dr. Robert Abbé was with us and exhibited with pride a tiny bit of radium, not so large as a pea, which he assured us was the first bit of the newly discovered mineral imported to our country and was worth many thousands of dollars. There were some incidents connected with this trip of peculiar interest to me. I found that the beautiful park in Lexington, Kentucky, was named Gratz Park, perpetuating the name and memory of its leading citizen, Benjamin Gratz. His niece had married my uncle. His daughter, Mrs. Henry Clay, was a cousin of my first cousins, which made a bond between us. Mrs. Desha Breckenridge, a granddaughter of Henry Clay, took us to the old family homestead to see the many relics and souvenirs of the distinguished statesman.

Walter Page was asked to thank Mr. Ogden in the name of the men of the party for his generous hospitality. I was delighted to extend the same courtesy in the name of the women. Mr. Ogden always remembered with amusement that on this occasion I called him a veritable "Lord of Hosts!"

In my capacity as chairman of the Committee on Industry of the General Federation of Women's Clubs, it was my privilege to preside over two sessions of the Convention which was held in St. Louis in 1904 at the time of the St. Louis Exposition. As chairman of this committee it was my duty to provide speakers for the two sessions allotted to me. I was fortunate to secure experts on different phases of industrial conditions.[1]

Being chairman it was not in order for me to give an address, although I had been urged to do so. Therefore, I was given a place on the program at a later session. It was remarkable that despite the beautiful exposition which had attracted thousands to St. Louis that summer, our meetings were crowded, not only with delegates, but with visitors, who, to our amazement, were enormously interested in the meetings.

We had two nieces with us, so in addition to my duties as chairman of the committee, I had to play the part of chaperon. This was very delightful, but, as my charges were beautiful young girls, my position was not a sinecure. There were dinners, luncheons, receptions to attend, and always the exposition to be visited. It was a very full ten days. We returned to New York just in time to close the house, pack up for Europe, and prepare my address for the International Women's Congress which was to be held

[1] Anna Garlin Spencer of Providence; Mary McDowell of Chicago; Sarah Platt Decker of Denver; Dr. John Graham Brooks of Cambridge; Dr. Thomas Darlington and Dr. Ernst Lederle, the one Commissioner, the other ex-Commissioner of Health, of New York City.

Rebecca Gratz

Tradition has it that this beautiful woman was the one love of Washington Irving's life, the difference in faith prevented their marrying. Her bible, with her name inscribed on the fly-leaf, was close beside him when he died. He had written of her to his friend, Sir Walter Scott, and she became the prototype of his Rebecca in Ivanhoe. One of her nieces married a son of Henry Clay; another niece married my uncle, Jonathan Nathan.

in Berlin that season. As I write of it now, twenty-eight years later, it seems very strenuous, but at the time I took it as a matter of course—all in the day's work. My energy and wonderful vitality never flagged. I brought a fresh enthusiasm to every new experience.

After the close of the Berlin Congress, of which I have written at length in a previous chapter, we began our real holiday. We went to Marienbad for a "cure." Here we met many of our compatriots. We enjoyed Marienbad so much that we often revisited it on our subsequent trips abroad. So, year after year, we were apt to meet the same friends who frequented this well-known Bohemian resort. Marienbad was the favorite watering place of King Edward, where he faithfully took the cure. We often met him on our way to and from the springs, or at the Golf Club, and occasionally we had adjoining boxes at the little opera house, where light operas were presented. He invariably gave us a polite bow of recognition.

Once I was an eyewitness of an amusing incident in which King Edward was the principal figure. It happened at an open-air Wagner concert at the Café Bellevue. The King's table was placed on the terrace, *hoi polloi* sitting literally at his feet. The garden was crowded, not a vacant seat to be had. A large, fat German woman appeared at the entrance, looking about for a chair. As she stood there, the King's Aide-de-Camp left his chair next to the King's to speak to the conductor of the orchestra. The woman spied the empty chair and calmly walked forward and appropriated it. Great commotion in the garden, the waiters rushed toward her and nearly pulled the chair from under her in their excitement. The woman had a bewildered expression. She evidently had no idea that she was almost touching shoulders with King Edward VII of Great Britain and Emperor of India. The crowd broke into a roar of laughter at the woman's confused discomfiture. The King laughed as heartily as any. He looked toward our table—which was right in front of him—and catching my eye, he actually winked. I am now immortalizing that wink on this page, as a proof of my intimacy with King Edward VII!

That was the year of the Bayreuth Wagner Festival. My husband and I—after leaving Marienbad—made the pilgrimage to the little Bavarian village held sacred to the memory of the great musician. There we heard *Tannhäuser* as we never had heard it before. It was given in its entirety without the usual omissions. The ballet in the Venusberg scene was the most voluptuous I ever saw. It was at Bayreuth that we heard *Parsifal* for the first time—a memorable experience. A spirit of reverence hovered over the audience. It was an audience of genuine music lovers, who came to listen, to gain inspiration from the master. At the signal for the opera to begin the house was darkened and the silence was so absolute that one could hear a pin drop. No distraction was allowed. The doors were closed upon those who were late. They could not enter until the end of the act. The Germans are essentially a music-loving people and although these large audiences were composed of many nationalities, they listened with soulful attention. They were all touched and penetrated by the spirit with which the Germans imbued their music festivals. It was not a fashionable, social function. There was no brilliant horseshoe glittering with jewels. The operas began in the early afternoon and time was given during one of the entr'actes for dinner. Richard Wagner's son, Siegfried, wielded the baton and the widow, Frau Cosima, was very much in evidence—a bustling self-important figure.

One summer we planned our trip to include the Passion Play given every ten years at Oberammergau. Just as in Bayreuth, the village life centers around the Opera House, so in Oberammergau, the peasants live only for the presentation of the story of the life of Jesus of Nazareth. I am not going to give a description of the Passion Play. It has been done over and over again and I could add nothing to it. I merely wish to note my own reaction to it. I was drawn to Oberammergau, not from curiosity or religious feeling, but by the artistic impulse. I wanted to see how these simple peasants, untrained by outside influence, could interpret and present this tremendous tragedy. I was not disappointed. If art consists in expressing in the simplest form the truths which we see and conveying these truths to others, then these simple Oberammergau peasants were artists of the highest type. I was impressed, deeply impressed, by the reverent spirit which imbued the entire performance—by the colorful costumes and tableaux, by the tragic climax. As I came away, however, still under the spell of the story that has influenced the world for nearly two thousand years, I could not help but wonder whether such a vivid presentation did not make for—and keep alive—religious prejudice and persecution. I live over the impression as I write of this today and I still wonder.

The first time we went abroad in 1880, summer travel in Europe was not the usual vacation trip for Americans that it has since become. I remember at a ball given at the Préfecture in Nice by the Prefect and his wife, the Count and Countess de Brançion, my husband and I heard on all sides the whisper as we passed, "Americana." [1]

Few Americans at that time spoke foreign languages and, because of this, many amusing incidents occurred. I remember seeing an American—who, by the way, was a well-known New Yorker—in a French restaurant, enjoying a dish of lamb chops and peas. He wanted some more and didn't know how to ask for it. He kept one pea on his plate, stuck it on the end of his fork, and, calling the waiter, said, "Garçon, encore de pea"! And he got it!

[1] Italian was frequently spoken by the Savoyards even after Savoy no longer belonged to Italy.

On another occasion when in Germany, my husband—who was nothing of a linguist—said, "Kellner, bringen sie mir die Bille." I said, "You should have said, 'der Rechnung'." To which he replied in a superior tone, "Oh, he'll understand." However, the waiter did not understand. He interpreted "bille" as "bowle," a white wine cup, and insisted that it had been ordered. My husband paid for it without any further discussion and *I* asked for "der Rechnung" and it was immediately presented. However, my German was far from impeccable. One day at a restaurant, I found myself asking, "Was für Kaiser haben Sie?" It was only the astonished expression on the waiter's face that made me realize that I had asked him what kind of an Emperor he had, instead of asking what kind of cheese ("käse") he had. It was a wonder I was not arrested for lèse majesté.

If Americans were unfamiliar with foreign languages, foreigners were certainly unfamiliar with American geography. The extraordinary questions I've had put to me! An Englishman once questioned my accuracy when I referred to Washington as the capital of the United States. He said, "You mean Atlanta, don't you?" He went on to say that he had met a charming American who had told him that she was from Georgia and had been born in the *capital,* Atlanta. Another Britisher, this time of my own sex, upon learning that I was a New Yorker, said she had always been anxious to meet some one who could tell her about the Amazon River. She knew New York was on a river. What difference whether it was the Hudson or the Amazon!

The American tourist's idea of European geography is sometimes quite as vague. As for instance, I overheard a young American woman say, "Now we are at Stresa—but when are we going to get to Italy?"

Our fellow-Americans were often amusing in other ways besides their lack of knowledge of the language, or of geography. Once, on the steamer, we noticed a very self-important couple. We didn't know who they were, but we heard the lady frequently refer to her husband as "the Senator." Later on the train, they occupied the same compartment with us and we had a good view of their hand luggage. All the valises were tagged "Senator Blank." I looked for a Washington, D.C., label, but to our amusement we read, "Borough of Bronx." He had evidently been elected from that district to the New York State Legislature. They were making their first trip abroad and he was prepared to overpower effete Europe with the dignity and importance of his Senatorship. Sometimes the ignorance of our compatriots was most mortifying, as, for instance, when a young American lad asked a fellow-traveler if there was anything worth seeing at Oxford!

One year we began our vacation with a motor trip through the Cathedral towns of England. When we went over the proposed itinerary with the agent who was providing the automobile for us, I said it would be impossible for us to cover so much ground within the three weeks at our disposal. He assured us that we could easily visit the abbeys, cathedrals, and castles, as well as the Dukeries and the Lake Country, within the specified time. He was right. We did it comfortably without fatigue. We never motored more than one hundred and fifty miles a day and sometimes we went only fifty miles. We also visited Cornwall, Surrey, and Devonshire before returning to London. It was only after the completion of this tour that I realized what a compact little island is England in comparison with the huge wide spaces of our country.

The agent, when making arrangements for our tour, asked us whether we preferred a "gentleman chauffeur" or an ordinary chauffeur. We were puzzled by the distinction made and hardly knew how to answer. We certainly did not want a chauffeur who would be ungentlemanly. It was explained that many of the university students were glad to do work of this kind during the summer vacation if they were treated as equals. They expected to eat at the same table as their employer and occasionally join in a game of bridge. Having a pretty young niece with us, we decided *not* to take the "gentleman chauffeur."

My diary gives a very full record of this trip and of my impressions of England's cathedrals and abbeys, so closely interwoven with the very fabric of English history. But travelers' impressions are apt to pall and I shall only refer to the old "George Hotel" at Salisbury and to the "God Begot House" at Winchester. These two inns are made memorable to me, because my imagination was so quickened and stirred that, like Mr. Wegg, I "dropped into poetry." At Salisbury I slept in the old Tudor bed where, tradition had it, Shakespeare had slept. This nonsense rhyme was the result:

Nathan the prophet was a lucky old seer,
She slept in the bed where once rested Shakespeare;
Inspired by memories of that most famous of bards
She wrote this poem—thus gave him spades and cards.

She dreamed of a "Hamlet" far away,
'Twas a "Midsummer Night's Dream"
Just "As You Like It" let us say;
A "Merchant of Venice" was "Taming the Shrew"
Which "The Merry Wives of Windsor" said he would rue;
On the "Twelfth Night" she dreamed "The Tempest" did appear
And "Othello" arrived in the midst with "King Lear,"
With "A Winter's Tale" they tried to regale
The spirits that hovered around the bed.

Now Mr. Shakespeare
Were you a fakir
Or did Mr. Bacon
Your dramas write?

I'm not a muck-raker
But the butcher and baker
And candlestick maker
Say this is right.
The butcher knows bacon,
The baker knows bakin',
And they both be stakin'
On Bacon their mite.
To know the truth I'm achin',
My body is quakin',
My heart is breakin',
So tell me this night!

The "God Begot House" was even older than the Old George Hotel at Salisbury. Its walls were covered with lines of cheer and comfort inscribed by former guests. The Proprietress asked me to add my word of greeting to the wayfarer. The following lines I handed her the next morning. They are framed and hang on the wall, together with messages from many a distinguished pen.

God Begot House! Blest thy name!
Far and wide has gone thy fame,
Sweet repose beneath thy gabled roof
Bring dreams of magic warp and woof.
The traveler here finds true repose
And hastes to tell his neighbor what he knows
And thus the guests arrive from far and near
And all delight much in the goodly cheer.

While motoring in Somersetshire, we passed through the sleepy little village of Frome, the birthplace of my ancestor, Simon Nathan. We stopped at the Town Hall to look over the records in order to copy some dates in reference to this ancestor. To my great disappointment, I found that the old records had been destroyed by fire, so my quest was in vain.

The new method of locomotion—the automobile—enabled us to see a great deal of the country within a short space of time, but we did not always take with us to Europe the American sense of rush and hurry. We often preferred to feel a sense of leisure, of *dolce far niente,* and deliberately chose a slow method of locomotion. One summer we drove at a crawling pace through the Dolomites behind a pair of heavy, slow-moving horses. We climbed the hills between the highly colored rock-ribbed mountains—mountains the ruggedness and coloring of which reminded me of Colorado's mountains. In no haste, we were glad to linger as long as possible at Misurina, watching the deep blue of the lake. When we reached the outskirts of Cortina, the Austrian *kutcher* claimed that his contract had been fulfilled. He vociferously proclaimed that he could not take his weary horses up the steep hill to the Hotel Falosia. He threatened to dump our trunk on the village street and said emphatically that we could hire another carriage to take us to our hotel. I calmly told him that in that event he would not receive a pfennig for *trinkgeld.* We would pay the amount we agreed on, but not a cent more. He suddenly changed his mind and discarding his former peevish, insolent manner, decided that the hill, after all, would not be too much for the horses.

When I visited England, it was always delightful to renew old acquaintances, to see a little of the River life on the Thames, to take tea on the terrace of the House of Commons, surrounded by men who were making history, to enjoy the hospitality of English country homes.

One year, we spent a day with Mr. and Mrs. Israel Zangwill and their three lovely children, Peggy, Ayrton, and Oliver. We lunched under the trees on their lawn. Mr. Zangwill met us at the railway station, leaning on his bicycle. We all took a short cut through the woods to his house, Zangwill pushing his bicycle along. As we reached the pretty English cottage, Mrs. Zangwill came forward to greet us and presently the charming children gathered around us. At the luncheon, our host spoke of his forthcoming play. This interested my traveling companion, Jane Manner, as she was anxious to have an opportunity to present it at one of her future drama recitals.

After luncheon, we were taken to Mr. Zangwill's study, a low-ceilinged, pleasant room, crowded with books and photographs. His writing table was in the window which gave a wide view of the distant sea. There was a slight mist which lent poetry and mystery to the scene, an outlook which could not fail to be an inspiration. The next time I saw Zangwill, it was again with the sea as a background. It was three years later. We were fellow passengers on *La France*. I thought at that time that he had aged considerably and looked far from well. It was not many months later that the world learned of his death.

The summer of 1913 promised to be a busy one for me. I was appointed a delegate to five international congresses. I could not attend all, but I did attend three of them. From Budapest I went to The Hague to represent the New York Peace Society at an International Peace Congress. I gave my address in French as that was the language understood by the majority of the delegates. At the close of the Congress, an opportunity was afforded the delegates to inspect the Peace Palace before its formal opening.

This Temple of Peace, erected by Andrew Carnegie, had as its forerunner the little "House in the Woods," where the ill-fated Czar first called together a conclave of the nations to consider international arbitration and peace. Today, when Geneva is the center of international conferences on peace, it may be forgotten that fifteen years ago the eyes of the world were focused on The Hague. The Palace of Peace was dedicated in 1913 to the good will and mutual understanding of the nations, Andrew Carnegie's contribution toward the ideal of world peace. It was recognized as an international event and as such the world looked forward to it with interest. Invitations to attend the opening ceremonies naturally had to be limited to the official representatives of the various countries and to the members of the royal family of Holland, to court officials, high dignitaries, ambassadors, and functionaries of the Dutch army and navy.

I was fortunate enough to be one of seven Americans present at these opening ceremonies. The Daughters of the American Revolution had voted to present two peace flags to the Peace Palace as an offering symbolic of the desire of American womanhood for universal peace. I had been singularly honored by being appointed the official representative to make this presentation. Is it any wonder that I felt almost overwhelmed by this great honor?

It had been requested that all gifts to the Peace Palace should be presented before the formal opening, so that they might be in place before the dedication. Therefore, a few days prior to the date of the opening, I presented the flags to the Committee at the Palace. These flags were large and heavy. I was obliged to accept the offer of a colleague—an American gentleman—to carry them for me. The ground of the flag was of white silk, with a brilliant border composed of the colors of the nations of the world. These colors were so skillfully and harmoniously blended that they were called "Rainbow Flags." The ceremony of presentation was very simple. I had prepared a short address in French, giving the name of the organization that made the gift and the few necessary data concerning it. This was written with much thought and care, as it was to form the official record of the gift. It was clearly stated that the flags were presented by the National Daughters of the American Revolution as an expression of the desire on the part of American womanhood for world peace. And it was requested that the flags be given a permanent place in the Peace Palace.

It was considered a great compliment that the Committee in charge decided to accept this gift. Many other organizations were desirous of expressing sympathy and interest through gifts, but the Committee limited its acceptance to a very few which were considered typically representative of their nation.

After I had read the presentation address, I handed it with the flags to the Chairman of the Committee for preservation in the archives. The Chairman accepted the gift in a few graceful words. The simple ceremony was over. On the day of the grand opening, I had a thrill when I saw those beautiful flags unfurled and draped near the Court bench in the small Hall of Justice, there to remain for all time, as an evidence of the will for peace on the part of the Daughters of the American Revolution.

On the day of the dedication, as I sat facing the Queen of Holland, the Queen Mother, and the Prince Consort, but a few feet away, I was deeply impressed with the significance of the occasion. The addresses were given in French—all but Andrew Carnegie's. He confided to me later that he would have given one million dollars to have been able to speak French and German fluently that day. And while I listened attentively to what was said, I was, on the whole, more interested in the splendid spectacle.

The setting of the beautiful hall flooded with sunlight, the allegorical picture which dominated one end of the room, the full dress of the foreign ambassadors, the uniforms and gold lace of the army and navy, all made a remarkable background for the quiet little Scotch-American gentleman whose ideal for peace had evoked this building and the wonderful assemblage.

I am not going to enumerate all the gifts presented to the Peace Palace by the various nations, but I must dwell on Chile's gift, because of an interesting incident in connection with it. Chile's gift was a replica of the beautiful "Christ of the Andes," bearing a cross, which had been erected on a high peak of the mountains on the boundary between Chile and Peru. It symbolized the hope of perpetual peace between these two countries.

This replica, placed in a niche on the beautiful stairway, was the innocent cause of the first note of discord struck in the Temple of Peace. Turkey protested. If the cross, the symbol of Christianity, were given a prominent place in the Peace Palace, then the crescent, the symbol of Islam, must be given equal prominence!

The incongruous note for me was struck by the glittering swords of generals and admirals. A spirit of resentment rose within me. What place had swords in a Temple of Peace? Why had not these symbols of warfare been left outside the portal? Through all the speeches pleading for peace, for justice, for fellowship, decrying the brutality of war, I could hear the clanking of those swords.

After the ceremonies, we all strolled through the Palace viewing the various halls. Then a collation was served in the beautiful garden surrounding the Palace. There was peace in the atmosphere, peace in our hearts, but I still heard the clanking of those swords! We left the grounds through the wrought iron gates—Germany's offering to the Palace of Peace. The gates clanged and alas, the dove of peace was imprisoned within!

From those peace meetings at The Hague, I went to Antwerp to attend an International Conference of the Consumers' League. The carillons of the Cathedral chimed us a welcome. Antwerp was happy, gay, secure, interested, and ready to further any movement which might benefit mankind. But one short year later, all this vibrant life was paralyzed. The city was in the grip of the invader.

As I write of these happy summer vacation days, full of activity, of color, of inspiration and of responsibility, my mind harks back to the earlier years when summer vacation days meant sitting in a rocking chair on a Saratoga hotel piazza, with a bit of embroidery in my hands.

## CHAPTER XIII

### THE SUMMER OF 1914

WHEN the great cataclysm, the World War, burst upon us, who can say that he was not astonished, bewildered, amazed, that in our Twentieth Century of progress, of civilization, we could be overwhelmed by such a vortex of bloodshed, of bombing, of poison gas, of cruel, wicked, and willful destruction of life and property! Yet there had been omens of this impending calamity. Vague whispers, strange rumors of trouble brewing. We had shut our eyes to the gradual approach of the war-cloud, had turned our backs to it while we watched the sunshine play over the Temple of Peace at The Hague.

As far back as 1905, an incident occurred on the *Princess Victoria Luisa,* the steamer on which we made our cruise to the North Cape, which proved to me that the Germans were not the friends of the Americans that they professed to be. It was the Fourth of July. The captain of the ship had the salon decorated with a large American flag, and on each table was a standard bearing a small silk flag—the red, white, and blue of our country. At the table adjoining ours, there was a party of eight Germans. They seemed to be the only passengers who were annoyed by the display of national colors. We could hear them muttering about the fact of not being in the "Vereinigen Staaten" and, therefore, they did not see the necessity for celebrating our national holiday. They showed their displeasure by placing the stars and stripes that decorated their table at half mast, then growing bolder, they turned the flag upside down. I, at once, sent a message to the captain, saying that this discourtesy to our flag would make trouble, and he immediately sent a steward to remove the flag and standard from the adjoining table. Only a few Americans had observed the incident. My husband wanted to go to their table, take the flag away, and slap the face of the man who had lowered it, but as my husband spoke no German, he would not have known whether any retort would have been an insult or an apology. Besides he was not as young and strong as the German men and I did not wish him to provoke a fracas. We told all of our American fellow-passengers of the disagreeable incident and from that day not an American spoke to the German party. Even when we found some of them in a rowboat, ready to go ashore to visit some picturesque village, we refused to go in the same boat with them and preferred to wait until we could get places in another. They never apologized. For the rest of the trip they were ignored and isolated and they seemed crestfallen and morose. What a contrast was their attitude to that of the Norwegian driver of the "Stolkjerre" in which we drove through the beautiful Romsdal valley to Horgheim on July third. He had visited the United States and spoke English quite well, had returned to Norway to marry and settle down on a farm. He gathered a bunch of red, white, and blue flowers and presented them to us while extending his best wishes for a "happy Liberty Day."

Apropos of this boorishness of the Germans, I recall that when we were at Cortina, the Austrian innkeeper told me that she would not take any German clients. She claimed they were so rude, so insolent, that invariably they antagonized their guests from other countries. This statement coming from an Austrian astounded me. Had she been French or Italian, I would have been merely amused.

We had gone abroad in June of 1914, planning our usual summer holiday of relaxation and leisurely travel. How differently it all turned out. We had about four weeks of the planned-for rest. After that, tumult, confusion, grave anxiety, greater than I had ever experienced or even dreamed of. I speak of myself only in this connection, because my husband—so much older than I—had been in the war between the North and South and knew what war meant. His experience made his apprehension even greater than mine. We went to Paris first this year. The city was as gay and sparkling as ever—not the slightest suggestion of warlike preparation anywhere. The press, which always reflects the humor of the people, gave no sign of any motive that could possibly lead to aggression. I was a faithful reader of the French papers, but during these days there was no indication of impending trouble. On the contrary, much space was devoted to the scandal of a divorce case which involved some prominent statesmen. We left Paris for Marienbad on July 13th, intending to remain there for several weeks to take the cure.

We had been there only a short time when the shot that killed Ferdinand at Sarajevo "sounded round the world." When we strolled on Kaiserstrasse that evening, we saw the notice posted on the bulletin board. Groups of serious, anxious-looking people were studying it carefully. We Americans—unaccustomed to European imbroglios—could not understand why the announcement gave such grave concern to the crowd composed of many nationalities. Had the victim of this assassination been a reigning monarch we would naturally have felt the serious import of the occurrence. We were, therefore, unprepared for Austria's ultimatum to Serbia, which was posted a few days later. The effect of this ultimatum upon the huge crowd gathered around the bulletin board proved to us the gravity of the situation. I heard a Russian say: "That means war!"

Almost over night, the character of this gay, pleasure-loving little Bohemian watering place changed. All the visitors from Russia, Poland, Serbia, Germany, Roumania,

Bulgaria, and the Austrians themselves packed up quickly to return to their homes. We had some American friends at Marienbad who made their home in Paris. They were not alarmed, nor were the English visitors or the Italians. The Burgomeister, realizing that such an exodus meant a monetary loss to the community, had posted bulletins exhorting the "Kurgäste" to remain and finish their cures, there being no cause for alarm. We felt no special need to leave Marienbad, even when at the breakfast table our little waitress, with red swollen eyes, served us haltingly. We realized that, as she was an Austrian, it was natural that her brothers had been called to arms. We sympathized with the young Bohemian woman who assisted me in the bath-house, when she burst into tears and told us that she knew her husband would be sent for to join his regiment and she didn't know how she could support her babies. All this appealed to our common humanity, but war, actual horrible war, though imminent, seemed far away from *us*.

Later the Russian boy who ran the elevator in our hotel told me in confidence that the proprietor intended closing all but one wing of the hotel because it would be difficult to get fuel and supplies. He also told me that the trains were to be used exclusively for soldiers and that, if we didn't get away soon, we might be compelled to remain many weeks or months waiting for transportation facilities.

This boy had been sent to Marienbad to learn the German language. He—like most Russians—spoke French fluently. He was so delighted to have me talk to him in that familiar tongue that I often lingered in the elevator to discuss the topics of the day with him.

Following his burst of confidence, an American friend told me that she had received a telegram from her son, who was one of the secretaries of the American Embassy in London, urging her to leave at once and go straight to England. The next day, July 31st, I met Bishop Johnston of California. He told me that he considered the situation very grave. He had decided to give up his contemplated trip through the Dolomites and would go north at once and try to reach England as soon as possible. After these warnings, our better judgment caused us to come to a prompt decision. We did some packing that afternoon, having determined to leave Marienbad Sunday, August second. There were persistent rumors, however, that there would be no more trains leaving Marienbad after Saturday, August first. On hearing this, we sat up nearly all night to complete our packing in order to get away a day earlier. I was about to purchase second-class railway tickets, as usual, when my husband intervened and said that at such a time—when the train would be overcrowded—it would be better to take first-class tickets in order to insure our securing seats. I am always amused when I recall this incident, because although we paid nearly double for this luxury, I sat in a third-class compartment, where I was able to get a last vacant seat, and my husband sat on his valise in the corridor of the train. Moreover no conductor appeared to take our tickets and we could have traveled *free* that day. The baggage agent who had promised to send for our trunks failed us and we were obliged to bribe two coachmen to take them down in the carriages which we commandeered in the street. These trunks had to be weighed and inspected by the Custom House inspector, and it took one hour and a half to get this accomplished, so great was the crowd of would-be passengers and so great was the confusion and excitement. We reached our train only a couple of minutes before the hour of its departure. Many of the people in line behind us were unable to catch the train at all. Our destination was Frankfurt-am-Main. We had been advised to go north and get near the Atlantic seaboard, so that in case of trouble an American transport could reach us to convey us home. On the train I sat next to an American woman who had married a German and whose home was in Frankfort. She told me that if we could not get accommodations at any of the hotels there, to come to her house and she would give us shelter until a room could be found. She also shared her sandwiches with us. At Nuremberg, we sent a telegram to one of the leading hotels in Frankfort, asking that a room be reserved for us. That telegram, we learned later, was never received. The man to whom it was given no doubt realized the futility of sending it and pocketed the money instead.

The train moved along at a snail's pace. We were compelled several times to leave the train with our hand luggage and go single file through the doorway of some station, where we and our bags were inspected. There were no porters to be seen and we were obliged to handle these heavy grips ourselves. I learned later that the inspectors were looking for bombs. There had been a rumor that there were Russian spies on board the train. At the time, however, we were at a loss to understand the reason for this annoyance and our patience was at the breaking point. Once, after one of these inspections, when we had been in the train but twenty minutes, we were again ordered out with our luggage. It was a hot day and the effort of dragging the valises the length of the platform added to our discomfort. When I reached the narrow doorway of the station, I could scarcely pass through it—with a dress-suit case in one hand and a hat box in the other. Half of the double door was closed, so that single file could be maintained, and this narrow entrance was guarded by two officials, one on either side. When I passed through, the inspector gave me a keen, searching look, and then, without asking me to open my bags, told me to pass on quickly. But by this time my amiable disposition had been spoiled! I asked him why in heaven's name I had been compelled to break my back toiling from the train to the station with heavy valises if he didn't want to inspect them. I ended my querulous complaint with the query, "And where am I to go now?" The inspector smiled good-naturedly and answered, "Go out on the lawn, sit down calmly, and cool off!" In my temper, I would have liked to box his ears, but I followed his suggestion and now I realize how unreasonable I must have appeared to him. At this distance of time I can appreciate his patience and good humor under such trying circumstances.

The suspicion that Russian spies abounded everywhere seemed to be an obsession with the Germans. One day in Frankfort, my husband and I were nearly trampled to death by the most unruly mob I ever saw. We were on our way to the railroad station to look for our missing trunks. We heard the distant mutterings of the crowd, which, rushing nearer, swelled into a long roar. We only had time to get our backs against the wall of the building when the mob surged wildly by us, yelling to stop the man who was dressed in Prussian uniform and who was trying his best to escape from them. Two policemen finally captured him and took him off to the police station. Afterward we were told that somebody had recognized him as a Russian, disguised as a German soldier, and he was shot as a spy. The poor man may merely have donned the uniform in order to get away, but in those days no mercy or leniency was shown to visitors belonging to any enemy nation. On another occasion I saw a Frenchman arrested in the streets of Frankfort—his only crime being that he was overheard speaking his own language. This incident made such an impression on us that my husband and I decided not to walk together lest we might be arrested for speaking English. So, in our daily walks from our hotel to the American Consul's office, he walked ten feet behind me. I recall, too, with amusement, one day when we were walking to a restaurant. We spied an open carriage, Dr. Alfred Hertz, the former orchestra leader of the Metropolitan Opera House, and more recently and for several years leader of the San Francisco Symphony Orchestra, was in it. He did not see us. As we knew him very well, we called to him, "Aren't you going to stop and greet old friends?" He stopped the coachman and said in a loud voice, so that the curious crowd which quickly gathered could hear him: "Aber, warum sprechen Sie nicht Deutsch?" That saved the situation.

But I have run ahead of my story. To go back to our trip from Marienbad to Frankfort. Instead of arriving at nine P.M., we arrived at three A.M. the following morning—six hours late. This delay was largely due to the fact that as we approached the city our train was sidetracked in order to let train after train pass on the main line. We could see these trains packed to overflowing with soldiers. They were being sent to the Belgian and French frontiers, *Saturday night, August first.* When finally our train pulled into Frankfort station, our eyes met a never-to-be-forgotten sight. The confusion and excitement were indescribable. Trunks were piled up everywhere on the platforms, so high that it seemed as though they must topple over. Handbags were strewn everywhere. Tired-looking women and children were sitting or lying on valises and carry-alls. Uniforms everywhere. Clinging to the men were their sweethearts, wives, mothers, sisters, and children.

Just as our train came to a standstill, three sections of a train, filled with soldiers, pulled out of the station. Waving to them from the platform were weeping, sobbing wives and crying babies. From this Bedlam, we managed to escape and got the last cab at the station. Then we went to one hotel after another in our quest for shelter. The same answer greeted us everywhere—"Kein Zimmer" (no room). We had almost decided to take advantage of our traveling companion's kind offer of hospitality when we found that there was one more hotel, the Imperial, on the list she had given us. We drove there in a discouraged frame of mind, expecting the same reply. When the night clerk came to the door and said he had one double room with private bath vacant, I could have embraced him. It did not take us long to tumble into bed after our wearisome day. We had had no sleep for two nights in succession, so it was natural that we slept all through the following morning. During the two weeks that we were obliged to remain in Frankfort, not a day passed that we did not make strenuous efforts to get away. We did not find our trunks, which had been sent from Marienbad, until four days after our arrival. We spent our mornings searching for them at the station. When we finally discovered them, we took them to the hotel in a carriage, not daring to lose sight of them again.

We made daily excursions to the Consul's office, endeavoring to get a passport from our American Ambassador in Berlin, Mr. James Gerard. For up to this time (1914) Americans did not bother to procure passports before leaving for Europe. They were not considered necessary. Our passports never arrived. Many packages of them were sent from Berlin, but ours was not among them. It was most disconcerting. We had to be satisfied with a Consular passport and, to prevent a possibility of being detained in Germany, we also secured a "laissez-aller" from the Police Department and a passport from the Military General Kommando. This last one required two trips on successive days. The first time, the important-looking official who questioned me seemed suspicious because my maiden name was identical with my married name. When he asked me what my maiden name was, I naturally said, "Nathan" (pronounced in German Nar*ton*). He retorted brusquely, "I didn't ask you for your husband's name, I asked for your maiden name." I replied, "Ich weiss, Herr General Kommando, Ich habe geantwortet, 'Nathan'." I explained that I had married my cousin. He looked dubious and told me to return the following day.

So we had to take the long drive to military headquarters again the next day. I do not know what research he had made. He could not have cabled to New York to get the filed record of my marriage, as the cables had been cut. I asked no questions when the military passport was handed me. I left at once lest it might be taken away from me again. Having secured the necessary papers to leave Frankfort, the next step was to make arrangements to get away. Every day we called at the Reisebureau to ascertain whether we could get a train to Biberich and whether luggage was accepted on trains. The officials there became so familiar with my question that eventually they would call out to me, "Noch nicht," as soon as I appeared in the doorway. Tales had been brought to us of people who left Frankfort in taxicabs to get beyond the frontier. These taxis had been commandeered and they had been forced to walk with their luggage on their backs. We were also told that railroad tracks had been torn up three miles from frontiers and passengers from trains were forced to walk that distance to get out of the country. My husband was not young enough, nor strong enough, for any such experience, so we determined to bide our time. All this excitement and worry were having a pernicious effect on his health.

Life during those two weeks in Frankfort was full of interest and excitement. Incidents either alarming or amusing occurred hourly. One day, hotels bearing foreign names were attacked by the mob. Windows and doors were smashed in both the Englisherhof and the Russicherhof and the proprietors were forced to change the names of the hotels. The police warned our proprietor that the mob would consider "Imperial" too French, and he was advised to change the name. The name, however, was cut into the stone façade of the building in large letters and the only thing he could do was to hang a large rug over it, which completely covered the name. Another day, we found that all the shop windows displaying a foreign name or sentence had been ruthlessly smashed. One evening while we were at dinner, a policeman entered the dining-room of the hotel, and snatching up a menu card from our table sent for the head-waiter and told him in future to use "speisenkarten" and not menu cards. The word "menu" being French was anathema! It was surprising to find a nation ordinarily so phlegmatic, so philosophical, a nation that prided itself on conduct ruled by reason, showing itself so childish, so hysterical. One might have expected such evidence of excitement among the Latin races, but not among the quiet, heavy, beer-drinking Teutons.

Perhaps the calm, phlegmatic characteristic of the German is, after all, merely on the surface, while underneath there is seething. On the other hand, the excitable ebullition of the Latin races is apparently on the surface and their steady poise during the war proved that beneath is the steadfastness and strength of steel.

While in Frankfort, we frequently met a young American couple who were quite congenial. He was a doctor and they had gone to Frankfort so he could pursue his studies. He was a nephew of the famous Baltimore beauty, Théo Robinson, whom I, as a bride, years before, had chaperoned at Monte Carlo. One day, after lunching together, we four strolled to the Zoological gardens. We had become somewhat careless in regard to speaking English on the street, and were carrying on an animated conversation. When we reached the gardens, I noticed a man who had been following us for some time. I turned in time to overhear him tell the keeper of the gardens to watch us as we were *English.* I suppose he feared we might poison the animals.

One night we were awakened from our sleep by the noise of firing; firing which sounded perilously close. We did not know what it meant. Could it be possible that part of the French army had reached Frankfort? Or was it a riot? We could distinctly hear the Colonel giving his orders to shoot, as volley upon volley deafened us. I hastily arose, and catching up my wrapper, ran into the hall. As I approached the staircase, I saw a man—disheveled and breathless—bounding up the steps, two at a time. I called to him, "Aber, was ist los?" (What's the matter?) He tried to explain—the words would not come, and finally he spluttered, "Oh, can't you understand English?" He was an American who had just escaped from the railroad station where pandemonium had reigned when the shooting began. An airplane had been sighted over the tracks and the German soldiers were trying to wing it. They thought it was a French plane and that bombs were to be thrown on the tracks to prevent trains from taking soldiers to the frontiers. The following day it was whispered about that there had been no French airplanes. The soldiers had been firing at one of their own aviators!

There were so many disturbing rumors floating about, it seemed impossible to learn what was mere gossip and what was the truth. We were told at a steamship agent's office that no English steamers were leaving for the United States, all their boats having been taken over by the British Government for the transportation of soldiers from Canada, Australia, and New Zealand. This seemed plausible. We had taken our passage on the *Olympic* of the White Star Line for an early date in October and as we were assured by the Frankfort agent that we would never be able to get home that way, we secured through him a cabin on the *Rotterdam,* of the Holland-American Line. He guaranteed that we would get our deposit back in Rotterdam if we found when we reached there that he had made a mistake and that the English ships were taking passengers. When we reached Holland we learned that the English ships were making their regular trips between England and the United States and that we could return on the *Olympic* as we had originally planned. I may say, before leaving the subject, that the Holland-American Line refused to refund the money we had paid on deposit, refused to permit us to transfer our cabin to friends who would have gladly paid us for it, and the officials behaved in such a disagreeable, grasping, avaricious manner that never since then have I crossed the ocean on one of the steamers of that line.

As an evidence of the difficulty to learn the truth, I was shown in Frankfort a German newspaper which had an account of the fall of Nancy in France. It contained a picture of the fortress there, which had been taken by the German forces. The same article stated that within a few days the victorious German army would reach Paris. It was only after we had left Germany that we learned that Nancy had never fallen. As we could not get anything but German newspapers in Frankfort, we were only able to get such news items as the Germans published. Regulations and ordinances for citizens and for foreigners were posted on bulletin boards daily. These I scanned diligently. One day I read that all foreigners in Frankfort were to appear within twenty-four hours at the Police Headquarters, and if they failed to obey this injunction, they would be arrested. These orders were posted only in the German language. Therefore, a foreigner not understanding the language of the country was liable to arrest. We went at once. There was a very large group of us. We all stood in line and each one was led to the chief's desk where we were questioned. One question was, "Do you wish to remain in Frankfort, or do you wish to leave?" The eagerness with which I responded, that I wished to leave the very minute I could get away comfortably with my luggage, made even the chief smile. He gave me a paper which would facilitate our departure. Some foreigners were not as fortunate as we were. One Russian woman who had married a German officer could not go to her home in Russia, as she was legally a German. She could not go out in the streets of Frankfort without being insulted and threatened by a mob, because they considered her a Russian. She was forced to remain indoors until the darkness of night shielded her and she then emerged stealthily from her room, heavily veiled.

At the American Consul's office one day we heard an American youth begging the Consul to let him have a passport for himself and his mother to enable them to return to the United States. He claimed that his mother was ill and could not come to the Consul's office herself. The Consul explained that it would be impossible to issue a passport for his mother, unless she appeared in person. He said she could wait until her health permitted her to come. The boy pleaded and sobbed, but the Consul was obdurate. The next day we met the boy and his mother at the Consul's. It was then apparent to us why the boy had not wanted his mother to accompany him the previous day. She could not speak a word of English—she was a German. Her son claimed to have been born in the United States. His parents were not Americans and, therefore, the Consul was unable to procure a passport for the boy's mother. This was just one of the tragedies that came to our notice. There were many others. We often wondered what became of a young boy we occasionally met in the park. He always wore the American flag conspicuously on his coat, yet he could not understand a word of English. We thought he was a Russian.

We had no difficulty in getting money, as fortunately my husband had plenty of American Express Company checks, which were readily cashed. Those who had only letters of credit on English banks were in a plight. None of the German banks would pay any money on these letters of credit.

The German tradesmen and restaurant keepers were

trying to get their patrons to pay them in gold and silver and were repudiating their own paper money. I read on the bulletin board, however, that this was illegal and that patrons could insist upon paper money being accepted. So we decided to pay our bills in paper money, notwithstanding the protests. After eating dinner at a certain well-known restaurant one day, my husband drew from his wallet a large bill. The waiter said he was not allowed to take it. The proprietor would accept only gold and silver. "Very well," I replied, "if he doesn't accept paper money, we will not pay at all. Moreover, I shall report the matter to the police." The waiter—without another word—took the bill and brought us the change.

We took tea with an English friend who had married a German and lived in Frankfort many years. Her sons had been born and educated in Germany. She sent affectionate messages to her sister in London, begging us to explain with what sorrow and anguish she saw her two sons leave with their regiment to take up arms against her countrymen. When a few weeks later, we took dinner with her sister in London, we met *her* three sons who had received commissions and were shortly to leave for the front. Would these cousins fire upon each other from opposite trenches? Who could tell? Their mother had tears in her eyes as she told us that our message from Frankfort was the only one she had received from her sister since the declaration of war.

Finally we grew weary of waiting in Frankfort for the special train which the consul assured us would carry Americans to France. I made some inquiries at the Dutch Consul's office and found there was a line of small Dutch steamers carrying a few passengers and a large amount of freight which plied between Biberich, Germany, and Rotterdam, Holland, making the trip once or twice a week along the Rhine. There were only a few cabins and these had been taken on all the boats for many weeks ahead. However, we were told that the boats only traveled by daylight and we could go ashore each night, securing rooms at inns. I got the schedule of each day's trip from the agent, telegraphed to the various inns (with reply prepaid) to know whether rooms could be reserved for us, and when favorable replies had been received, we engaged passage on one of these boats. I was obliged to be reasonably sure of accommodations before starting, because my husband—who had not been well—was by this time almost on the verge of nervous prostration. In the meantime, we were told that Holland was on the eve of war, the Dutch steamers were not sailing for the United States, and stranded Americans were sleeping in the streets without shelter, food, or money. Believing that these reports were greatly exaggerated, I wrote a letter to our Ambassador at The Hague, Dr. Henry van Dyke, whom we knew well, asking him for the facts. This letter was enclosed in an envelope belonging to the American Consulate Department and stamped accordingly. The letter was opened by German officials and returned with the injunction to write the letter in German and leave the envelope unsealed in order to insure delivery. I was obliged to translate my letter and send it unsealed. It may seem that I am making too much of this incident, but the point I wish to emphasize is that this was a communication from the American Consulate in Frankfort to the American Ambassador at The Hague. Both the United States and Holland were at that time neutral countries, yet the official correspondence between an American Consul and an American Ambassador was subject to German censorship. I was so indignant at this piece of insolence that, I, for one, was ready to go to war at once with Germany!

The Consul received the following telegram in reply from Dr. van Dyke: "Advise Mrs. Nathan, Imperial Hotel, Holland, ships run regularly, Hague not crowded, money obtainable here." This telegram was posted on the bulletin board of the American Consulate. We ascertained that the first outgoing train carrying luggage would leave on Monday, August seventeenth, so we planned to leave Frankfort that morning for Biberich-am-Rhein. We took tea with Dr. and Mrs. Howe—our young American friends—at their apartment on Friedrich Strasse, Saturday afternoon, August fifteenth, to bid them good-by. They seemed loath to see us go. They suggested that we dine together the following day at the Kaiser Kellar and we were delighted to do so. They surprised us by joining us at supper that evening at the Schauspielhaus Restaurant and accompanied us afterward to our hotel. Because of Dr. Howe's studies, they felt compelled to remain in Frankfort. I know, however, they bade us good-by with heavy hearts. Our train took two hours to get to Biberich—a distance of but twenty-three miles. Despite the fact that I had telegraphed for a carriage and luggage van to meet us at the station, no vehicle of any kind was there. We telephoned, but received no satisfactory assurance in regard to the possibility of getting a carriage. The trunks were put on hand trucks and wheeled to the boat landing, while we walked to the Kaiserhof opposite. The room which had been reserved for us was a small single one, but we managed to get another bed—a cot—placed in it. The boat was not to leave until Wednesday morning, August nineteenth. We spent the intervening day, Tuesday, at Wiesbaden, a ride of twenty minutes in the tram from Biberich. There we met friends who piloted us to a lingerie shop where the entire stock was being sold out at bargain prices. The owner was panic stricken because of the war, and knowing American tourists were leaving the country as rapidly as they could, she offered everything in her store at such ridiculously low prices that the American women could not withstand the temptation and bought recklessly. The more so, as they obtained everything on credit. The owner declared she would rather have a check after they returned home. Of course, I did my share in helping this distracted shopkeeper to reduce her stock.

On Wednesday we rose at five A.M., as the *Hollandia,* the little boat of the Netherland Steamship Line, was scheduled to leave at six-twenty A.M. However, it was an hour later before we left the dock. We gave a sigh of relief. We had actually left German soil. We were sailing under the Dutch flag. Our desperate efforts to get away with our belongings, our difficulties over passports, the annoyance, the anxiety, were all in the past. We had a wonderful sense of security. This feeling of safety, however, lasted only until we reached the first pontoon bridge, then again we faced anxiety. A signal was given the captain that he would not be allowed to pass. We were all in despair when we were told that the captain would have to return to Biberich and give up trying to make the trip. We stayed in the stream for two hours, communications being sent back and forth between the captain and the officer in charge of the pontoon bridge. Finally the bridge was opened and the signal was given to pass. At each pontoon bridge there was a delay. There were misgivings. There were hopes that seemed about to be crushed, but each time the signal at last was given, which permitted us to continue our journey. All these delays prevented the captain from keeping to his schedule. My elaborately planned forethought for each night's accommodation had been useless. We never tied up for the night at any port where rooms had been reserved for us. The first day we reached Neuwied about five o'clock. The captain intended rushing on to Linz, but he was informed that the hotels were poor and, moreover, were crowded with soldiers, so he decided to remain at Neuwied for the night. The inkeeper's wife was at the dock looking for customers. She had been to the United States and spoke

English well. She took several of the passengers, including my husband, to her hotel—Hotel Zum Wilden Mann—not a very propitious name! And my husband, finding it cleanly and quiet, engaged at once a large room with twin beds. He took the precaution, upon leaving, to lock the door and put the key in his pocket. Then he returned to fetch me and the bags. When we reached the corridor of the hotel, we found the landlord in a great state of excitement. "Wer hat diesen Schlussel genommen?" I heard him say in stentorian tones. He was shaking the door knob of the room engaged by my husband and was incensed because of his inability to open the door. My husband explained in English that he had the key in his pocket, as he had taken the room for the night. The landlord protested. It had been rented by *Herr Nathan* and here were the gentleman and his wife—pointing to a couple of our fellow-passengers, who were waiting in the corridor, ready to take possession of the room. "But *I* am Mr. Nathan," protested my husband. "No, that is *my* name," said the other man, equally emphatic. We thought the man had appropriated our name so as to procure the room. The landlady was called to settle the dispute. She at once pointed to my husband as the man to whom she had given the room. So the other couple had to go elsewhere for their night's lodging. On the boat, the next day, my husband discovered that there was indeed another couple by the same name as ours. They were from Georgia and, after explanations ensued, the two Mr. Nathans enjoyed a hearty laugh over the incident.

At Neuwied, we dined in a garden at long tables laid on a terrace. One of our fellow-passengers told us afterwards of an exciting experience he had had at the dinner table. He was an American who had been living in Paris and was a correspondent of the Paris edition of the London *Daily Mail.* He had been sent to Frankfort to get news. After he had been there a short time, he found he was being followed. One day he had reason to believe that his room had been entered and a search made for incriminating papers. He decided it was time to get out of Germany. At dinner, he was placed at the left of a German officer in uniform, who was occupying the head of the table. They bowed and then the officer opened some mail, which he had brought with him to the table. As he opened an official looking letter, he turned one page so that its contents fell directly under the eye of his neighbor on his left. The newspaper correspondent could read his own name plainly. It was written clearly and seemed to stand out boldly on the paper. The name seemed to burn itself into his consciousness. He knew at once that if the German officer suspected who he was, he would be arrested as a spy. He tried to eat, but he could scarcely swallow. He feared that if he left the table before dinner was over, the act would be deemed suspicious. He was worried lest the handbags in his room had already been ransacked for papers. After dinner, he went to his room and destroyed every vestige of correspondence and everything that could lead to his identification. He tried to find some train by which he could escape that night, rather than wait until morning for the boat. But there was no train and he was forced to spend a sleepless night and take his chances of being arrested in the morning. Before we left Neuwied, soldiers came on board to search for him, but didn't find him. When we reached the Dutch frontier, no one on board that little boat was as frenzied with joy, as hilarious, and as thankful as was that poor, distracted correspondent, who had fully expected to be thrust into jail before he got out of Germany. He asked me for my address in New York, so that he might call to see me. I gave him my card and on it I wrote, "Fellow-passenger, with Charon on the Styx—in journey from *Hades* to Holland."

The first time we made the trip on the Rhine, it took us

only one day, but our journey in 1914 was one of four long days, days that seemed like years, so fraught were they with danger and anxiety. We saw an airplane on the second day of our trip and suddenly we heard shots and the alarm on our little boat was intense. We thought the German soldiers were firing on us. However, they were firing at the airplane—for practice. We saw two Zeppelin airships, reconnoitering. At Cologne, we were told that the boat would not leave for two hours, so we walked to the Dom Hotel and had unch there. Two German officers were enjoying a very lavish meal at the table next to ours: hors d'œuvres, many courses, and plenty of champagne. I could not help wondering whether they were saying to themselves, "Let us eat, drink, and be merry, for tomorrow we die!"

We visited the beautiful cathedral and in the semi-darkness, the quiet and peace of my surroundings, I prayed to God from the depths of my soul for the enlightenment of mankind. I prayed to Him to bring more kindness and humanity into the hearts of the leaders of all nations. I prayed fervently, passionately, that men should see the folly, the wickedness of strife, of slaughter, and there might be instilled into their minds more humane, more just, more rational principles and ideals, so that war might cease from the earth. Was I praying to the God of the Germans—seated as I was in their marvelous place of worship? Was I pouring out my soul to images of saints in whom I had no faith? It matters not. The silent prayer gave me strength—strength and fortitude for whatever I was to endure.

My husband returned to the boat and I strolled a couple of blocks away in order to buy some fruit. When I reached the gangway and was about to go on board, two soldiers pointed their bayonets at me and demanded my passport. I explained that my husband had it and he was on the boat. A woman was not considered an entity—

merely an appendage to her husband ("Frau-gemahlin"), so the one passport was considered sufficient. The soldiers were obdurate. Either I had to show my passport or I could not go on board. Fortunately, my husband saw from the railing of the deck that there was some controversy, so he came to the rescue with the passport. Only then were the bayonets reversed.

A party of two men and four women, very obviously English, came on board at Cologne. They brought with them six steamer chairs to sleep on at night, to obviate the necessity of leaving the boat and showing passports. They had been at Hombourg, taking a cure, when the war burst upon them, transforming them from peaceful aliens to dangerous enemies. The English Consul had left Hombourg, but their passports had been issued by the General Kommando. The hotel proprietor had asked them to leave at once. When they reached the railroad station, they found a bulletin announcing that no aliens would be given transportation. They were not allowed to remain and not allowed to leave. They finally left under cover of the night, in a carriage. Then they managed to get on board a train and after enduring insults, after being buffeted about, they arrived at Cologne, exhausted from lack of food and sleep. They hoped to escape further vicissitudes by remaining on board the boat until it crossed the frontier. Alas! We had only proceeded as far as Wesel, when soldiers came on board and arrested them, marching them off to the "Polizei." They were told to take all their luggage with them. The captain told them he would delay the boat as long as he dared. My heart sank when the order was given to pull away from the dock, and the party had not returned. One of the men was at least seventy years of age. He had white hair and would not have been likely to take up arms in defense of his country. The other man was younger and there might have been some excuse for putting him in a detention camp. But certainly there seemed no valid reason for detaining the women.

As we left the little landing, we wondered what fate had befallen this quiet, inoffensive party. Strangely enough, when we crossed the Channel later on, from Flushing to Folkestone, almost the first faces I saw on the boat were those of the two women of that party. One was Miss Aspinall, the daughter of the older man; the other Mrs. Edgerton Stewart-Brown, the wife of the younger one. Our anxiety concerning them had been so great that we greeted them with the fervor of old friends, eagerly inquiring about their experiences and asking where the men were. We learned that the two men were held in a detention camp in Germany. They were given straw to sleep on and the coarsest kind of food. Before we sailed for home that autumn, we spent a day at Liverpool in order to dine with Mrs. Stewart-Brown and learn further particulars about her husband and Mr. Aspinall. It was many months later that they were released and that I was able to hear directly from Mr. Brown. Mrs. Brown and I had kept up a brisk correspondence and, indeed, even now I always receive a line of greeting and a pretty card of remembrance at holiday time. It was a pleasant episode to have met her twice since the war, at Geneva and at Rome, where she was one of the delegates from Great Britain at the International Congresses.

I have written of the warlike appearance of the soldiers with pointed bayonets, who seemed to spring up everywhere during our memorable trip down the Rhine. There was one soldier who accompanied the captain from Wesel to Emmerich, standing alert with his gun on the bridge next to the captain all the way. We even had an escort of soldiers on a police boat part of the way. But I have said nothing as yet in regard to the war of words among the passengers on the boat.

At one time it looked as though a battle would be

fought on deck. There was a group of German-Americans on board—the kind of hyphenated American that remains loyal to the Vaterland. They were loud in their praises of Germany. In their estimation, the war had been forced on Germany. Germany would wipe France and Russia off the map and would humiliate England. Germans were superior in *all* the arts and sciences. They excelled in literature, in philosophy, in industry! I was unable to remain silent. Although I was not acquainted with any of them, I broke into their circle and began tearing their statements to pieces. How could they claim superiority over the French in art, in invention; over the English in literature? As for superiority in industry, I quoted a German woman, Elsa Müller, who had said, at an International Conference in Antwerp the previous year, that the output of German cottage industries was cheap and nasty. She claimed that the Germans competed in international markets by turning out an inferior product, produced by the poorly paid labor of women and children. She begged the delegates from other countries to refuse to buy these products until Germany raised its standards in industry. This group of German-Americans also whispered stories of brutality and of horrors perpetrated by the enemies of Germany, but later we were told that these stories were circulated in order to make the German soldiers fight with more vindictiveness, with more hatred in their hearts.

The boats bringing back the maimed and wounded were never permitted to tie up to the dock during daylight hours. In the darkness of the night, these helpless victims arrived. One evening, at our port for the night, there was a large crowd of women on the dock, waiting for the hospital ship to arrive. Some of them were bitter. Their sons of seventeen and eighteen were taken from them. They wanted to be sent to the front themselves. "Can't we fight as well as boys of seventeen?" they said to me.

In my best German, I gave them an impromptu speech on the futility and senselessness of war and suggested "frauenstimmrecht," as a means to prevent such man-made madness. Some of the women were on edge and half-hysterical, and I wonder as I look back why they allowed me, a foreigner, to preach to them at such a time.

When we finally crossed the frontier and drew up to the little village of Nijmegen at seven forty-five P.M., to stay there overnight, there was wild cheering among the passengers and a great display of enthusiasm. I remember how the men cheered for a quarter of an hour at the convention when Theodore Roosevelt was nominated for Governor of New York—how they threw their hats up in the air and marched around the hall like schoolboys. But that demonstration was no more sincere, no more filled with spontaneity and light heartedness than was the demonstration on that little Dutch freighter. Our excitement was apparently infectious. The huge crowd of men and boys on the landing was equally excited, but their shouting and yelling was caused by their eagerness to get the generous tips of the exuberant travelers. They were pushing and shoving each other in their endeavor to be first to snatch our valises from us. It was such a rough mob that some of the men among our passengers quailed and admitted afterward that they had been completely unnerved. We missed the rigid military discipline of Germany. We almost longed for German soldiers with bayonets to preserve order! There were a few policemen on the dock looking on complacently, but they did nothing to check or control the aggressiveness of the money-hungry crowd. We were scarcely able to push our way off the gangplank. We held on to our satchels tenaciously and finally succeeded in reaching a cab and were driven to the Hotel Boggia. Here we found an English paper—the first we had seen in over three weeks. We pounced upon it and learned of the recent deaths of the Pope and of

Mrs. Wilson, President Wilson's first wife. We also read that the *Olympic,* the steamer on which we had secured a cabin for our return voyage, would not sail during July, August, or September, but that passengers would be transferred to other steamers of the same line.

We were glad to be able to write letters again in our own language. While in Germany, I had been forced to write all letters in German. As only one member of our family understood that language, German was far from satisfactory as a method of communication.

Our boat left the next morning at seven o'clock, so we rose at five, breakfasted on bread, butter, and Dutch cheese, then wended our way to the dock. Fortunately we had fine weather during our trip, but when it seemed long and wearisome, I stretched myself on a steamer chair and read a French novel, which I had managed to keep despite the fact that the German soldiers had confiscated all French books when they found them. I imagined I was taking a delightful cruise on a private yacht. This was to be our last day on board. We had made a few pleasant acquaintances and when we reached Rotterdam at noon, we were sorry to bid them good-by.

In Holland we found hundreds of our compatriots, all desperately eager to get passage to the United States. The Holland-American Line could not accommodate them all. Rough cabins were built even in their steerage quarters, full prices being charged for them, and still the company could not meet the demand of the clamoring, homesick Americans. When we called on Dr. van Dyke at the Embassy at The Hague, we did not remain long, as he was very much occupied. The American transport *Tennessee* had just arrived with gold for Americans who had been stranded in Germany.

On our Channel steamer, the *Mecklenburg,* we met, among others, Mr. and Mrs. Archer Huntington. He told us of his terrible experiences in Germany. He had been suspected of being a Russian spy. He had unfortunately traveled in a French automobile and had a French chauffeur in Germany. His automobile was confiscated and his chauffeur was taken a prisoner. He never heard from him again and feared he had been shot. There were many other tragedies related to us. One couple had left their children in Wiesbaden with a French nurse who couldn't speak any language but her own. They had gone to Russia on business. When the war broke out, they were able to leave Russia only with the greatest difficulty. They went to Lapland, traveling twelve days to reach Biberich, and only stopped over one night to rest. They were obliged to walk part of the way with their hand luggage. They finally reached their children in Wiesbaden.

Another couple had left their daughters in a school near Brussels. When the Germans invaded Belgium, they were frantic. They were delayed in reaching them and didn't know whether they would find them alive or dead.

All these accounts, besides the story that Mrs. Edgerton Stewart-Brown and Miss Aspinall told us, made us feel that indeed we had been fortunate. My husband and I had not been separated, we had not been suspected of being spies, and we had had nothing confiscated. It is true that we had left Marienbad too hurriedly to enable me to get my Brussels lace, which I had left to be repaired, but I got it eventually through our American Ambassador in Vienna, Mr. Penfield. We had also left other articles in Marienbad and in Paris, but later everything was sent to us. While we were in Holland, we thought that each day would bring the news that this sturdy, industrious, peaceable little country had been forced into the war. It was sorely in danger of having its neutrality invaded, its citizens were greatly excited, the streets were filled with soldiers, the noise of artillery and cavalry going through the streets was heard all day and late into the night. We were sure that Holland would soon be a participant in the war and we were glad to get away.

When we reached England, we were surprised at the tranquillity to be found everywhere. Was this country really at war? One short week before we had been in the midst of the turmoil of war. We sensed it on every side—in the regulations that pressed upon us, in the faces of the people we met on the street, in the sense of insecurity, in the undercurrent of alarm, fear, anxiety, that we felt all the time we were in Germany.

Only a short twenty-four hours before, we had been in Holland, a neutral country, yet the atmosphere was charged with war. There was an electric feeling—what will the next hour bring forth?

In England, there was calm. Except for the training of recruits on the green, we would hardly have suspected that this country was engaged in what was felt to be a life-and-death struggle.

Under the apparent calm and placidity could be sensed the grim determination, the steadfastness of the British character. The flower of British youth had answered the first call. The ever-lengthening lists of those who would never return were crowding the space in the newspapers. But as a nation, the British only set their jaws more firmly, determined that those who had gone before "should not have died in vain."

"Business as usual" was one of the slogans seen everywhere. The theaters and concert halls were crowded, the idea being that the spirit of the people must be kept up. We saw the anti-aircraft guns placed on some of the high buildings. We saw the people scrutinizing airships which hovered over the city. They did not know whether these were German or English airships, but they maintained a calm exterior—however fraught with anxiety they may have been.

It did not take the women in England long to organize

for war relief. The American women residing in London wanted to do their bit, too. A large mass meeting was held in Shaftesbury Theater, under the auspices of the Women's Coöperative Union. The Duchess of Marlborough presided. She had written to me, urging that I attend the meeting and suggested that I enter the building through the stage door in order to avoid the crowd. She also stated that a seat would be reserved on the stage for me. I had been lunching with Miss Winifred Holt (now Mrs. Rufus G. Mather) at the Albemarle Club. She had been trying to persuade me to remain abroad and assist her in establishing a "phare" in France for blinded soldiers—similar to "The Lighthouse" in New York which she had founded. We were so engrossed in our talk that we did not realize how rapidly the time was passing. When I reached the Shaftesbury Theater, the meeting had already been called to order. The Duchess of Marlborough came forward, however, shook hands with me and indicated a vacant seat near her, which had been kept for me. She asked me to take tea with her the following day at Sunderland House. There she suggested that I remain in London to help her organize a committee of American women to undertake war relief work. It was gratifying to be asked to help in such a crisis both for France and England.

How gladly would I have done it, but I felt that my first duty was to my husband, who seemed to be failing in health. He was anxious to get home to the United States and I was anxious to have him in the peace and comfort of our own home. As I put aside the temptation to do my bit in this war against military domination, I never dreamed that, two and a half years later, my own country would be in the struggle.

Our daily pilgrimage to the office of the White Star Line reminded us of our daily visits to the Reisebureau in Frankfort. The uncertainty was maddening. One day we were told that the *Olympic* would surely sail on a certain date. We would make our preparations accordingly, only to be notified later that the sailing had been postponed. After much suspense, we finally were assured that September twelfth would be the definite date.

We left London a little ahead of the sailing date, in order to stay at Liverpool a day and dine with Mrs. Stewart-Brown at her father's castle-like home. London had always been so kind and hospitable to us, it seemed almost cruel to turn our backs upon her in her distress. However, even in those early days, the question of food supply was a serious problem, so perhaps it was after all a kindness to leave.

We were fortunate to have delivered to us—at the very last moment—our trunk, containing our steamer rug and fur-lined coats, which we had left at Cherbourg, having expected to board our steamer there. We had been told that it would scarcely be possible to get the trunk as very few boats were crossing the Channel. We had received so little encouragement from the London White Star Line office and from the American Express Company that we had despaired of getting it in time and I had already purchased a warm cloak in London. We happened to hear of an agent who was going to France on other business. We entrusted him with the key and asked him to bring our trunk back with him if he could. It arrived a few hours before our departure, after we had given up all hope of seeing it.

We left Liverpool on September twelfth. As we stepped on board the *Olympic,* the relief was so great that we felt almost as though home were in sight. There were many anxious days, however, before the Statue of Liberty loomed up before us. Portholes were darkened, no lights allowed on deck, and the danger of the submarine—that new sea monster—was constantly in our minds.

All sorts of vague rumors were afloat. This vagueness

and uncertainty added to the general unrest. We were within twenty-four hours of New York, the taut nerves were beginning to relax, when suddenly something happened. We were taking afternoon tea in the saloon, when without warning a sudden lurch sent the dishes flying in every direction. We felt ourselves being swirled about, yet the sea was calm. We rushed on deck and could see from the position of the sun that the ship had completely reversed her course. We were headed toward Fastnet Light. When we went to the stern of the ship, we could easily distinguish with our field glasses a man-of-war flying the Union Jack. This did not seem cause for alarm, but we were told afterward that our captain had been warned of a German cruiser flying the British colors. He didn't propose taking any chances. However, he was later reassured, presumably by signals, and again our ship changed its course and the Statue of Liberty was once more its goal.

Only those Americans who were caught in the war during that summer of 1914 can appreciate how we felt when finally we set foot on American soil. No dread of Custom House inspectors shadowed this home-coming! My own feeling of relief, of thankfulness, was such that even the eager welcoming faces of friends and relatives did not stir me as much as the sight of my native land. I wanted to throw myself down on the ground and embrace its very soil.

# CHAPTER XIV

## WHAT CAME AFTER

WHEN we had left New York in June, 1914, we had no thought but that we would return in October to take up our usual life with its duties, its interests, its pleasures. When on that memorable July day we stood before the bulletin board in Marienbad and read of the assassination of the Austrian Archduke, it never occurred to us that the shot which killed him would so reverberate that in our own city, thousands of miles away, it would change the entire current of life.

Yet this is exactly what happened. All the way over, on that darkened steamer, while we sat quietly on deck, listening to the rhythmic splash of water, dreading at any moment the unknown horror of the submarine, we felt that when at last we landed in New York, war, danger, and dread of aggression would be left behind. At last we would be secure and at peace. It seemed as though these hopes were realized as we stepped on the dock, saw the dear familiar faces, and were warmly greeted by our loved ones. The war-clouds seemed to have rolled away and the past was but a shadowy dream. Alas! we were soon awakened to a sense of reality, for as we drove home, there were reminders of the horror we had left behind—flaming posters pleading for the Belgians stared at us from shop windows. Large photographs were displayed of Queen Elizabeth and King Albert, whose features, heretofore almost unknown to the average passers-by, were to become so familiar to us all. The Red Cross flag was flying conspicuously and appeals for help were plastering the city.

At first these signs and appeals impressed me as witnesses of war, later I came to see in them a far deeper significance. Were they not rather evidences of deep human sympathy, of the sense of brotherhood, and of admiration for Belgium's heroic stand, for the courage and patriotism of the French *poilu,* for British loyalty and honor? This sympathy, this feeling of brotherhood stretching across the water, gave to these nations our help and encouragement.

My husband had not been well all summer. The anxious weeks in Frankfort had taken more out of him than perhaps we realized. The relief of being at home was so great that for a few weeks he seemed almost like his old self. This, however, was only temporary. In December the break came, and the sadness that was overshadowing so many homes entered ours, too. I had no sons to send to the war, but I've always felt that my husband's three long years of invalidism was the result of what he had lived through during that summer of 1914. He was as much a victim of the war as though he had fallen, going over the top.

And now my life changed. Many of my former activities had to be put aside. My first duty was to my husband. Everything else was subordinated to this. So I was able to continue only such outside responsibilities as did not conflict with helping him through the long tedious hours of illness. Suffrage work, which had hitherto claimed such a large share of my time, sank into the background. Invitations to give addresses outside of New York had to be declined. I retained the Presidency of the Consumers' League, but there came a time when I felt that even this work, close as it was to my heart, had to be given up, too.

I did what war relief work I could at home. As I sat by my husband's bedside, I knitted mufflers, or sewed on hospital garments. I tried to do my share of Red Cross work, going to headquarters of an afternoon or evening when I could be spared. It was now that I found my facility for French could be put to practical use. The American Society for the Relief of French Wounded collected clothing to distribute among the sailors of visiting French warships. I was one of the volunteers to attend to this distribution. The clothing donated to the society was of all kinds, the idea being to send to the women and children of France necessary warm garments. It was amusing to see how these sailors cast eager glances at the heaped-up piles of women's coats, capes, and suits that lay on the tables ready for distribution. We naturally gave the preference to married men. This was soon discovered and, after that, every sailor from sixteen years up claimed to be married and the father of a large family!

I was often called upon to act as interpreter and to direct these French sailors, thronging the streets, to the club houses which had been thrown open to them. One evening I came upon a group of three, surrounded by quite an interested crowd. The sailors were gesticulating, holding up five fingers, and the crowd stood by, eager to assist them, but helpless. I joined the group and asked in French whether I could be of assistance. The sailor boys nearly hugged me in their delight at hearing their own language. They explained that they wanted to reach a certain club near Fifth Avenue from which they had received an offer of hospitality. It was easier to pile them all into a taxi than to get them by direction from Columbus Avenue across the park to Fifth Avenue.

A new word was coming into our vocabulary—preparedness. Its significance was sinister. For what were we to prepare? Was it possible that we were ever to hear the thunder of enemy guns on our shores? Were we to "prepare" our young men for the art of war, and was militarism to become a part of our national policy? The sentiment of the country was divided. There were those who felt that preparedness for war meant an invitation for war.

They argued that peace at any price was preferable to having the youth of our nation trained for "cannon fodder." On the other hand, there were those who realized that adequate training might mean an enormous saving of life. With all Europe ablaze, what certainty was there that the conflagration would not reach our shores? Although I had been for some years a member of the New York branch of the American Peace Society, and although I had been the delegate of the Daughters of the American Revolution to present the peace flags to the Peace Palace at The Hague *only one short year before,* yet I appreciated that with lawlessness on the high seas, our own flag not being recognized as a protection to our nationals or our commerce, with bridges being blown up close to our borders and treachery exposed in Washington, this was no time to expound the doctrines of peace.

I resigned from the Peace Society, not because I was converted to militarism, but because I felt that General Leonard Wood and his followers were right at that time. And whenever I heard the *Star-Spangled Banner* or the *Marseillaise* played at theatrical performances or at concerts, the spirit of patriotism flamed within me so high that more and more convinced I became that Theodore Roosevelt was right when he said, "There can be no true peace with dishonor."

The Officers' Training Camp, established at Plattsburg, was the first of its kind. It was not long before similar camps were established in other parts of the country. It was with a heavy heart that I saw my nephews leave for these camps, yet I would not have held them back. There is a curious psychology about this which the following story will illustrate. I was walking down Fifth Avenue one beautiful spring day in 1917, just after we had gone into the war. Suddenly my arm was clutched and, looking up surprised, I recognized a friend in khaki—an officer in the United States Army. He said, "You are just the woman I need. You must make a speech at once for recruits." I protested I had important engagements that I was on my way to keep. He insisted that nothing was of importance compared with the necessity of stirring the youth of the country to volunteer for service. We were in front of the Public Library at Fifth Avenue and Forty-second Street. Without another word, he lifted me—almost bodily—to the stone parapet and I found myself facing a curious crowd. My military friend had kindled my patriotism into a leaping flame and I spoke with a fervor and passion of which I had not thought myself capable. When I finished, several of the lads whose faces had been upturned toward me came forward and enlisted at once. Then suddenly an awful weight of responsibility descended upon me. My mother-heart yearned to protect these boys. In the sudden overwhelming emotion that filled me, I almost cried out, "Don't do it! Don't do it!" The captain told me that more men had signed up as a result of my speech than had enlisted during all the previous hours of that day. He insisted that I come down to City Hall Park the next afternoon and again make a plea for patriotism. Still in a state of bewilderment, and torn between conflicting emotions, I agreed to meet him the following day and rushed off to keep my engagement. Again I made an impassioned speech, and again when I had finished volunteers filled the tent. But it was the last time I did this. The reaction was too great. I went home to weep hysterically, feeling that every mother whose son had joined the ranks through my persuasion could point the finger of reproach at me.

Belgium's plight pulled at our heartstrings. I had seen some of the Belgian refugees during the few weeks we were in London and had done what I could for them. A friend from Antwerp wrote me of the distress of the Belgian refugees in France. France was bleeding and could do little for them. She asked my help. This appeal came to me at the time of my husband's illness, and I, too, was flat on my back suffering from an attack of sciatica. But I felt the urge to do what I could. So, with the help of my secretary, I arranged for an entertainment to be given at the Automobile Club of America. The entertainment was very successful and I was able to send a draft of several thousand francs. Mme. Belpaire wrote me that this was the first sum collected in our country for Belgian refugees in France.

When Queen Elizabeth of Belgium visited New York, she expressed a desire to meet the women who had worked especially to help her people. The Committee for Belgian Relief tendered her Majesty a reception and I had the honor to be included among the small number invited. This reception was unique. Queen Elizabeth, instead of merely bowing as we were presented, greeted us cordially and said a few words of friendly appreciation to each one.

Fifth Avenue to the New Yorker has always spelled color, movement, brilliancy. From its strategical position, running north and south through the center of the narrow city and its freedom from car tracks, it has been from early days the parade avenue par excellence. But never was it so colorful, so full of movement, so brilliant as during the war years. The long vista of the Avenue fluttering with banners and at night illuminated by miles and miles of looped garlands of colored lights; the picturesque uniforms of the French officers, mingling with the kilts of Scotchmen, and the khaki of our own men, gave a strangely cosmopolitan appearance to the familiar thoroughfare. As I think of the Avenue in its relation to the events of the past fifty years, the pageantry of its processions passes in review before me.

Decoration Day parade with its hallowed significance; the Fourth of July parade with its blare of trumpets, sounding the note of freedom; Evacuation Day parade, celebrating local history; St. Patrick's Day parade with the waving of the green and the Shillalah conspicuous; the solemn funeral pageants of the two great Civil War leaders, General Grant and General Sherman; the joyous welcome to Admiral Dewey when he returned from his signal victory in Manila Bay; the Civic parade of the police force, the "White Wings" and the business men's associations; the weird torchlight processions of political campaigns; the suffrage parades, picturesque and unusual, because for the first time women marched; the Preparedness Parade with its grim suggestion of possible war; the Red Cross parade, the Avenue filled with marching, white-garbed women, veils floating, following the red cross held aloft; the wild tumult of Armistice Day, the sparkling sunshine bringing out the colors of the flitting confetti, the entire length of the Avenue a dense mass of shouting humanity, swaying and surging beneath the flags of all the nations that floated from every window and which lined either side of the street waving from high flagpoles; then the return of the 77th Division from overseas—I have been a part of them all. As a child I had stood by the hour on the steps of the brownstone houses to see the parades go by. Later I guided my little girl to the hospitable Fifth Avenue home of a friend where she could proudly watch her father march by with the veterans of the Seventh Regiment Association or the Lafayette Post. Then I left the ranks of the spectators and joined the marchers in the suffrage parades, and again in the Red Cross parade. I was one of the turbulent, cheering crowd on Armistice Day. Then when the 77th Division marched up the Avenue, it seemed the climax of all. I saw my nephew—one of General Alexander's aids—riding immediately behind the General. The thrill of varied emotions brought the tears to my eyes, while we cheered and waved with abandonment. This boy that I watched so proudly had come home. The ranks for me were not empty, but many of the wives and mothers who watched that home-coming regiment—with its thinned ranks—also had a glow of pride, because their husbands and sons were among the missing. We lived intensely in those days, so intensely that the trivialities of life seemed to drop away from us. There was a leveling of social barriers, a wiping-out of prejudice. It was as if the common tie of humanity, of brotherhood, bound us together in the one desire to help. There is no incident more beautiful than that related by the Jewish chaplain who—on the battlefield—held a crucifix before the dimming eyes of the dying Catholic soldier. In all the horror and agony of war, this spirit, in some strange paradoxical way, permeated the world. We felt its influence and were better and nobler because of it. It was this spirit that led the crowds watching one of the parades to cheer the little band that carried aloft the flag of Zion—the Star of David—together with our own stars and stripes. Again this spirit prevailed when Cardinal Hayes—at the steps of St. Patrick's Cathedral—greeted the return of the 71st Regiment with General O'Ryan at its head. The tragedy came after, when these crumpled walls of prejudice which we thought had disappeared forever were gradually rebuilt, stone by stone, until today they seem to be higher and wider and stronger than ever.

During those war years, I had been fighting my own private battle, fighting the approach in our household of that grim conqueror to whom we must all yield at last. So these years freighted with tragedy slowly passed, years so different from those filled with happy activities and loving companionship. My husband died in the first month of the year 1918. For the first time in my life, I found myself alone.

# CHAPTER XV

## READJUSTMENT

PERHAPS there is nothing more difficult than the readjustment of one's life within the familiar environment. The necessity came to me at a time when the whole world was facing this readjustment. It may be because of this fact that my personal problems seemed easier of solution. I was but a tiny atom in this world maelstrom. In a measure my life seemed empty. I was no longer President of the Consumers' League, and although my interest in the work continued, the compelling duties involved by such a position had ceased for me. The struggle for equal suffrage seemed to be nearing its goal. The happy incentive of home-making no longer existed. The home that my husband and I had made together seemed so big, so lonely, that I fled from it to a small apartment. Kind words and kind deeds from loyal friends helped me through these dark days.

I always remember, with a pull at the heartstrings, the first meeting of the Consumers' League Board I attended after my husband's death. As I entered the room, every member of the Board spontaneously rose to her feet, thus paying me a tribute of sympathy and affection, and honoring the memory of one who had stood at my side in all my work. Perhaps it was merely a gracious formality, but I like to make mention of it here, because of the comfort and solace it brought me.

When the spring of 1919 came, I was very glad that I had been elected one of the delegates to attend the Woman Suffrage Convention which was to be held in St. Louis. It was my first long journey alone—a trying experience.

When the Convention was called, the Federal Amendment for Woman Suffrage was before the country and a large number of States had already ratified it. We knew that before long the required quota of thirty-six States would be secured and our goal reached. It was felt that it would be advisable to hold together the large national organization of women, which had taken many years to build up. It represented a powerful group whose force was recognized—not only in our own country but also in foreign lands. It was agreed that the organization must be held together, but under a new name. We felt that although we were nearing our great goal, the battle still had to be fought in other lands and our own organization must help. A number of titles for the new organization were suggested and voted upon. The name suggested by me—"The League of Women Voters"—received the largest number of votes and was adopted. The American National Woman's Suffrage Association went out of existence and the League of Women Voters was born.

It was as a delegate from the League of Women Voters that I made preparations to attend the International Suffrage Alliance Convention which was to be held in Geneva in June, 1920. I was fortunte in having a friend accompany me to Europe. I had not yet grown accustomed to traveling alone. Many of the delegates were to sail on the *Royal George* of the Cunard Line on May nineteenth, so we booked passage on that steamer too. Among our fellow-passengers who were to attend the convention were Mrs. Carrie Chapman Catt, President of the International Suffrage Alliance; Mrs. Desha Breckinridge of Lexington, Kentucky; Mrs. J. Hamilton Lewis; Miss Constance Drexel; Senator Robinson of Colorado, one of the first women to sit in a State Senate Chamber; Mrs. Josephus Daniels, wife of the Secretary of the Navy. Mrs. Daniels had been appointed a delegate at large to represent the United States. Her stateroom was directly opposite mine, and this gave me the opportunity of knowing this generous-hearted woman in a more intimate way than would have been possible under other circumstances. Among the other passengers crossing, but not to attend the Congress, were Baron and Baroness Huard. The Baroness was a daughter of Francis Wilson the comedian, and was the author of the widely read book, *My Home on the Field of Honor.*

As I was to give my address in Geneva in French, I took advantage of the opportunity to brush up my French by chatting with Baron Huard and also with Monsieur Saint Hubert, a French artist who was returning from Minneapolis where he had received a medal for work he had done for the Art Museum in that city.

Dr. Raiguel, the lecturer on international affairs, was traveling with his friend, Burton Holmes, the well-known travelogue lecturer. He and Mr. Holmes were most kind in looking over the slides which the Women's Suffrage Association had loaned me to illustrate my lecture, and they gave me the benefit of their judgment as to which ones to use.

Upon our arrival in Paris, from Havre, we realized what a change the war had made. All the former sparkle and gayety of Paris streets had vanished. The only men to be seen who were not crippled or maimed were either very old ones or very youthful—mere boys. To see so many one-legged and one-armed men was most depressing. The men who took us up in the elevators, who opened taxi doors, and even those who carried our hand-luggage had, in many instances, but one arm. It was difficult to find taxis. None had been constructed since the war and the old ones had done all the service of which they were capable during those terrible war days. The streets were not so brilliantly lighted; the cafés and restaurants had plenty of vacant tables; the menus were not elaborate, unpalatable war bread was still being eaten. The amount of sugar allowed the individual was limited. It was difficult to get change. Paper money, dirty, torn, pasted together, was being used and postage stamps were given as change. These postage stamps were given everywhere to tourists, but chauffeurs and shopkeepers were unwilling to accept them. Caustic arguments often ensued. Once I purchased some cheese in a small shop and the *marchande* reviled me because I only could give her stamps. Although the cheese had been cut especially for me, she preferred to keep it rather than accept the kind of change which was considered perfectly legitimate for her to give her customers. All chauffeurs—in giving change—would give as many postage stamps as they could collect from their pockets, but if they received stamps as tips, their insulting remarks could be heard by all passers-by.

Many of the theaters were closed. Attendance at the few that were open was made difficult because of the scarcity of cabs. Even when we were able to secure one, the chauffeur was often insolent, demanding to know where we wanted to drive before he was willing to accept us as fares. One evening, leaving Le Grand Guignol, we started to walk to our hotel, not a taxi being in sight. Suddenly I felt as though we were walking in the wrong direction. I was bewildered. Seeing a British officer in khaki, I asked him if he could direct me. He was in doubt, so he crossed the street to ask some Frenchman. He learned that we were headed in the right direction, but that it was a long walk to our hotel, which indeed I knew full well. He very gallantly offered to accompany us and we accepted his offer with alacrity. We felt much more secure in the dimly-lighted streets of Paris at midnight accompanied by an unknown English officer than had we been alone—an illustration of the confidence inspired by both the Union Jack and the British uniform.

Loving France as I did, my heart had been torn in two when during the war I had read of the terrible devastation of that fair land. But if my heart had been torn reading the account of it, what words can express how I felt when I actually saw the complete wreckage in the war zone? From Soissons to Rheims we passed battlefield after battlefield, a desolate country, no villages, no life. Ruins of chateaux stood out against the landscape here and there, mute witnesses of man's wanton destruction. There was a hillside of charred, gaunt, twisted stumps of trees, as bare as telegraph poles, etched against the sky. All the beauty of the country which the centuries had helped to build up to fruition had been cut down at one fell swoop. A few cellars remained of former farmhouses and to these cellars had returned the owners. They had come back to all that was left of their homes. It was pitiful to see an occasional man with a hoe, trying to go over the surface of this arid waste land. There were volcano-like mounds, the result of the explosion of mines. The guide on Cook's motorbus, on which I was making the tour of the devastated region of France, was a French war veteran who only spoke enough English to enable him to repeat—parrot-like—phrases of explanation. Most of the passengers were English and American tourists. As I had spoken to this guide in his own language when I joined the party, he seemed to take it for granted that I was a compatriot of his. After every halting English sentence, he would turn to me and in rapid fluent French give me a vivid and dramatic account of what we saw. His English was so poor that I could hardly understand it, and his French was so delightful that it added to the interest of the trip. But feeling that it was imposing upon him to make him repeat his descriptions, I finally told him that I understood English as well as French and that it wasn't necessary for him to translate for my benefit. He was amused afterward when he found that I was an American and not a Frenchwoman as he had supposed.

The shell of the Rheims Cathedral seemed to me the

climax of all the wicked waste and destruction we had seen. Workmen were at work, trying to restore the beautiful building. I felt a sense of personal affront at the outrage of it all. And oh, the futility!

Souvenirs were on sale close by the Cathedral, the profits of which were used in the work of restoration. A notice printed in French to this effect was posted conspicuously in the booth. I suggested that in order to attract English and American tourists, an English translation should also be printed. The woman in charge said, "Il n'y a personne ici capable à faire la traduction." I was very glad to be able to make the translation for them.

Three years later, when I was in Paris, Miss Anne Morgan asked me to spend a day visiting the district where her "Association for Devastated France" was helping in reconstruction work. It was a most interesting experience. It gave me an opportunity to measure in a way the rapid progress that had been made in three short years. Miss Morgan had kindly arranged to have her chief director meet us at the station with a car. After lunching at headquarters, we drove to various points in the district, stopping to visit a crèche and to greet the village priest whose home had been unroofed by a shell and who was cheerfully living in his garden.

We also visited one of the Health Centers and had tea with the Director. We heard many tales of sacrifice, of heroism, of simple faith and courage. There was one story, which I shall call "The Rape of the Bells." The little village church had a particularly beautiful set of carillons. The village loved the bells and took great pride in them. One bell was specially dear to them; into the making of it, women had thrown their cherished silver ornaments. The silvery tone of the bell rang out to them in loving cadences. It was the smallest bell of the set and they named it "Petite Jeanne." When the Germans entered the village, they at once proceeded to take these bells from the tower to melt them down. The priest, followed by his flock, went to the commanding officer and pleaded with him not to destroy these beautiful bells, the music of which meant so much to the entire countryside. When he found that the German officer was obdurate, the old priest said, "We are helpless. We cannot prevent your soldiers from taking the bells, but spare the little one, our 'petite Jeanne.' Leave her to us that we may hear her sweet voice calling us to prayer." Petite Jeanne went with the rest into the melting pot.

The date of the Convention to be held in Geneva was drawing near. But traveling was not easy in those early post-war days and we had difficulty in securing accommodations. The railroad equipment was poor, no cars had been built since the war, and wagon-lits were scarce. I used all my ingenuity, but only through the influence of an acquaintance—a French business man—were we able to secure two berths in a "couchette." I had never traveled in a couchette before and I hope I shall never be obliged to do so again. It is a compartment, containing two upper and two lower berths. Occupants lie down without undressing. Pillows and blankets are provided at a small additional cost. We were fortunate in having as fellow-travelers a lady and her brother. We might have been shut into the compartment with two bandits.

We almost lost the train because of difficulties with baggage. War regulations were still in force. No one was allowed to have excess baggage. My trunks were overweight. I could not get them registered. The baggage master refused to allow me to pay extra for them. I needed my gowns for the many entertainments I knew would be given for the delegates and speakers at the Convention. I rushed to the ticket booth to buy an additional ticket which would enable me to carry additional baggage. The porter accompanied me and tactlessly told the ticket agent that I required only a third-class ticket as I merely wanted it to enable me to take excess baggage. The ticket agent thereupon refused to sell me another ticket. I was in despair. It was train time. Was I to leave without any clothes (clothes so necessary to a woman's peace of mind) or was I to remain in Paris and lose the opportunity of getting to Geneva in time for the opening session of the Convention? I gave the porter a generous fee and told him to send the trunks the best way he could and I'd pay for them at the other end. I had been told that France could not accept payment for overweight baggage, but Switzerland could and would. We just caught the train by rushing and arrived in a breathless condition at the platform with our small pieces of luggage. I wondered whether I would ever see my trunks again. At the frontier I gave the chef de Douane the numbers of the trunks and the keys to open them. I explained the situation to him and he assured me that the trunks would without doubt arrive the following day and would be sent to Geneva with my keys. I then wondered whether in the event of receiving my trunks I would find anything in them. Many tales were told of tourists getting their trunks with everything of value stolen from them.

When we reached Geneva, we were not reassured by the accounts we heard on all sides of missing pieces of luggage belonging to delegates. Some of the women had been waiting over a week for their trunks. I waited one day. Then I telegraphed to an official, whom I knew, of the Paris, Lyon, Mediterranée Railroad, gave him the numbers of the trunks and asked him to have them searched for and forwarded to me. He wired that they could not be found at the station and therefore they must have been sent. The very next day our trunks arrived with the keys and not an article missing from the contents of those trunks. Our relief was great. In contrast to my fortunate experience, some of the delegates never received their pieces of missing luggage until after the close of the Convention.

This Convention at Geneva was the first to be convened since the war. It had been originally scheduled to be held in Madrid. The Catholic authorities, however, objected to our use of the Royal Opera House for our meetings, stating that our organization was opposed to the tenets of Christianity and Catholicism. As the Spanish delegates contended that the Opera House was the only building sufficiently large in which to hold the Convention, it was decided to make Geneva our meeting place instead. I was asked to be one of the speakers and to give my address in French, because that was the language of Geneva. And as the Swiss women were not enfranchised, we wanted our arguments to have full effect upon the native audience. The Convention was to convene on June 6th. It had been fully expected to have the thirty-sixth State ratify the Federal Amendment by that time. So when I was asked for the title of my address, I gave it as "Comment les Americaines ont obtenu le vote." But as the date grew nearer and nearer, it became evident that we would be disappointed. As a matter of fact we did not get the thirty-sixth State until the autumn of 1920. Therefore, at the last moment, the title of my address had to be changed and I gave it under the caption of "Les moyens employés par les Americaines pour obtenir le vote."

Before the Convention convened, Mlle. Gourd, President of the Swiss Suffrage Association, gave a tea and garden party as a welcome to the visiting delegates. It provided a pleasant opportunity for the exchange of greetings among those of us who had attended previous congresses and who had formed international acquaintances. The delegates came many thousands of miles—some from Turkey, Greece, India, Japan, China; others from Australia, New Zealand, and South America. These women were among the most intelligent of their countries.

On the Board of Directors of the International Suffrage Alliance were two German women whom I had met before on several occasions. One of them I remembered as a handsome, buxom woman who before she had retired from the stage had been the idol of her countrymen. She had been with us at Budapest in 1913. At that time, she was still a fine looking woman, graceful and gracious, with a rich, sonorous voice. At this garden party at which Mlle. Gourd was hostess, she came forward in a deprecatory way to greet me. I was shocked at her haggard appearance. She was lean and hollow-eyed, her cheeks sunken in, her eyes had a haunted look, her hands seemed cadaverous, she leaned heavily on her cane. She must have suffered untold agony during those fearful war years. I could scarcely believe it was my erstwhile radiant friend. The tears sprang to her eyes as I put my arms around her. My heart was too full for utterance. She clung to me, appreciative of my sympathy. Then, later on, she came to me and asked whether I had made any arrangements to sit at any special table for tea. If not, would I sit with her and Frau L., the other German delegate? She explained haltingly that many of the delegates from other countries would not wish to sit with representatives of an "enemy country" and she and Frau L. dreaded being ostracized. I had not made any previous arrangement and even had I done so, I would have withdrawn from it, so as to sit with these two forlorn, embarrassed, humiliated women, who were in no way responsible for whatever brutality or aggressiveness or crime had been wrought by the military party of their country.

This first meeting of the women of "enemy countries" was a wonderful test of character. The German and Austrian women were shunned by many who could not forget and would not forgive. We could scarcely blame the Belgian Suffrage Association for refusing to send a delegation if Germany were to be represented. An official of the International Association was a Belgian and she left the platform when the German officer took her seat there. It was a most dramatic moment when the French officer went up the steps to the platform. Her seat was on the right of the President, Mrs. Carrie Chapman Catt. Mrs. Catt stood with her usual dignity and poise. Every one knew her views on peace. The German official was on her left. Mrs. Catt turned and pleaded with her eyes, if not with her lips. The delegates held their breath and gasped—what would happen? Suddenly, spontaneously, the German representative and the French representative held out their hands and clasped each other's fervently. The auditorium was in an uproar. The delegates from the forty countries applauded and cheered; handkerchiefs, like small flags of truce, were waved. There were tears shed and bravos heard. Women stood for peace, the mother-heart of every delegate could sense the agony of the mother-hearts of those who had given their sons for their respective countries.

This incident of the meeting of delegates from enemy countries was a forerunner of what happened at the League of Nations Council, several years later, when Germany was made welcome by her former enemies.

The business sessions of the International Suffrage Alliance convention were held in the Municipal Building at Geneva, but the important public evening meeting was held in the large Salle de la Réformation. Here in this setting, so soon to become historic, as the first meeting place of the League of Nations, I gave my address. The auditorium was a dense mass of men and women. It was computed that there were between two thousand and twenty-five hundred people present.

It had been announced that all the addresses were to be given in French, so the Geneva populace turned out in force. My address was the last on the program and was illustrated by stereopticon views. It was so well received that I was asked to repeat it in Paris, Basle, and Berne. However, this I could not do, as I had made other plans.

Earlier in the evening, Lady Astor had given a dinner at the Hotel Beau Rivage in honor of the English and American delegates. Lady Astor begged me to tell the English delegates the story of my having knocked on the doors of Parliament and having them thrown open for me when the Shop Assistants' Act was under discussion. It is a coincidence that Lady Astor, an American, should have been the first woman to have been elected to the House of Commons, and that I, an American also, should have been invited to give testimony before a Committee of the House of Lords before the passage of the Shop Assistants' Act.

Many entertainments were given for the members of the Congress. The Dalcroze School gave an exhibition of rhythmic dancing for us, which was most poetic and artistic. The Geneva and Swiss Government authorities gave a tea and garden party at the Palais Eynaud. The officials received us at the top of the stairway leading to the beautiful garden where tea was served. Many of Geneva's leading citizens were brought up to be presented to me.

Mrs. Stanley McCormick, who, at Budapest, had been elected a member of the National Board of the International Suffrage Alliance, arranged a delightful automobile trip for the English and American delegates. We motored to Coligny, the summer home of the well-known American composer, Ernest Schelling, where Mr. and Mrs. Schelling received us. My husband and I had been entertained by them years before, and I was delighted to renew the acquaintance. Tea was served in the spacious music room, which was a separate building from the rest of the villa. Mrs. McCormick, Lady Astor, and I were called upon for speeches. But these were very brief, for most of the time was given up to the appreciation of the delectable refreshments provided for us. On another day, we were taken in the late afternoon in motor boats to Coppet to visit Mme. de Staël's château and park. Afterward we had supper at the hotel near the lake. I was asked to be the spokesman for the American and English delegates, to thank the Committee for arranging the excursion and for giving us such an interesting time. I gave my little speech of appreciation in French, and was berated afterward for not having included the delegates from other countries as well. They all pounced on me and begged me in future not to leave them out, as they too wished me to be their representative.

It is with a sense of pride that I recall the fact that at the Budapest Convention in 1913, I was the candidate of the French, Italian, Swiss, and Roumanian delegates, to serve as one of the Board of Directors. At Geneva, in 1920, I was nominated as a candidate by the delegations from Finland, Germany, and Austria. That I failed to be elected by *one* vote means nothing to me. The fact that so many foreign delegations showed their confidence in me by wanting me to be their representative was an honor that I am proud to record.

One of the most interesting entertainments given for us was the tea and garden party at Villa Marguerita, given by Professor and Madame Eugène Borel. There were always some brief speeches at these entertainments, as such gatherings provided good opportunities for the spread of propaganda. In the garden of the Villa Marguerita, Madame d'Arcis spoke of her work in organizing the "World Union of Women," for good will and better understanding between the women of all nations. Her dream, she said, was to abolish all race hatred and prejudice. She was followed by another officer of the society—an English noblewoman who spoke specially of the needs of the women of Slovakia. Twice in the course of her remarks she spoke bitterly of the "Jew Profiteers" as being the cause of much of the post-war suffering and misery she had seen. These remarks aroused my indignation. For I knew that while some Jews had been profiteers, many non-Jews were also in this category. I immediately sought Mme. d'Arcis who had shortly before asked me to join the World

Union. I told her that Lady M.'s references to "Jew Profiteers" were scarcely consistent with the object of the association of which Lady M. was an officer. Such unfair discrimination was not calculated to break down racial hatred. Therefore, I asked to have my name withdrawn as a member of the organization. Madame d'Arcis protested that she was sure Lady M. had not meant to be unfair and she would ask her to retract her statement and make an apology. I returned to my seat, quivering with indignation. I waited to hear the promised apology. In a few moments Lady M. appeared again in the bow window which jutted out into the garden. She made no direct apology for the covert insult tendered the entire Jewish race, she merely glossed over her former statements, saying she feared she had given a false impression. The profiteering in central Europe had not been done by any one class, but by all classes.

These vague remarks did not satisfy me. I felt that some one ought to take up the cudgels in behalf of the Jewish race. I looked about me—there seemed no one there, except myself, to do it. It was not an easy thing to do in that gathering—to stand alone as champion of a downtrodden race. It was quite a different matter to make a similar protest to Bishop Potter in the quiet privacy of his study. As Lady M. finished, I cast self-consciousness aside and rose from my seat. I protested against the injustice of having designated one particular group as profiteers when the whole world knew that such action had been common to all self-seekers. Fortunately I happened to have in my handbag some newspaper clippings showing how general profiteering had been in several European countries. I was able to quote statistics and to read the names of many non-Jewish men who had made large fortunes through the need of others during the war.

I told about the Chicago packers and their profits of 300% and of their indictment. I said, however, that when they were denounced from public platforms, they were not referred to as Episcopalians, Presbyterians, or even as Christians. I had a few statistics at the tip of my tongue in regard to the small proportion of Jewish criminals in comparison with that of Christian criminals, and I finished by appealing to my hearers for fair play. Was this sort of race discrimination going to aid the desire for world peace? I sat down trembling with excitement. I had spoken with heat and had flung myself into the fray, knowing that I was in the minority, that probably the majority were opposed to my line of thought, and the only result would be that I would find myself unpopular—perhaps even ostracized. Much to my amazement, however, I was heartily applauded and at once surrounded by a crowd of people who voiced their approval of the sentiments I had expressed. Instead of being shunned, I seemed to be the central figure of the afternoon. My hosts, Professor and Mme. Borel, insisted upon my remaining to dinner and I was placed at the right of my host and made to feel that I was the special guest of honor. Monsieur and Madame d'Arcis motored me back to the hotel later.

Among those who congratulated me upon my fearless presentation of facts was Julian Grande, the Geneva correspondent of the New York *Times.* He was so impressed with the incident that he cabled a concise account of it to that paper, where it appeared the following day prominently on the front page. Mr. Grande also called at my hotel the following day to interview me, and to bring an invitation from his wife, the daughter of a New Zealand ex-Governor, for me and my friend to take tea with them at their villa. We spent a delightful hour there and they presented each of us with a copy of the book they had written together on the history of Geneva. This was a delightful souvenir of a charming acquaintance formed under unusual circumstances.

I cannot refrain from dwelling on this incident. It is

typical of what is occurring all the time, not only in Europe, but in our own country. The prejudice against the Jews, of which one was not conscious fifty years ago, has become so serious that today it is a burning question and is frankly spoken of as "The Jewish Problem." To the sensitive spirit this discrimination which affects the social life has a disastrous effect. It induces bitterness and counter-prejudice. It hampers spontaneity and restricts freedom of choice. Jewish people find themselves banned from certain neighborhoods, but I have yet to see the merchant refuse to sell his costliest wares to a patron because he is a Jew. Socially the Jew suffers the humiliation of enforced segregation and ostracism, yet when a great civic movement is afoot, he is asked to do his share.

When Bishop Manning conducted the "Cathedral drive" many Jews subscribed and subscribed liberally. They felt that while the Cathedral would be sectarian in character, it would stand for noble uplift work and would be a spiritual force in the community, as well as a beautiful architectural monument. As loyal citizens they were ready to support it. I was asked to serve on a committee. This I declined to do, but I sent a small contribution. I inclosed with it a personal letter to Bishop Manning, stating that I was willing to do my share in helping to build the Cathedral, but solely on one condition: that there would be no collection ever taken up in the Cathedral for the conversion of the Jews. Bishop Manning promised me that during his administration no such collection would ever be asked for. This assurance of Bishop Manning's is befitting the spirit of a building upon the portals of which one reads the inscription: "A House of Prayer for all People."

## CHAPTER XVI

### GLIMPSES OF THE ORIENT

I HAD longed for years to visit the Orient. In the spring of 1921 the opportunity came. I had crossed the Atlantic many times. I thought the glamour of the unknown had vanished. But now as I stood on the brink of the Pacific —the very name holding romance and mystery—a thrill which is in reality the love of adventure tingled through me. I was to sail to the "Land of the Rising Sun."

Of this trip to the Orient, I kept a very detailed diary. On turning its pages today, I find so much of interest, the names of so many distinguished people to whom I had brought letters of introduction, accounts of native entertainments, of unusual opportunities, that I feel the telling of this story would make a book in itself.

My desk and pen are beginning to have a lure for me. So, perhaps, some day I may tell the story in full, but there is only space in this chapter to touch upon the highlights.

At Hawaii, it was not the greeting with "lei," it was not the wonderful aquarium with its strange brilliantly colored fish, it was not the romantic garden of the luxurious Hotel Moana, it was not the famous sport of surf-riding, nor was it even the impressiveness of the great volcano that gave me the deep emotion that I felt when I realized for the first time that the United States had become a world power. Our stars and stripes were being carried as the proud possession of men decidedly Asiatic in features.

After leaving Hawaii, we had the experience of wrestling with the tail of a typhoon—what the full body of it might be, I hardly dare to imagine. Sailing through the turbulence of this convulsion of nature into the calm and brilliant sunshine of Yokohama harbor, my one thought was—shall we see Fujiyama? Will she unveil herself to us? I was not disappointed. As we approached, I first saw Fuji as a vast cloud on the horizon gradually assuming its conelike shape. We drew nearer, and then I understood the feeling of awe with which the Japanese regard this mountain. It rose serene, aloof, majestic. It dominated the scene. Later when we visited Miyanoshita, Fuji showed herself to us again in a never-to-be-forgotten way. We had motored over the Long Tail Pass, near the foot of the mountain overlooking the plain of Sengaku. On our drive the clouds hung low and we feared that we would be disappointed and the peak obscured. Just as we emerged from the mouth of a tunnel, the clouds separated and there was Fuji. It was so dramatic that it seemed as though the clouds were a curtain that had been parted for our special benefit. We gazed and gazed, awed, enthralled by the beauty of this solitary snow-clad peak that pierced the blue. Then as we still gazed, the cloud curtain slowly fell together and Fuji was but a memory. Again when we made a trip to Kyoto, we were fortunate in gaining another impression of Fuji. All day long as we traveled we could see this queen of mountains, first through the window of one side of the car, then from the other. It was a clear day, the slopes were vivid green, and the snow-covered crest seemed suspended above the green in mid-air. Many travelers have lingered in Japan for months in vain for a glimpse of Fujiyama. We, therefore, were particularly fortunate in seeing the mountain in such varied aspects.

However, it is not of the usual tourist sightseeing that I want to write, though the beauty of the Cherry Blossom Fête, the Temples of Nikko, the Emperor's Garden Party, sorely tempt me to let my pen run on at will. Rather it is of the unusual opportunities I had for personal contacts that I would write.

I found, to my surprise, that my work along the lines of economic and political justice for women was not unknown in the Orient. I was invited to address groups of women on these subjects. Japanese women whom I had met at international congresses offered to be interpreters. One address was on "The Position of Women Throughout the Centuries." Mrs. Asano loaned her home—considered one of the most beautiful in Tokyo—for one of the meetings. When I came to the platform that afternoon, I faced an audience strange indeed to western eyes. The dainty little Japanese women, hatless, in kimonos and obis, with zora and tabi as footgear, sat on cushions on the floor, although a few availed themselves of chairs, which had been placed in the room. They gave me rapt attention, while Miss Taka Kato translated my words into their native tongue.

This meeting was followed by one that had been arranged by the Foreign Women's Club. The audience was made up largely of American and English women. I was amused and interested to note that my Japanese audience lingered on through this second meeting, although they could not understand a word. The little ladies did not seem in the least bored and their rapt, interested faces proved an inspiration.

Mrs. Carrie Chapman Catt had been much interested when she learned of my proposed visit to Japan. She felt that I would be able to help the Japanese women to form an organization which would become affiliated with the International Suffrage Alliance. A meeting was arranged and many of the most advanced Japanese women attended. The new organization was formed along the lines of the American Women's Suffrage Association.

My interest in industrial conditions led me to accept an invitation from a worker of the Y.M.C.A. to visit with her the largest department store in Tokyo—Mitsukoshi. Needless to say, the object of my visit was to compare conditions under which Japanese clerks worked, with conditions of work in our own country. The manager of the store met us at the entrance and we were first invited to have tea. Then he showed us all over the different departments of the store, but when I asked him to take me to the quarters where the saleswomen were domiciled and ate their meals, he seemed greatly astonished, saying that such a request had never been made before and, because of its unusual nature, he felt it would have to be submitted to the Board of Directors, to be considered at their next meeting to be held the following month.

It was surprising to find the small, delicate looking women of Japan doing heavy work side by side with the men. We saw them working in the paddy fields, ankle deep in water, with their babies strapped on their backs. At Nagasaka, we saw them helping to coal our ship, and although they did exactly as much work as the men, I found, upon making inquiries, that they received much less pay. On the Hodzu River, we saw them pulling the heavy boats back to the point where passengers embarked to shoot the Hodzugawa Rapids.

The letters I had brought introduced me to many prominent Japanese officials. They all called and showed great courtesy and hospitality. Baron Goto, later Viscount Goto, the Mayor of Tokyo, was among the first to call. Baron Ito, son of Prince Ito, former Governor of Korea, called and invited me to attend a classic Japanese play that was being given at the Imperial Theater. This was one of my most interesting experiences, as it included a visit behind the scenes and an introduction to the leading actors, Baiko, Koshiro, and Somosuke. We were shown their dressing rooms, the property rooms, and the room where all the various wigs and marvelous headdresses were kept in order.

Other distinguished visitors who called on me in Tokyo were Baron Takahashi, Premier of Japan, Mr. and Mrs.

Hanihara, who later were Japan's representatives at the Embassy at Washington, Mr. Kaneko, son of the former statesman, who was a friend and admirer of Theodore Roosevelt. Mr. Kaneko and his bride invited us to tea at their home and there we met Princess Tokugawa—her family is recognized as next in prestige to the royal family.

Mr. and Mrs. Hanihara took us to a reception given by Viscount and Viscountess Uchida. Viscount Uchida was Minister of Foreign Affairs. The Viscountess surprised me by greeting me in faultless English. She presently left her other guests and invited me to join her on a divan in a secluded corner of the room. Then I discovered that she was a graduate of Bryn Mawr College and was a classmate of my friends, Josephine and Pauline Goldmark, about whom she made friendly inquiries.

Mrs. Watson, wife of the American Naval Attaché, formerly Miss Hermine Gratz of St. Louis, gave a beautiful luncheon in my honor, inviting some of the most distinguished Japanese women to meet me.

At the Emperor's Garden Party—which I am *not* going to describe—I met Baron Takahira, whom I had first met in Washington at a White House reception, during President Roosevelt's administration, when the Baron was the Japanese Ambassador. He greeted me cordially and introduced several distinguished people to me. These renewals of acquaintanceship with Japanese ladies and gentlemen were very pleasant and made this land of the Rising Sun far less strange and unfamiliar than I thought it would be.

Indeed my experiences in Japan lead me to say that there exists in that nation a deep feeling of friendliness for the United States. It may not be affection, but certainly it is made up of admiration and respect.

With the influx of English and American tourists, the Japanese are feeling more and more the necessity of acquiring the English language. This is shown by the growing number of street signs printed in English—as she is spoken in Japan! Some of these signs were most amusing. For instance a ladies' tailor announced on a swinging sign: "Respectable ladies have fits upstairs." A dairy window held the following: "We sell responsible and irresponsible milk. The responsible milk comes from cows constantly supervised by Mr. ——" The "irresponsible" milk proved to be cans of condensed milk, the label showing that they had come from California. At the door of a theater, the price list of seats was posted on a bulletin board and read as follows: "Soldiers half a yen, human beings, one yen"!

I have given a few instances of amusing English translations of Japanese signs. The phrase books from which the middle classes gain their knowledge of English are often responsible for these mistakes. A Japanese guide who had learned his English from a guide book greeted me courteously one day with the following phrase: "Good morning, Sir or Madam, whichever the case may be"!

The mistakes made by foreign tourists in regard to Asiatic languages and customs are quite as amusing as those made by Asiatics in regard to our language and customs. The East and the West look at life from different angles. It is not alone that we do not speak the same language, but it is also that we do not see things in the same way. Here are a few stories by way of illustration: An American woman bought an attractive Japanese umbrella with large Japanese characters painted in vivid colors on top. Whenever she opened it on the street, she was followed by a jeering, hooting crowd of little gamins and she could not understand the reason. Finally she showed the umbrella to a friend who had lived in Japan for many years and understood the language. To her horror, she learned that the characters spelled, "I am the Emperor's concubine"! Imagine the mortification of a New England lady, a descendant of the Puritans, gayly sallying forth under this flaunting caption! This tourist was covered with confusion by reason of her mistake, but a certain United States senator arriving in Japan swelled with pride when he heard shouted from the dock the greeting, "Ohayo, Ohayo" (Japanese for good morning). He turned to a fellow-passenger beside him on the deck and said, "Now, how did they know that I was a Senator from *Ohio?*"

I cannot resist telling two more anecdotes and they have a more personal character than the previous ones.

A Japanese gentleman is permitted to have as many wives as he can support, but modern opinion frowns on this custom. However, the following story will show that it is apparently not unusual for a man to travel with as many as three wives. When we arrived at Shimonoseki, the conductor of our party—who was young enough to have been my son—was asked for his passport. I and the Misses H. stood close beside him and as he produced his passport, we were prepared to show ours. The inspector, after glancing at the paper, returned it to him and with a sweep of the hand—indicating us—he asked quite as a matter of course: "Your three wives?" We burst into a peal of laughter and the inspector seemed amused at our hilarity. He doubtless thought that there was much sympathy and congeniality among the wives of this harem.

The second anecdote has a far deeper significance, inasmuch as it is a fair illustration of the seeming impossibility of the Occidental mind to grasp the spiritual ideals of the Oriental mind, and also of the insolent cocksureness of the average American and British tourist.

We were visiting a certain Japanese temple, in which were many wooden images of the gods. Some of them had been defaced by flood. The guide in a painstaking way explained the cause of their disfigurement. One of the ladies in our party interrupted, saying, "If they were gods, why didn't they have the power to prevent the flood?" The guide looked distressed and helpless. I, filled with indignation, turned to the young woman and said: "How can you ask such a question? Does *your* God prevent floods and earthquakes and deaths by lightning?" She replied curtly, "That's entirely different, it is not at all the same thing!" But alas, it's *not* entirely different, and it *is* exactly the same thing. But is not Christendom apt to assume too much the attitude that it holds the *only* light and that all who live outside its radiance are in darkness?

It is true that the Japanese have no weekly Sabbath, but this does not mean that they never worship. We never entered a temple on any day of the week without finding some worshipers in reverent attitudes. They have a spiritual feeling for beauty which we hard-headed Americans might do well to develop. This peculiar spiritual quality in their love of beauty is expressed in the way in which they regard works of nature. I have seen an entire family group kneeling in silent adoration before an exquisite cherry tree in full bloom.

We had the joy of seeing the wonderful wisteria in bloom, draping itself over pergolas, the long and pendulous clusters swaying in the breeze. We also saw with delight, later on, the beautiful lotus flowers, their brilliant purple and pink coloring reflected in quiet pools.

I haven't tried to describe Japan, because it is indescribable. There is something about it unreal, not part of the ordinary, work-a-day world. It was not only the difference in architecture, in costume, or the physical aspect of the natives that produced this effect. It was as though I were visiting a different planet, where there was mystery, charm, a magic spell thrown over the country. I felt this most deeply when we visited the Inland Sea with its picturesque water torii near Myajima.

I am going to resist the traveler's temptation to fall into the guide-book trap. And so Korea, with its beautiful scenery, its temples, its tombs, its interesting customs, I shall leave to Baedeker. But I must say a word of the shock we received at the extraordinary costumes worn by the native Koreans—men and women. It was, perhaps, more of a shock because we had come directly from Japan where our artistic sense had been delighted with the colorful beauty of the native costume.

As we landed from the small steamer at Fusan, we were met by crowds of native Koreans, the men in long white garments that looked for all the world like long nightgowns, and perched on top of their heads were small black contraptions that looked like nothing so much as mouse traps. It was to our eyes an odd looking costume, but as it covered the entire body it had at least the recommendation of modesty. The women's costumes, on the contrary, left much to be desired in this respect. They wore a skirt that hung from above the waistline and extended to the ankles. Above this was worn a short Eton jacket fastened at the throat, but leaving the breasts exposed. It was explained to us that the Koreans consider it unhygienic to have the bosoms covered. The effect to our eyes was startling and very ugly. Pierre Loti called the Japanese women, "Mesdames Chrysanthème," and I dubbed the Korean women, "Mesdames Hiatus." This cognomen was adopted by all of our party. As Madame Hiatus I always remember the Korean woman. It may be that the women of higher class dress differently, but we did not see them. I marveled at the general cleanliness of the men's white garments. I soon found, however, that to keep these white robes spotlessly clean seemed to be the chief occupation of the women. Everywhere we went we saw the women kneeling at the brink of brooks and rivers, washing diligently. As we passed their homes, we heard a strange, rhythmic noise that kept up all day long and far into the night. It was so general, so ceaseless, so unvarying, that it could not fail to attract the notice of the foreign passer-by. We asked the meaning of this tom-tom like sound and were told that it was produced by the beating of the men's garments on a flat stone with two sticks—this was the Korean process of ironing.

From Korea we went to Mukden in Manchuria—the most God-forsaken place, it seemed to me, that we visited in all our travels. There were vast, desolate areas that had been stricken by war. The streets were narrow, muddy, dull. There were a few palaces and beautiful ancient tombs, and the American Consulate resembled a museum, but the general effect of the town was sordid, gray, and forlorn. We were glad to leave for China to visit Tientsin and thence to go to that wonderful cosmopolitan city, the Chinese capital, Pekin.

Bourget has said, "Never resist temptation, it's bad for the nerves." At the risk, however, of becoming a nervous wreck, I am going to resist the temptation of giving my trip through China in detail.

I found it the most interesting of all the countries I have ever visited. To do justice would require a volume. I shall only try—as with my account of Japan—to keep to the more personal experiences.

Pekin! One pictures it as a city of pagodas, of mandarins, of coolies with long pigtails and bowlshaped hats, of women with dwarfed feet and moon-shaped eyes. One's imagination conjures up all the familiar scenes on Chinese screens, on vases, on fans, on the porcelain used on our tables. It was all there and more besides. However, with all the color and picturesqueness of the Orient, we enjoyed the comfort and luxury of the Occident.

From my window of the Grand Hotel de Pekin, there stretched out before me the Forbidden City with its roofs of green, blue, and gold tiles, the palace, and the Temple of Heaven. When I first saw this view with the sun bringing out the colors on the roofs, I thought there could be nothing more wonderful. But I had an opportunity to modify this opinion when I gazed from the window at the Forbidden City, lying under the glamour of moonlight.

We spent many hours at the summer palace built by the Dowager Empress with the money appropriated by the government for the building up of a large navy. When I spoke to Dr. Yamei Chin, whom I had known in New York, about the ethics involved in diverting funds appropriated by the government for a specific purpose, in order to gratify desire for luxurious living, she replied: "You must admit that the money was spent for something constructive, rather than destructive." The old Empress may have been lacking in a sense of ethical values, but she certainly was not lacking in a sense of esthetic values. The bronze kiosk used as a summer house, the white marble bridge with its delicate carved lacery, the open loggia with fine frescoes, all testified to her love of the beautiful.

It was in Pekin that I first saw caravans of camels treading the streets in slow, supercilious fashion. They came from the Gobi desert, laden with strange burdens and they seemed to bring with them all the mystery of the silent desert. Dr. Yamei Chin, wanting to entertain me, asked if I would like a dinner cooked and served in true Chinese style. This, of course, delighted me. Dr. Chin took me at my word. The table was set with chopsticks instead of forks and knives. These I could not manipulate and after vainly trying, my hostess provided me with a fork. I was then able to enjoy the delicious food, which was entirely Chinese in character. We had soup, duck, the tubers of the lotus plant farcis, pickled eggs, hoary with age, watermelon seeds blanched and salted as we do almonds, jasmine flower tea. At each place was the usual individual bowl of rice. Two or three different kinds of soups were offered. One was expected to help oneself with the spoon provided with the bowl of rice. This I did, pouring the soup over the rice, as I saw the other guests do. My neighbor whispered, "If you don't care for the flavor of the soup you've taken, try another." "But I've already used my spoon," I said. "That doesn't make any difference," was her reply.

It was through the kindness of Dr. Yamei Chin that I was asked to be a guest of honor at the Annual Banquet given by the Alumni of American Colleges and Universities. About five hundred graduates, men and women, gathered in the large banquet hall of the Grand Hotel. On the walls hung the banners of our various colleges. Between courses the different college yells were given and the after-dinner speeches were all in English. It was thrilling to look around the hall at this crowd of Orientals, bringing to their native land the spirit of Harvard, Yale, Williams, Columbia, Pennsylvania, California, Wellesley, Bryn Mawr, Barnard, and Vassar.

I was delighted to find Dr. and Mrs. Dewey installed in an apartment at Pekin. He had been granted a leave of absence from Columbia University in order to deliver a course of lectures in the Orient. At Dr. Dewey's suggestion, I received an invitation to give an address at the Pekin College, which I was very glad to accept. Dr. and Mrs. Dewey arranged that I lunch with them before giving my address. Professor Li, of the college, who was to be my interpreter, called for us and took us there in rickshaws. Dr. Dewey congratulated me upon being able to have such an excellent interpreter. He told me the following story of an American lecturer who had not been so fortunate. The interpreter in question was accustomed to the conventional opening sentence of thanks for a cordial reception. When the lecturer, starting in without this usual preamble, said: "These are the facts which I wish to bring to your attention," the interpreter was puzzled, but not allowing himself to be floored by the unusualness of the opening phrase, turned to the audience and smilingly translated it: "He says he is glad to be with you and thanks you for your kind reception."

Again I faced an Oriental audience, but one that looked

different from that which I had faced in Tokyo. This audience was composed of both young men and girls, the former in much larger numbers. Instead of sitting on cushions as in Japan, they used the chairs which filled the hall. But indeed the audience was greater than the seating capacity, for many stood in the aisles at the rear and even crowded the windows. It takes a long time to give an address when there must be a pause after each sentence to allow for translation. This address took an hour and a half, but the students seemed interested up to the very last word. Not one of them, not even those who were standing, left the hall. It was difficult for me to judge when the interpreter had finished a sentence. The Chinese language sounded so sing-song to my western ears that I had to watch the interpreter's lips for my cue to proceed. I remember an interesting incident in connection with this lecture. I had told an amusing story and was curious to see the effect on the Oriental mind. I was not sure whether the students would get the point. The interpreter apparently gave it to them in their own tongue, and there was no response. Then he quickly turned to a blackboard on the platform, picked up a piece of chalk, and swiftly drew a few characters. There was an immediate outburst of laughter.

We had the opportunity of seeing in Pekin the famous Chinese actor, Mei Lang-fang, the great impersonator of women's rôles. It took no stretch of imagination to picture him as a woman. It was far more difficult to imagine him a man, so tiny were his hands and feet, so small was he in stature. His voice was high pitched, with all the quality of feminine tones. We sat in a box, thus having a good view of the stage and the audience. The audience really proved more diverting than the play. I watched with interest and amazement a unique custom. Up and down the aisles went the ushers, the boys bearing trays piled high with towels which had been wrung out in hot water. These were presented to individuals in the audience, who would take one, mop the brow, wipe the hands and return it to the boy who put it in a bag which he carried for the purpose. When this bag was full, he tossed it over the heads of the audience to another boy on the opposite side of the theater, who returned the compliment by throwing back a pack of towels which had been freshly wrung out in hot water. It was an astonishing sight to see these packages of towels hurtling over the heads of the audience, sometimes even crossing the front of the stage. I was in a nervous tension lest the actors be hit. But nothing happened, and both actors and audience took the whole thing as a matter of course.

From Pekin we made a trip to the Great Wall and the Ming Tombs. The Great Wall of China stands today as a monument to a labor that cannot be computed in terms of years, as a sacrifice of countless tens of thousands of human lives. It is a monument to man's age-old fear, a witness to the futility of stone laid upon stone as a barrier to man's urge for conquest. From the point where I stood, the height of the wall looked insurmountable, and its thickness made it seem impregnable. To the modern airplane, its height would seem as an ant-hill. The modern gun would crumple its thickness as though it were paper.

The Ming Tombs did not greatly impress me, but as I gazed on those grass-covered pyramids and mounds, I could but muse on what was sealed within them. Like the Egyptians, the Chinese buried with their rulers priceless treasures. I was told that lest the tomb be robbed, the slaves who placed the treasures beside the departed monarch were themselves entombed alive for fear they would divulge the secret of the door leading to the treasures. This was but one instance of what impressed me through my entire trip in the East—the cheapness of human life.

We visited the tomb of the great Chinese philosopher, Confucius. To reach Confucius' tomb from Pekin, we had to travel through Shantung. At Tsinan-fu, we stopped at a hotel which had been kept by a German for many years. There we found the Chinese boys speaking "pidgin" German, just as at the Grand Hotel in Pekin we found them speaking "pidgin" French.

When I stood in front of the simple monument erected to the memory of the man whose code of ethics has become the religion of at least the half of China I felt that the effort had been well worth while, although I had found the journey both fatiguing and difficult.

Confucius' tomb, in the beauty of its simplicity, seemed an expression of the beauty and simplicity of his religious faith. There is no complicated system of theology in this religion of Confucius. It is a simple belief in right living, in the feeling of brotherhood toward one's neighbor, in acts of service.

Matthew Arnold called conduct three fourths of life. The philosophy of Confucius might well be summed up as, "conduct is the whole of life." His tomb is near the temple where he expounded his philosophy to his disciples.

There are also other tombs in close vicinity—the resting places of members of his family including women, which is not usual in China. There was a wooded path leading to the tomb. There was a setting of trees which made for seclusion. In the distance was the holy mountain of Tai, to which pilgrimages had been made since the days of Abraham. I brought away with me a sense of peace, of rest, even of inspiration, that one does not usually capture in visiting the ancient tombs of the Orient.

In Nanking we were taken to see the old university, a part of which has fallen into decay. This university was famous for its rigid civil service examinations. Not only were examinations held here for government positions, but for any position in arts or letters. We boast so much of our western civilization, yet here existed centuries ago—at the old University of Nanking—a system the value and importance of which we are only just beginning to realize.

I had always wanted to see something of the much-talked-of river life of China, and a trip of four days and five nights on the canals and the Yangtse Kiang formed part of our itinerary.

It was a delightful leisurely trip. We sat on deck and watched the panorama of the river unfold itself before us. The chug-chug of our motor boat was sufficiently unusual to draw the natives to their doors to see what the strange sound could mean. As we passed slowly along the narrow canals, we could see the intimacies of family life within the homes that stood close to the banks. The junk-boats were an unending source of interest. There were so many of them that at times they were huddled together and formed a jam.

They were curiously colored and had painted eyes on either side of the bow, for, as the Chinese say, "If boats have no eyes, how can they see where to go?" We stopped at Soochow, Hankow, and other villages before reaching Shanghai, our last stopping place on this river trip. Shanghai seems to belong to every nation in Europe as well as to the Orient, the Chinese note, however, *not* being the dominant one. The Bund was policed by stalwart East Indians in native costume, subjects of Great Britain. The buildings along the Bund are European in character. As we walked along the streets, we heard English, French, Portuguese and Japanese spoken. In the center of the city there was an enclosed park reserved exclusively for the use of foreigners. This word "foreigner" had a wide interpretation. It included every resident of the city, every visitor, every tourist, *not* a native of China. I saw the Chinese, as they strolled by this reservation, stop, glance at the sign conspicuously posted at the entrance: "No Chinese Admitted," and then peer through the iron railings at the Japanese, the East Indians, the French Singhalese, the Portuguese mariners, enjoying themselves on Chinese soil —forbidden them.

It impressed me as an arrogant attitude to assume toward a hostess nation. Of course it was explained that the foreign concessionaires had purchased the property and therefore had the right to make their own rules. But I could not help but wonder if we would allow foreign nations to purchase, for instance, Madison Square, rail it off, and place a sign near the gates, excluding native-born Americans. Such an act is inconceivable. Two years later, when I was in England, I met at a dinner an English lady who had spent many years in Shanghai. We were discussing Chinese unrest with its recurrent revolt against foreign domination. I instanced the park at Shanghai with its affronting sign as an example of one of the causes of irritation, provocative of this spirit of revolt. The Englishwoman turned on me fiercely, saying: "We British could not have lived in Shanghai had we not had such a reservation where we could send our children with their nurses and be sure that they would not be interfered with by Chinese coolies." A characteristic British retort, but not an answer to the argument. Since the writing of this, I understand that this park has been thrown open to the Chinese. We stayed at the Astor Hotel within the American concession. The clerks were Americans, the Chinese boys spoke "pidgin" English. One day when I asked for stamps, I was given our familiar United States stamps. I thought the clerk had made a mistake and handed them back, saying, "I need Chinese stamps to send these letters home." He laughed and said, "You are on American soil and American stamps will carry your letters home." This was a situation entirely new to me. In all my travels I had always used the postage stamps of the country.

I had been given a letter of introduction to Judge and Mrs. Lobingier. He was the Judge of the United States Court located at Shanghai. At that time—1921—litigation between an American and a Chinese was not brought for settlement before a Chinese Judge, but before the Judge of the United States Court. Since then the Chinese have insisted upon a modification of this ruling. It seemed to me at the time unjust that the law of the land should be superseded by the law of the foreigner. Is it any wonder that young China, men who have graduated from our Universities, imbued with the western spirit of culture, progress, and national independence, should rebel at this gesture of contempt toward their law and institutions? The Chinese are not a subject race, but because they have granted foreigners valuable concessions and because they are a peaceful people, they have found themselves placed in an anomalous position.

I could not resist the temptation of the famous silk shops of Shanghai. I was showing my purchases to a friend in her room at the hotel, when her tailor came in with some finished work. Picking up my silk, he said, "Missy want dress?" I explained that my steamer was leaving in thirty-six hours and there would be no time to make a dress. He assured me that he could do it and deliver it to me before the ship sailed, only as it was a rush order it would cost me much more. "How much?" I asked. He shook his head deprecatingly, "Oh muchee, muchee more!" "Well, how much?" I repeated. He named a price equivalent to five dollars of our money. As the Chinese cannot design gowns, but can make a faithful copy of anything, I gave him a gown that I liked as a model. Before he left he spied the piece of silk I had bought for pajamas for my nephew and he asked to make these up, too. He came the next morning to fit me. On the second morning he brought both garments completed, even to the monogram embroidered on the pocket of the pajama coat, and a small patch under the arm—a faithful copy of the model I had given him!

As I begin to write of Canton, memories throng my mind, for Canton was one of the most interesting, the most colorful of all the Chinese cities we visited. In connection with our orgy of shopping at Canton, it is natural to think of the custom house. We learned that an export duty was imposed upon everything taken out of Canton, so we trembled, fearing we would have to pay dearly for our shopping revelry. However, we had made up our minds to be honest. We had had our fun and were willing to pay the piper.

As we were about to board the steamer to leave Canton, the first member of our party to be interviewed by the customs inspector was a gentleman who had made but one purchase, a small China bowl. This he carried wrapped in paper. He showed it to the inspector, who passed him on, exacting no duty. I, standing at his side, was prepared to open my valise filled with purchases. But the inspector impatiently waved me ahead, saying, "I told the gentleman you could go on board." I was mystified, but I needed no second invitation. When the other two ladies of the party joined me, we compared experiences. None of us had been asked to pay a cent of duty. The situation was so puzzling, that at my first opportunity I asked the captain of the ship for an explanation. He smiled and said, "Don't you know that all custom duties must be sent to Pekin? Pekin and Canton are at war, therefore, Canton exacts no custom duties to be sent to Pekin. Such moneys are turned into ammunition to be used against the Cantonese." It was an interesting explanation. I almost wished that San Francisco and Washington might be at war by the time I arrived at the Golden Gate!

When I reached Canton I found that Mrs. John Dewey had written to the principal of the Girls' College, suggesting that I be invited to give an address. The principal called upon me shortly after my arrival and, as she could not speak a word of English, she brought with her a young Chinese student—a girl of about thirteen years of age—who spoke English fluently. Her name was Dorothy Li. She was a typical looking Chinese girl, in Chinese dress, her long black hair braided and hanging down her back. I asked her how she had learned to speak English so well. She drew herself up proudly and said, "I am an American. I came to China to study the Chinese language." When I asked her further details, she told me that she had been born in Minneapolis, where her father had owned a Chinese restaurant. When her father died, his body had been sent to China to be buried with his ancestors. When later her mother died in Minneapolis, it was considered too expensive to send the body to China, so *she* was buried in the new world. When Dorothy reached her teens, her brother-in-law thought she ought to have a knowledge of her ancestral tongue, so she became a student at the Girls' College in Canton. I accepted the principal's invitation and gave an address on "Women as Political Factors," with one of the faculty serving as interpreter.

China is full of curious customs which have their origin in what we call superstition. The fear of demons enters very largely into Chinese life. The entrance gate to a Chinese home is guarded by a screen. With the poorer classes, this screen is often merely a roughly made fence. In entering the gate, it is necessary to turn either to the right or to the left to approach the dwelling. The reason given for this was that such a screen is a protection to the home from visits of demons. Demons can travel only in a straight line! Chinese boy babies are often dressed as girls, their hair tied with bright ribbons, bracelets on their tiny arms, and chains and lockets hung round their necks to befool the demon. It is not conceivable that even a demon would desire to carry off a girl! Hence the deception to protect the treasured baby boy from harm. Many babies are born on the junk-boats and live their entire lives on the water. I was told that if perchance a girl baby rolls off the deck into the water, those on neighboring junk-boats call out: "Don't try to save her, else the demons will take a boy!"

Everywhere we went in China, there were swarms of children. Apparently they sprang up from the ground and surrounded us on all occasions. Once on a shopping expedition they called out to me, "Tsai Yen." I had been told in Pekin that "Tsai Yen" meant good-by. In fact, even Americans used the phrase there. So when in Canton the children thus greeted me, I waved my hand and called back to them, "Tsai Yen, Tsai Yen!" This made them most hilarious. I learned afterwards that the language of Canton is different from that of Pekin. While "Tsai Yen" meant good-by in northern China, it meant, "foreign devil" in southern China. No wonder the children were amused at my calling them foreign devils in their own country.

One of the most ludicrous experiences we had on the trip comes to my mind as I write of the children. We were waiting at a small hamlet on the Yangtse Kiang for our launch. There were a few poor looking shacks near the wharf and I discovered a chair outside the door of one of them. I was tired, so I promptly appropriated the chair. At once children and babies sprang up from nowhere. They clustered around me, interested in the great curiosity of foreign dress and appearance. In the meantime the others in the party were looking vainly around for seats. A woman came out from one of the houses and the conductor of our party tried to make her understand that he wanted two more chairs for the other two ladies. He gesticulated wildly, pointing toward me, surrounded as I was by children, and putting up two fingers he gave her a few coins. She nodded as though she understood and rushed off to a distant house. She returned *not* with the chairs, but with two babies, one on each arm. Did she think that we wanted to take home two Chinese babies as souvenirs of our trip? Did she think we had bought and paid for the two funny little, yellow-faced, parchment-like creatures she held out to us? We never knew.

I have spoken of the impression made upon me in various Chinese cities of foreigners seeming to own the city. In Macao they actually do own it, as the island belongs to Portugal. It is called the Monte Carlo of the Orient. Portugal sells the gambling privileges to the Chinese and the most beautiful gardens we visited were those which had been laid out with the profits of these Chinese gambling dens.

Our itinerary allowed but three days for the Philippines, but as I think back to those full days, they were as crowded as any three days in hectic New York. It was a somewhat breathless experience, covering a speech before the Women's Club, a reception given me by its members, an address at one of the public schools to native school children and teachers, an inspection of factories where women's white underwear was made, sightseeing, shopping, a visit to the Navy Club, a drive at sunset around the Lucarno, a visit to the famous fort and waterworks, a glimpse of the old market and of a Spanish convent with its beautiful, characteristic garden, attendance at a Rotary Club luncheon where General Leonard Wood was the principal speaker, and a dinner at Malacanan Palace, winding up with a dance in the open loggia of the hotel, with the moonlight glimmering on little waves gently lapping against the sides of the loggia. Certainly I had not been infected by the microbe of Oriental indolence!

General Wood, who was then Governor General of the Philippines, tendered me every courtesy. It was his car that called for me to take me to the dinner which he gave in my honor at the Malacanan Palace. General Wood had invited some of the prominent Filipino men and women to meet me, as well as some distinguished Americans living in Manila. It was a brilliant dinner, served in a tropical setting—soft-footed, white-clad Filipino servants passed the unfamiliar dishes and strange fruits. Coffee was served on the balcony. The fragrance from the tropical garden enveloped us.

The Southern Cross gleamed above the tree tops. This was the last time I ever saw General Wood. In 1927 he returned to his native land, was taken ill, and the end came swiftly. A memorial service was held for him at Roosevelt House, his admirers feeling that no more appropriate setting could have been found.

The glimpses I had of Japan, China, and the Philippines only whetted my appetite for a wider experience of these Eastern countries. In 1923 I made a trip to Egypt. I had a friend who lived in Alexandria, a Pasha, a man of wealth, influence, and social standing. He was eager to show me the beauty and mystery of his country, and, delighted at the opportunity to play the host, had written me to leave all details of arrangements in his hands. We arrived at Alexandria late in the evening, having been delayed by a storm. My companion was not well and could take no responsibility. I was suffering from an attack of neuritis in my hand which made me almost helpless. The crowded wharf, with the porters in their strange dress, gesticulating and shouting in an unknown tongue, the bewildering hurry and confusion which always attend the arrival of a ship seemed particularly overwhelming on this occasion. I looked for my friend and didn't see him. My heart sank. For a moment I must confess I longed for the cozy, safe retreat of my library of Seventy-fifth Street, where I could have gained the glamour of Egypt through a book, without a sinking sensation of being alone in a strange world—and then at the foot of the companionway I saw the Pasha. I felt for an instant that never before in my entire life had the sight of a friend brought me such a sense of comfort. He immediately assumed all responsibility. He handed the keys of our trunks and valises to his man servant, telling him how many pieces we had and instructing him to attend to the custom house. Then he hurried us to his waiting limousine with chauffeur and footman in Egyptian livery and whirled us away to the hotel where he had engaged our suite of rooms. For the following day he had planned a sightseeing tour with his son as escort and in the evening a dinner at his palace. The day after, he was to escort us to Cairo, where he had been thoughtful enough to engage rooms for us and had so arranged his business affairs that his time was to be at our disposal in order to show us Cairo life. In years gone by, my husband and I had been accustomed to meet the Pasha at Marienbad, where he came annually for the cure. He was never accompanied by his wife, although he himself led a continental life and his language was French. At the dinner, which he gave in my honor, it was his married daughter in European dress and wonderful jewels who played the part of hostess. His wife had been brought up under the old régime and was secluded in the harem. The dinner was according to the Egyptian cuisine, delicious and beautifully served. However, when I noticed the particularly fine apples displayed in the fruit dish, I was told that they had come from *Oregon!* In Alexandria I was interested to find French almost as much a national language as Arabic. It was spoken in all the shops. I heard this language on the streets and in the hotel. In Cairo we heard more English on the streets, but French still remained the dominant language. It is the strange mingling of the new and the old as seen in Cairo that is so fascinating—a group of British officers in khaki, Arabs from the desert in flowing abayehs and turbans, women garbed in black, wearing yashmaks and anklets, European and American tourists, strings of camels, heavily burdened, elegant limousines, donkey carts filled with women, the strange cries, the brilliance of the bougainvilleas, and, over all, the marvel of the Egyptian sky, and the peculiar softness of the air which envelops one. Of course, I did the usual sightseeing—to the pyramids and the Sphinx by moonlight, to the bazaars, to the museums, to the mosques, to Luxor to visit Karnak by sunset and by moonlight, to the Valley of the Kings, and to the desert of Saccara.

I had been appointed a delegate to the International Suffrage Congress which was to meet in Rome in May. The Congress was the ultima thule of my trip. I, therefore, was much interested when I read in the paper that three Egyptian women were to be sent as delegates to the Congress. It was the first time that Egypt was to be represented. I was fired with the idea of having the Queen of Egypt send a message through these delegates to the Congress. There would be something picturesque in this, the Queen, representing, as she did, the oldest civilization, and Mrs. Carrie Chapman Catt, who was to preside over the Congress as President of the International Suffrage Alliance, representing the youngest civilization. I wanted the opportunity to suggest to the Queen that she send such a message. The American Minister arranged that I should be received by the Queen. It was a most interesting experience.

Queen Nazli had a French grandfather, so she was perfectly at home in the French language. The twenty-minute interview was conducted in that tongue. The Queen was gowned in European costume and, as she talked, she waved a large feather fan. Her manner was most gracious. She asked me to take a chair close to her sofa, which was on a slightly raised dais. It was pathetic to note with what eagerness she asked me to tell her of my country and of the various countries I had visited. Her evident longing to travel, to escape from the walls of her harem, made me think of a bird beating its wings against its gilded cage. When I read that she accompanied King Fuad on his recent trip to Paris I recalled this interview and I well appreciated how keen must have been her enjoyment. Etiquette forbade my introducing any topic of conversation. This is the prerogative of royalty. Therefore, I was on pins and needles lest the opportunity would not be afforded me to make my bold suggestion. My opening came when her Majesty asked me how long I would remain in Cairo. I replied that I would be obliged to leave very shortly as I was a delegate to the International Congress which was to meet in Rome within a few weeks. Her Majesty then expressed her gratification that there would be three delegates to the Congress from Egypt, and that all three were representative, enlightened women. I then pleaded for a message from her Majesty. She intimated that much as she would like to send a greeting, she would be obliged first to consult the powers that be, and would let me know later whether she could accede to my request or not.

The message was not forthcoming, so evidently such action was considered too radical. The room in which the Queen received me was very long and as I backed out when leaving, it seemed interminable. In my endeavor not to turn my back to royalty, I nearly knocked a screen over, but it merely swayed a little and I succeeded in making an exit without disaster.

From Egypt I made a flying trip to Palestine, leaving my friend who was traveling with me in Cairo in charge of a nurse to recuperate from an attack of bronchial pneumonia. My original plan had been to devote three weeks to a tour through Palestine, but because of my companion's illness, the tour was cut down to four days. However, I saw so much of interest in those four days that I am glad to have taken the journey even for so short a time.

I stayed with a friend who had a house in the American colony in Jerusalem. Her sister met me at the railroad station and after refreshing myself at their home, after my all-night journey from Cairo, we fared forth for a day's sightseeing. I felt indeed that I was walking on holy ground. In my day dreams of travel I had never dared to hope that I would have the opportunity and privilege of visiting the Holy Land. In reading the Bible, the places mentioned seemed so remote, almost mythical. But here I was on the roof of a house watching the sunlight play over the Mount of Olives, visiting the historic places of worship, the bazaars, looking down into the Dead Sea, treading the Via Dolorosa. I lunched with the British High Commissioner, Sir Herbert Samuel. I took tea with the Governor, Mr. Storrs. I motored to Bethlehem to visit the Church of the Nativity. I was taken to Rachel's tomb and to the well which the Virgin Mary frequented. I motored to Tabgha, on the Sea of Galilee, where we passed the night at the home of a hospitable German monk. The moon shone over the peaceful Galilean Sea and peeped through the flowered lattice of the balcony which led to our room. Mount Hermon reared her stately brow in the distance. There was no jarring note. I felt at peace with the world; yet there were echoes of jarring antagonism and race hatred shown at times by the Arabs against the Jews. Everywhere were evidences of nature's at-one-ness and man's belligerency.

On our motor trip I was amazed to find such a large variety of wild flowers. I counted over one hundred various specimens. I visited two of the Zionist colonies which had been established, and was greatly interested to find the work being carried on with a coöperative spirit which in its zeal and enthusiasm made for uplift and inspiration. I visited the industrial school established for orphans in Jerusalem. Everywhere I noted the fine and noble spirit of self-sacrifice which led men and women to leave their homes in the new world in order to be of service to their co-religionists who had fled to the land of their forefathers from their torn and persecuted homes in eastern and central Europe.

My visit to Palestine was of such short duration and the whole question of colonization is such a complicated problem that it would be presumptuous on my part to make deductions and draw conclusions. I must dwell, however, upon the beauty of this land. I had expected to find a barren, arid country; instead, I motored through smiling valleys, the hillsides covered with wild flowers. The mountains reminded me of California. Jerusalem, like Rome, was a city of hills—picturesque, scintillating, colorful. I was surprised, enchanted. I had many delightful memories to keep me company on my all-day journey back to Cairo.

When we left Egypt, we went directly to Venice, from there to Florence, thence to Rome to attend the International Congress.

We remained in Rome one month. The same interesting experiences I had enjoyed at previous conventions were repeated in Rome—only with a different environment. Mussolini gave an address of welcome at the opening session, and a few days later we had a suffrage parade through the streets of historic Rome to the Palazzo Chigi, where Mussolini received us in his office and a petition requesting political enfranchisement for Italian women was handed to him. We were honored by receiving invitations from the highest officials for entertainments given at Capitol Hill, at the Museum, the Campidoglio, and at various Palaces. After giving my address at the Congress in French, I was invited to repeat it at the Sorbonne in Paris, on the occasion of the meeting of the French Association for Equal Suffrage. However, as in former years, I was determined to spend part of the summer in building up my health, so after the strenuous days spent in Rome, I joined some relatives at Salsomaggiore and gave myself up to the luxury of the baths and the delight of a *dolce-far-niente* existence. The effect of the rest was to be seen in the resultant energy which prompted me shortly afterwards to begin my book, *The Story of an Epoch-Making Movement,* in the beautiful garden of a friend, whose villa was on Lake Como.

## CHAPTER XVII

### TODAY

I HAVE followed the fairy tale from its misty beginnings —"Once Upon a Time" through all its adventures of stumbling experiment toward self-expression, through the experiences of travel, of home-making, of love, of joy, of deep sorrow, of loneliness, of readjustment. There were giants to overcome, dragons to subdue, wicked fairies to propitiate before the doors of the enchanted castle could be opened and the imprisoned happiness released.

So I come to the "Today" of my story. In the fairy tale, the present is the culmination, the fulfillment, and with its invariable "and they lived together happily ever after," the note of prophecy is struck. So the analogy of this human life with the fairy tales of old is complete, for having reached "Today,"I can see the fulfillment of many hopes and ambitions and this fulfillment gives the power of the peep into the future.

Looking back down the long road of life, how impossible it is to realize that the little *me* of "Once Upon a Time," who started the long journey, is the *I* of today. What is it that *I* have been able to carry along from that little *me?* As I look back upon the traveled road, I see mile posts that guided me upon my journey. I see stumbling blocks, too, that at times made my feet falter. If those mile posts can serve to guide others on their path, and those stumbling blocks can serve as a warning, let me point them out to the wayfarer who has been sufficiently interested to have wandered through these pages.

The rough places of life's journey have been smoothed

My home in the Litchfield hills; a New England farm house, built nearly two hundred years ago.

for me through love. First the mother love. I was blessed with a wonderful mother, the cherished memory of whom has abided with me through all my life. When my mother passed away in my early youth, it seemed as though the rest of my journey must be made in darkness, in sorrow, in gloom.

But the heart yearns for love. At a time when I most needed that solace, a great love was vouchsafed me. The lover who was to become my comrade, my pal, my knight, my husband, never failed me. His sympathy, his understanding, his readiness to champion my every cause, enabled me to continue my journey without falling by the wayside. Love so enriches life that even the few years that my little daughter journeyed along with me lit up with a wondrous light the rest of my path. The warmth and glow enkindled in my heart, from the magic flame of mother love, never became ashes. The love my baby engendered smoldered and spread until it reached out to others who needed help and sympathy.

The greatest stumbling block that confronted me—as I look back through the jungle of my memories—was the constant reiteration on the part of others in regard to the futility of effort to change conditions. So many, many people were not only willing to accept conditions as they found them, but decried any effort of the minority to change them. "It can't be done! What's the use of trying?" I so often found myself in the minority. I always persisted in protesting whenever I felt that a protest was due. I could not bear the thought of injustice. It seemed cowardly to me not to protest whenever I considered an act of injustice was being done to me or to others. Many a time when I was considered fearless, my actions were due rather to a sense of fear—fear lest I be weak and cowardly; fear lest I be weighed and found wanting.

When, for instance, Prince Henry of Prussia was visiting New York, he was given a luncheon at the University

Club, corner of Fifth Avenue and Fifty-fourth Street. I was on my way to pay a visit at a home on that street. The police tried to stop me from passing the club house—they wanted me to take another street and go far out of my way to reach the house in question. I refused. My democratic views led me to rebel against the fiat that because a German Prince was lunching at a club house, a peaceable citizen was not permitted to pass the door of the club, on a legitimate errand. I risked arrest and proceeded to walk through the street. It was not done in a spirit of bravado. I felt that I must assert my rights as a citizen if I were not a coward.

At another time, I refused to leave an excursion boat at Glen Island. I had been told before purchasing our tickets at the ticket office in New York that we would be permitted to make the round trip without leaving the boat at Glen Island. It was a very hot day. There were crowds of people waiting on the sunny pier for the gates to be opened. My husband and I had comfortable seats in the bow of the boat. The boat-hands said it was against the rules to remain on board. They wished us to leave and take our places on the crowded dock, to swelter in the sun, and then push our way on board and scramble for seats fifteen minutes later. I refused very firmly to do this, explaining that I had been told by an official of the company that we could make the round trip without leaving the boat, and we had bought our tickets with that understanding. A controversy arose. My husband, rather than have any further discussion, did as he was bidden and advised me to follow him. But the injustice of the proceedings made me the more obstinate. I refused to leave my seat. Two policemen were called. They threatened to take me off by force. I remained calmly in my seat and said that if they dared lay a hand on me I'd sue the company for damages and it would cost them more than they might care to pay. One of the policemen shrugged his shoulders and, turning to the deck steward, said: "I guess you'd better let her stay." And I stayed.

It was this same spirit of rebellion against injustice that led me to give up a meeting one day at which I was to preside, and accompany to the police station some girl pickets who had been arrested. I had seen the girls clubbed by policemen while peacefully engaged in lawful picketing. It seemed to me that the action of the police had been unjust and brutal. I gave up my entire afternoon to serve as a witness for those helpless frightened working girls. Another time, when I was present at a meeting of a patriotic society, a report was read, showing that a young woman, specially fitted for a certain position to teach manual work and having every necessary qualification, received the appointment. However, after learning that the young woman was a Jewess the chairman broke the agreement. Was no one going to protest against this unfair discrimination? Apparently not. Then, of course, I must. I rose to my feet and made an impassioned plea for fairness, for the kind of patriotism which is the spirit of our American constitution; freedom of conscience, liberty to follow one's religion without limiting one's business opportunities, one's civic opportunities, one's social opportunities. My protest made a sensation, but it was too late to reverse the decision in question. I wrote a protest to the President of the National Organization. She thanked me for bringing the matter to her attention. She assured me that such discrimination was contrary to the policy of the association, and the chairman who had been responsible for the action was asked to resign.

I have already given in detail the story of how, at a meeting in Geneva, I heard the Jewish people unjustly denounced as profiteers, as though there had been no other profiteers in all Europe. And I, the one Jewess in the large assembly, rose to voice a protest.

Are the majority right when they say, "What's the use?"

"Nothing can be accomplished by the protest of the minority. The weak, spasmodic effort of the few against the tide is worse than futile!"

Yet a stone is worn away eventually by the slow dripping of water, drop by drop.

Change in its deepest sense is restlessness—the restlessness of the innermost spirit seeking expression. This spirit exists everywhere, trying out, testing, eager to find itself. We see it in nature, in the material world. We recognize it in the moral world and its influence dominates everywhere.

Perhaps one of the most noticeable changes that the half century has wrought, is the attitude of the world toward women. Fifty years ago a woman was almost a cloistered creature and this not of her own volition, but because the world said, "Woman's place is in the home." The bars were put up and she was kept there. One by one she broke those bars, always despite protests and expressions of horror. First she gained the rudiments of an education and having tasted of the fruit of the tree of knowledge and finding it good, demanded more. Then the question came to her—how was this knowledge to be used? And it was here that she began to knock on the doors of the business and professional schools. She knocked with such persistence that the men who held the bolts grew weary and gradually one by one the bolts were withdrawn, until at last all doors were opened. Now the women saw that with knowledge and training came a new responsibility, so they demanded their share in the upbuilding of the nation. This, too, they have gained. The woman of today still carries the age-old responsibilities of wifehood, of motherhood, of homemaker. She has added to these the new responsibilities of bread-winner and of citizen.

This new woman is still young. She is only just beginning to learn how to walk along the new paths, how to handle the new freedom. She has the encouragement, the sympathy, and the understanding that we of the pioneer class, who blazed the trail for her, lacked entirely. The younger generation is the product of these women who felt it necessary to discard tradition in order to gain their end. The young girl of today is such an entirely new creature that we have to coin a new word to express her. Full of exaggerations, of extravagances, even of lawlessness, she finds herself loose in a world without the protecting hedge of tradition.

Despite her extravagances, her occasionally mistaking liberty for license, her lack of reverence and apparent disregard for the spiritual values of life, at heart she is a fine creature, frank and fearless, with a courage that keeps her eyes fixed on her goal, no matter what obstacles may be in her path.

Another great change of the last fifty years is a gradual shedding of what we call Puritanism. Today the Puritan Sabbath is fast disappearing and in its place has come the Continental Sunday.

Does the throwing off of formalism, of traditional custom and observance mean a death of spirituality? I doubt it. For all about us there are signs of a spiritual stirring, a hunger for the bread of life. How is this need being met? We decry the materialism of the age, but what spiritual values are we giving that have the force to combat it? On all sides we hear the older generation criticizing and condemning the younger people of the day. But is it not our part in this spiritual evolution to help our youth to find themselves, to encourage them in their efforts at self-expression, so that from all this friction there may arise a spark which will kindle the flame that will light up heights we have only faintly glimpsed? I have said that we have shed our Puritanism, but strangely enough, at the same time there has developed a medieval intolerance. When our country was fifty years younger, religious and racial differences were not the acute problems that they have become today.

There is a change, a change that has been so gradual, so subtle, that we have not realized the sinister problem that has finally developed. Into our politics there has been injected a question of a man's fitness for office if he belongs to the Roman Catholic Church. Discussion of the matter has invaded social circles, until a sharp division is found between the protagonists of either side. Like the children's game of London Bridge, members of society line up behind the leaders of each division. The press in its turn reflects the situation.

Into our social life has been injected the question of the fitness of the Jew to mingle freely on terms of equality with the dominant group.

These religious and racial problems are new factors in the life of our nation. Fifty years ago, such a book as Cosmo Hamilton's *Caste* could not have been written. For the Jewish problem that it frankly presents was not then a problem, and would have been no more understood than a novel which had for its motif the radio.

So, I must again raise my voice to plead for tolerance, to protest against the bigotry, the prejudice, the injustice of socially ostracizing Jewish people of culture and refinement. Such a protest may eventually wear away the stones of the walls of this social ghetto.

Social segregation emphasizes racial characteristics and racial pride. Prejudice produces humiliation which is not easy to bear. And the sad part is that the nature becomes warped and the spirit of kindliness and friendliness is changed into bitterness and resentment. To live in peace, there must be mutual confidence, trust, coöperation, no antagonism. How often, instead of mutual respect for differing spiritual values, there is suspicion, intolerance. Does not this intolerance find its final expression in the un-American principles of the Ku Klux Klan?

This country has experienced the horror of Civil War, when brother fought brother. Do we want racial and religious warfare with every man's hand against his neighbor?

Many of the fine women with whom I have been associated, whose names I have mentioned in these pages, are striving with all their splendid energy to educate the people as to the cause of and cure for war. Is it possible to eradicate international antagonisms so long as antagonisms exist at home? As expressed by a certain writer, "Does peace consist in all thinking the same thoughts, living the same lives, sharing the same interests? Is it not rather a harmonious, happy dwelling together of widely differing thoughts and actions? If the parable of the lion and the lamb means anything, it is not that antagonistic natures shall become similar in character, but that we shall curb our passions, restrain our prejudices, that love may lead us to a better understanding of each other and to a broad and kindly tolerance."

I feel all this very strongly, because I know that no constructive work can be accomplished without an environment of tolerance, faith, and confidence. Let no one who has read these pages think that the work accomplished was done without effort, without trembling, without handicaps. They were all there, as they must be in every life.

Never could I have carried on without the encouragement, the friendly sympathy, the enfolding kindliness of my co-workers. Given such an environment, we are strengthened to make our best efforts, and the weakening influence of self-consciousness is pushed aside.

I have learned one of life's lessons. One individual handicapped by sex and by having been born into a minority group, by having been brought up in a small country town, isolated from even that small minority group, has been able to make her protests count, because she persisted. She refused sheep-like to follow the majority. The world *does* change. Ideas change, sentiments change, characters change, nothing remains static.

So, as I look back, I feel that each mile post on my journey was a record of some little deed, insignificant, perhaps, in itself, but helping to build character. And as I look more closely, I find that the stumbling blocks became, in turn, stepping stones to the guide posts. What I thought at first were insurmountable pitfalls, were in reality the gateway out of the forest of confusion and struggle into the promised land of independence of thought and action.

I have covered some of the great changes of the last fifty years. But there is one—perhaps the greatest of all, certainly the most intimate one—that I have not as yet touched upon: the elimination of "old age."

It makes no difference whether we be sixty, seventy, or eighty, life still holds new interests, new possibilities. Voronoff's secret of renewing youth may or may not have failed, but the real secret lies in being ready to adapt oneself to new conditions as they arise, to engage in new activities, to use the wisdom that the years have brought, not to simulate a superficial youthfulness, but to form a sympathetic bond with youth that will enable us to glimpse new vistas, to explore with them new paths.

As I write the concluding paragraph of this book, two stories come to my mind. One of Julia Ward Howe, taking up the study of Greek at the age of eighty, and the other of the charming Frenchwoman of ninety who, when asked by her young grandson at what age a woman ceases to be interested in lovers, replied that she didn't know as she had not yet reached that age! Such souls never grow old. The birthdays may accumulate, wearing out the physical machinery, but the spirit of youth remains—that wonderful spirit with its zest for living, its eagerness to tread unknown paths, its courage and love of adventure; this is the spirit which, when the old paths are closed against us, will carry on and on and on to further heights, to further achievement.

## MAUD NATHAN

(Written on the occasion of her seventieth birthday.)

What is she like? I said—how best portray
This woman of courage, kindliness and beauty?
Where are the similes that will convey
The fire-flash wit, the rock-firm sense of duty?
The broad-winged mind, the poise that birth bestows?
Varied and quick the images arose:

Is it the swan?—No, not the swan I said,
Although the grace of that white-plumaged head
Is swan-like; but the soul of this self-giver—
Never the idle swan, vain-mirrored on a river!
The ardent eagle, mounting without fear?—
The will to dare, the heart to persevere—
No, not the eagle; the brave bird is cruel
And this heart burns compassion for its fuel.
Is she the clear lake's truth? the vigor of the brook?
The fountain's upward urge? the sea's far-reaching look?
Does the proud rose describe her? the goldenrod?
The human touch of clover? the sun-flower's faith in God?

They only glimmer forth
A shadowing of her worth.
Combine each metaphor
And she is ever vastly something more.

And all the words of praise are leaves on branches
Casting a patterned shade that cannot be,
Even remotely, in its wavering outline,
The contour of the great, full-fruited tree.

MAY LEWIS.

October 20, 1932.

# APPENDIX I

Simon Nathan, born in 1746 in Frome, Somersetshire, England, was a patriot of the American Revolution. At the risk of his life he supplied the Continental Army with canvas and gunpowder. He voluntarily provided $300,000 for clothing for the soldiers at Fort Pitt which was repaid in ruinously depreciated currency. He advanced $320,000 to the State of Virginia and was thanked by Thomas Jefferson and the Council of Virginia for his substantial help. He married in New York, August 29, 1780, Grace, a daughter of Isaac Mendes Seixas, who was born in Lisbon, Portugal, September 5, 1709, and arrived in New York in 1738. Isaac Mendes Seixas married Rachel, daughter of Moses Levy and Rycha Asher. Simon and Grace Nathan had one son (Isaac Mendes) Seixas Nathan, born in New York, May 24, 1785. Simon Nathan died in New York in 1822 and was buried in the old Bowery Cemetery, where in 1932 a tablet was erected near his grave by Manhattan Chapter, Daughters of the American Revolution, as a tribute to his patriotism.

Isaac Mendes Seixas Nathan was named after his grandfather, Isaac Mendes Seixas, who was the only son of Abraham Mendes Seixas and his wife, Abigail. As his will (see Appendix II for copy of will), still extant at Somerset House in London, shows his Marrano name [1] was Miguel Pacheco da Silva, and in 1737, in a petition to the King, he signed himself: Miguel Pacheco de Seixas. He was probably a descendant of Vasco Gomez de Seixas, whose family originated in Galicia, a province of the northwest of Spain, and who was knighted about 1385 by John I of Portugal.

My grandfather, Seixas Nathan, was one of the signers of the Constitution of the New York Public Stock Exchange Association and a member of the St. Nicholas Society, from its

[1] Marrano was the name given to those Jews who, in preference to exile, changed their names, becoming outwardly Christians, while in the privacy of their homes, adhering strictly to their own forms of worship.

organization in 1835. He married Sarah, daughter of Benjamin Mendez Seixas (who was a lieutenant in the New York militia in 1775), November 30, 1808, and they had fifteen children.

## APPENDIX II

REFERENCE: New York Historical Society Collections, 1896, Abstracts of Wills, Vol. V., p. 115.

Wills of Jews on file in the Surrogate's office at the City of New York, 1754-1780.

American Jewish Historical Society No. 12, 1904, page 163.

Liber 20, page 36—Certificate of Thomas, Archbishop of Canterbury, that the will of Abraham Mendes Seixas, otherwise Miguel Pacheco Da Silva, late of the parish of Dunstans, Stepney, County of Middlesex, was proved in London on April 7, 1738, and Letters of Administration granted to Rodrigo Pacheco and Daniel Mendes Seixas, executors.

"In the Name of the Eternal God, Creator of Heaven and Earth:

"I, Abraham Mendes Seixas, otherwise Miguel Pacheco Da Silva, being in my best understanding, though incapable of making my own will with own hand for want of sight, have caused these Presents to be made.

"I declare that I lawfully married once and had three children, all of whom are now living, towit, Judith, wife of Rodrigo Pacheco, Isaac, who is now a single man, and Rebecca, wife of Daniel Mendes Seixas.

"And as I have given to the husbands of my daughters their marriage portions, I give to each of my daughters 20 pounds as a token of love, and to my son Isaac only 50 pounds for reasons known to myself. I leave to Esther da Silva, who is at present in my company, 50 pounds. To my son in law, Daniel Mendes Seixas, 80 pounds. And I make my two sons in law executors, and they are to allow my son 30 pounds a year. If he marries with their approval and has children, they are to divide the estate between them, otherwise at his death I leave the whole to my two daughters.

"Done at Bethnel Green, March 6, 1737-8. Witnesses, Abraham de Mesquito, Premental, Isaac Messoptrix."

"Faithfully translated from the Portuguese original according to the best of my skill, this 10 of April, 1738.

"John da Costa."

Confirmed by Sir Charles Hardy, Governor, June 25, 1756, and letters of administration granted to Isaac Mendes Seixas, surviving executor.

(Note. The above-named persons were very important members of the Jewish Colony in New York and principal supporters of the Hebrew Synagogue Shearith Israel.—W. S. P.)

## APPENDIX III

FREDERICK NATHAN was the son of Benjamin, the third son of Seixas Nathan, and my father's older brother. Benjamin Nathan was named after his maternal grandfather, Benjamin Mendes Seixas. He married Emily Hendricks, a descendant of Joseph Isaacs who was made a freeman in New York in 1691. Her father was a member of the firm of Hendricks Brothers of Soho, New Jersey. Their copper factory was one of the oldest business houses in the country.

That Benjamin Nathan fulfilled the ideals of his ancestors for participation in civic life, is shown by these facts: He was one of the early members of the New York Stock Exchange, having been elected in 1836, and becoming its vice president in 1851. He was appointed aid-de-camp with the title of Colonel to Governor Hamilton Fish of New York State. He was a director of the Chicago and Northwestern Railroad, a member of the Union and Union League Clubs, and of the St. Nicholas Society.

Side by side with his duties as a citizen and man of affairs, he was known as a consistent Jew, a leader in Jewish philanthropies, a regular attendant at the synagogue, and a staunch upholder of Jewish traditions. He so strongly impressed these traditions upon his large family of sons and daughters, that they too felt the urge of carrying on these ancient racial customs. When his second son, Frederick, became my husband, his desire was to have the same Jewish home life which had formed his boyhood background. The Sabbath lights were lighted, the Sabbath day was a day of real rest.

Another of Frederick's ancestors was Abraham de Lucena who was in New York in 1699 as noted from Court Records, he having filed a suit in that year against John Basford. Abraham de Lucena was a merchant of prominence in New York and Rabbi of Shearith Israel Congregation during the first two decades of the 18th century. His will probated in 1725 is on record in New York. His daughter Rebecca was married to Mordecai Gomez, the son of Moses (Lewis) Gomez, a prominent merchant first mentioned in New York in 1702 and a member of one of the most prominent Jewish families in New York. This Moses (Lewis) Gomez was the son of Isaac Gomez who was born in Madrid, escaped from the Inquisition, and is said to have died in France.

My husband and I were both descended from Solomon Myers, our great-grandfather's grandfather, who was a member of the militia in New York in 1738.

It may seem curious that so many of my ancestors intermarried but the number of those from whom to choose was small in early colonial days. However, there was not always strict adherence to race and religion. Many of the descendants of my great-great-grandmother Rachel Levy Seixas' brothers and sisters were Christians. Her brother, Samson Levy, married Martha Lamply of Philadelphia, and their son Samson married Sarah Coats of Philadelphia. Her sister Abigail married Jacob Franks, and their son married Margaret Evans, while their daughter married General Oliver Delancey.

Thus from the earliest days of Colonial America there have been two divergent tendencies, often productive, no doubt, of conflicts in the minds of my ancestors and their relatives, one to remain loyal to the ancient faith of their fathers, the other to yield to the more insistent demands of love.

This ancient Jewish strain runs through many of our best known American families. Only recently a family connection, familiar with our genealogy, was calling at the home of a prominent Philadelphia churchman, belonging to an aristocratic family. The host pointed with pride to the portrait of his ancestor, Moses Levy, to whom reference has been made, and whose coat of arms our family is entitled to use.

## THE NEW COLOSSUS

Not like the brazen giant of Greek fame,
With conquering limbs astride from land to land;
Here at our sea-washed, sunset gates shall stand
A mighty woman with a torch, whose flame
Is the imprisoned lightning, and her name
Mother of exiles, from her beacon-hand
Glows world-wide welcome; her mild eyes command
The air-bridge harbor that twin cities frame,
"Keep ancient lands your storied pomp!"
Cries she
With silent lips, "Give me your tired, your poor,
Your huddled masses yearning to breathe free,
The wretched refuse of your teeming shore,
Send these, the homeless, tempest-tost to me,
I lift my lamp beside the golden door!"

This tablet, with her sonnet to the Bartholdi
Statue of Liberty engraved upon it, is placed
upon these walls in loving memory of Emma
Lazarus.
Born in New York City, July 22nd, 1849
Died November 19th, 1887

# APPENDIX V

THE following letter was sent by Mrs. Corinne Roosevelt Robinson after reading Chapter VIII:

Mrs. Douglas Robinson
147 East 61st Street
New York

Jan. 9th, 1928

DEAR MRS. NATHAN:

I cannot tell you how much pleasure it has given me to read the chapter in your book which you have entitled, "Recollections of Theodore Roosevelt."

I consider it a real contribution to the material about my brother, first because of the vividness of the portrait you paint, and second, because, though showing admiration of my brother's character and achievement, you never indulge in sentimentality; and therefore your opinions carry so much more weight than they otherwise would do.

Your vivid account of his, Theodore Roosevelt's, equally vivid and rapid manner of taking up the case of the delinquent policeman is more than delightful. Nothing could be more characteristic than his handling of the whole situation.

You show in every way his effort to understand any matters brought to his attention, and his invariable desire to give a "square deal" in his decisions.

Best of all I like your frank admission of his keen political sense and your conclusion that while he was often criticized for "political expediency," he specially, you felt, showed his independence by his "utter indifference to criticism following a decision which had political significance." I always felt that so strongly with my brother —the indifference either to being called too political, or not political enough. The cause for which he was working was the only point in which he was interested, and criticism of himself did not count.

I have reread your article with care, and I thank you for having written it.

It is interesting; it is fair; it shows the man as he was, the citizen as he was. It is almost the only article about my brother which I have not wanted to change in some respect.

I thank you for letting me have a copy, and I am gratefully and appreciatively yours,

(*signed*) CORINNE ROOSEVELT ROBINSON.

# INDEX